S0-BPI-556

op '90

25
IO

Essays in Economic Analysis and Policy

Essays
in Economic Analysis
and Policy

EDITED BY

Franz Gehrels, Henry M. Oliver, Jr.
and George W. Wilson

HB
171
·E77
West

INDIANA UNIVERSITY PRESS

BLOOMINGTON & LONDON

Copyright © 1970 by Indiana University Press

All rights reserved

No part of this book may be reproduced or utilized in any
form or by any means, electronic or mechanical, including
photocopying and recording, or by any information storage
and retrieval system, without permission in writing from
the publisher. The Association of American University
Presses Resolution on Permissions constitutes the only
exception to this prohibition.

Published in Canada by Fitzhenry & Whiteside Limited,
Don Mills, Ontario

Library of Congress catalog card number: 70–108217
ISBN: 253–31960–9
Manufactured in the United States of America

To the memory of

HENRY M. OLIVER, JR.

CONTENTS

Part 1. **ECONOMICS OF COLLECTIVE ACTION**

1. Economics and the Analysis of Government Behavior:
   The Mainstream Tradition and Recent Trends 3
   HENRY M. OLIVER, JR.

2. American Unionism: The Membership Problem 45
   BENJAMIN J. TAYLOR AND FRED WITNEY

3. Economic Externalities and the Justification for
   Collective Action 77
   H. J. KIESLING

Part 2. **RECENT DEVELOPMENTS IN MONETARY THEORY**

4. Is the Money Supply an Exogenous Variable? 103
   ELMUS WICKER

5. Applications of the Theory of Rational Choice to the
   Transactions Demand for Cash 122
   EDWARD WHALEN

vii

Part 3. **PROBLEMS IN THE ANALYSIS OF UNDERDEVELOPMENT**

6. Trade Policy and Allocative Efficiency in Underdeveloped
    Countries   165
    FRANZ GEHRELS

7. The Concept of Capital and Its Role in Economic Growth 192
    GEORGE W. WILSON

    Part 4. **KARL MARX REVISITED AND THE WORKINGS OF
    CENTRALLY ADMINISTERED ECONOMIES**

8. On Rereading Marx's *Capital*   219
    SCOTT GORDON

9. Macroeconomic Models and Central Price-Setting in the
    Soviet Economy   253
    ROBERT W. CAMPBELL

PREFACE

In 1948–1949 the Department of Economics at Indiana University sponsored a series of special lectures on economic theory. These lectures, delivered by James E. Earley, Lawrence H. Seltzer, Kenneth E. Boulding, and Allan G. Grunchy, were published in 1950 under the title of *Economic Theory in Review* as part of the Social Science Series at Indiana University.

Having in mind the sesquicentennial of Indiana University and the success of the earlier departmental venture, I proposed another departmental volume. This time, however, it seemed more appropriate to attempt a survey of some unsettled questions or current controversies and their origin in some of the major divisions of economics. At the same time, as part of the recognition of 150 years of existence, the contributors to the volume, I felt, should be scholars at Indiana University. Birthday celebrations may perhaps, excuse some degree of parochialism. Accordingly, I asked certain faculty members in the Department representing several of the major fields of economics to prepare original papers that summarized or surveyed the leading issues in their respective areas of expertise. The initial response was most encouraging. But as all soliciting editors know from experience, there is a long strugggle between initial enthusiasm and final product. The papers ultimately selected do not therefore represent the kind of consistency and uniformity that one would like any volume to possess. They do not, for example, constitute a complete convass of all the major areas of economics. Yet they do survey and analyze some of the leading issues in such important areas as economic development, the economics of collective action, and monetary theory, as well as portions of the history of economic thought and the functioning of Soviet-type economies. The papers generally seek to elaborate the current controversies and provide an evaluation of their respective merits. As such, they should be of interest to economists in general and usable in advanced courses where leading issues in economic analysis are presented.

All papers selected have gone through several substantial revisions and have benefited greatly from the meticulous and perceptive reviews and criticisms of Professors Henry Oliver and Franz Gehrels, who, along with myself, constituted the editorial committee for the Department. Thanks are also due to Professor George P. Adams, Jr., of Cornell University for his critical appraisal and to Professor Nicolas Spulber, who undertook the final preparation for publication of the paper by Professor Robert Campbell (then on leave). I should like to thank the Centro Studi e Richerche su Problemi Economico-Sociali for permission to use parts of Professor Campbell's paper, which was presented orally at its Florence International Seminar.

One should not add to the already cluttered literature on economics unless one has something of interest or importance to say. I am too close to the present papers to judge them on this score. Whether they merit all the efforts involved in getting them into present form is up to the reader to judge. In this connection, however, I believe the labor theory of value has some merit.

Since the above was written, the Department has lost Professor Oliver. The present volume owes much to his efforts and contains his last published work. It is only fitting that we dedicate this book to him.

GEORGE W. WILSON

Indiana University
Bloomington, Indiana

Essays in Economic Analysis and Policy

Part 1

ECONOMICS OF COLLECTIVE ACTION

1

Economics and the Analysis of Government Behavior: The Mainstream Tradition and Recent Trends

HENRY M. OLIVER, JR.

One of the general questions that economic analysts face is how to treat government behavior. When they pay attention to it, as they at least sometimes must, shall they talk only about its effects, or also about its causes? What choice shall they make with respect to policy decisions? With respect to the administrative, follow-up actions that so importantly govern policies' effects?

When talking about the future, shall the analyst make all statements about these variables conditional, say only what will happen *if* policies and follow-ups are thus-and-such? Or shall he make his conclusions less cautious—and more interesting—by not relying so heavily on these two kinds of "ifs"? What shall his practice be when he constructs abstract models? When he applies them in concrete situations?

When talking about the past, shall the analyst bring his cause-and-effect reasoning to a halt each time government appears upon the scene? When he records relevant changes—and constancies—in policy and administration, shall he *merely* record them, say nothing

Henry M. Oliver, Jr., was University Professor of Economics at Indiana University.

to explain? Again, what shall his practice be when he generalizes? When his analysis concerns particular past events?

Economists' writings show that they have given widely varying answers to these questions. In each of the kinds of analysis mentioned above, government actions of various types have played contrasting political roles, have served both as autonomous and as dependent variables. The nature and context of the writings suggest that complex mixtures of reasons have accounted for this variety, i.e., have led economists neither always to treat government behavior in the same general way nor to follow some other simple rule. This paper asks what have been the practices, and why.

Part I concerns mainstream economics, defined as the micro and macro analysis largely descended from nineteenth-century Cambridge, Lausanne, and Vienna forebears. Topics briefly discussed are, in the order listed, policy-making and mainstream theory, policy-making and mainstream economics as a whole, administrative behavior and mainstream economics, and reasons for the mainstream tradition.

Part II describes and discusses recent trends away from this tradition. After the initial, key section, "Causes and Types," which links Part II to Part I, its subjects are theses about government behavior in Soviet-type and other centrally administered economies, theses about government behavior in economically underdeveloped countries, theses about government in predominantly market, relatively advanced economies, arguments about some political fundamentals, and highly abstract theses about government behavior fairly generally.[1]

Part III asks how the trends fit into the history of economics and what they might indicate about the "discipline's" future.

I. THE MAINSTREAM TRADITION

Government Policy-Making

Mainstream economic theory has, until recently, said nothing about government policy-makers' behavior. Insofar as the Cambridge-Lausanne-Vienna heritage has concerned policy decisions, it has asked about their consequences, not their causes. Moreover, it has been selective in what it has said about consequences. First, the effects discussed have been only those on the familiar micro and macro variables, i.e., on specific inputs, outputs, and prices; on output and input aggregates and price averages, and on the distribution of income. Next, the channels through which these effects have been pictured as taking place have been quite limited. Mainstream theory has not asked whether market or other reactions to "initial," "independent" policy choices may not trigger later, derived policy choices significant for the micro and macro quantities studied. Its *ceteris paribus* has been so interpreted as to rule out economically influential political responses as well as economically influential autonomous political change.[2]

What has been true of mainstream theory has also very largely been true of mainstream economics as a whole. This, of course, is not to assert that nearly all economists who have generally stayed within the main tradition have nearly always refrained from statements about policies' causes. Such an assertion would be false. Nor would it be correct even if a closing date were supplied to keep it from applying to the last few decades. Policy debates and interpretations of economic history provide numerous exceptions.

Among the pre-1914 examples that can be cited are (i) the familiar argument that only a metallic standard currency is safe because, if policy-makers are free to alter the money supply as they wish, they will disastrously inflate it, (ii) the almost equally familiar thesis that, if country A imposes a tariff which injures country B, B will (in certain circumstances) return the favor, (iii) the generalization that, when an economy becomes wealthier and more complex, government's share of aggregate income will rise, and (iv) the argument that central planning plus state enterprise will so concentrate power that the executive branch of government will be able to, and will, put an end to political democracy and civil liberties.

Some of these statements about policies' causes (e.g., the second type listed here) amounted to narrowings of the very broad *ceteris paribus* mentioned above, or, in other words, to the insertion of economically influential government responses as intermediate variables in the micro or macro analysis. Others (e.g., the first, third, and last examples listed) either theorized about government actions ordinarily treated as initial, autonomous precipitants of market reactions or introduced unorthodox "terminal" (not merely intermediate) variables.

But, to repeat, such theorizings about policy-makers have not usually characterized mainstream economics. Although Marxist and various other analyses have fairly generally linked conclusions about causes and conclusions about economic consequences of policy decisions, the main tradition has been quite different. While his statement is too sweeping, Stanislaw Wellisz correctly described the *usual* treatment when, in his recent book on Soviet-type economies, he said of "the analytic approach developed by economists in capitalist nations":

> At most, economists investigate how government decisions influence and modify the market process. The decisions made by the government are taken as a datum; the investigation of the decision-making process is left to political scientists.[3]

Indeed, so strong has been the tradition of treating government policies as independent variables that mainstream economists have, fairly widely, slipped into the habit of talking about them as "causes" and of policy-makers as responsible actors deserving praise or blame, while simultaneously speaking of market actions as ("mere" or "natural") consequences and of utility-maximizing, nongovernmental buyers and sellers as automata, (neither commendable nor blamable). Thus, in his 1951 paper "Keynesianism and Inflation," Walter Morton argued:

> Prior to the recent popularity of the income theory of prices monetary theory sought to distinguish between the basic causes of

general price movements and price-making actions such as consumption, savings, and net investment. Of course, we could say, and some still do, that all who buy and sell "caused" prices to rise and then blame unions, profiteers, and farmers for the inflation. This confuses a process with a cause. Since, moreover, economists expect those engaged in the economic process to maximize monetary gains under whatever monetary conditions that may exist, we regard as the "cause" of inflation not the maximizing conduct but the limiting monetary and economic factors determining this behavior. . . .

The basic cause of postwar inflation was the release of idle cash balances created by the war. . . .

So far as the future price trend is concerned, aside from excessive demand arising from inadequate taxation in a war economy, I hold that ordinarily monetary and fiscal policy are responsible for inflationary tendencies. . . .[4]

(Policy-making, in other words, is not mere "process.")

Administrative Behavior

Mainstream economists have more frequently drawn conclusions about administrative behavior.[5] They have almost had to do this in order for economics to play its familiar advisory role, since the impact of a decision depends on follow-up administrative actions as well as on other, more narrowly "economic" causes of nongovernmental responses (to the policy choices plus the follow-ups). The alternative to conclusions about administrators' behavior is analysis with *ifs* that often rob it of much of its interest, and in much of the literature on trade barriers, public finance, price controls, and the like, authors have preferred not to make their argument so conditional.

Indeed, not only does much of the literature dealing with fairly concrete policy proposals clearly reflect this preference, but also much more abstract analysis may embody it. A possible, and not implausible, interpretation of mainstream theory is that, when it concerns the effects of legislation (e.g., excise taxes, minimum wage rates), it implicitly concludes that administrators are lawmakers' obedient and efficient servants; i.e., it theorizes about government without explicitly saying so.[6]

Mainstream theory, however, has offered at most a very limited account of administrative behavior. Moreover, it may not have offered even that. Another possible, and not implausible, interpretation of the Cambridge-Lausanne-Vienna heritage is that it treats administration as well as policy-making as given; i.e., when it explicitly assumes a particular policy decision, it does not draw any conclusion about follow-up actions but merely assumes that they will be suitable. In other words, the meaning of *ceteris paribus* is stretched to include this assumption also: "Other things remaining equal" implies that administrative actions are compatible with the theory's conclusions.[7]

Nor has applied mainstream economics (as defined above) gone very deeply into the matter of administrative behavior. Mainstream economists, although often ranging beyond the bounds of mainstream theory when discussing policy questions, have not usually appealed to general theses about administration. Instead, their analyses have presented conclusions about follow-up actions as explicit or implicit ad hoc judgments.

Quite a few exceptions can be pointed out, of course. Thus, when either actual or proposed legislation has delegated substantial policy-making authority, instead of chiefly instructing administrators to act as police, one type of general thesis has concerned planners' abilities to make necessary calculations, including predictions. Debates over stabilization schemes and socialist allocation provide examples here. And, both when the central topic has been administrative discretion and when it has been administrators as police, a second type of general thesis has concerned integrity (or corruptibility) and sympathies. Examples under the first heading (administrative discretion) include some of the writings on public utility regulation, other discretionary price controls, and various kinds of rationing. Examples under the second (administrators as police) include arguments about collection of tax revenues and enforcement of other statutes. But, as in the section on policy-making, the term *exception* tells the story. Explicit accounting for administrative behavior has not been the usual practice.

Reasons for the Tradition

If a single, sweeping reason is to be assigned for the tradition, it must, of course, be mainstream economists' conception of their function. Although most of them have been willing to theorize about government a little, now and then, or in areas of their special expertise, basically they have regarded themselves as analysts of market behavior, and the market participants they have had in mind have been private households and business firms, not governmental buyers and sellers. Or, to be more precise, they have regarded themselves as basically analysts of market behavior when they have thought of their role as social scientists, i.e., when they have not conceived of themselves as specialized logicians, whose special skills concern the mathematical calculations that optimizing choices logically require.[8]

Nor is this sweeping explanation as tautological, as repetitive, as it may initially seem. It both calls attention to mainstream economists' acceptance of their tradition (as distinguished from their conformity to it) and points to the equally general reason that may be assigned recent trends away from the tradition, namely, the changed conception of function in recent years. But to assign such a single reason is, obviously, only to postpone a more fundamental explanation. Causes must be found for mainstream economists' conception of their function as social scientists. In the case of the recent trends, causes must be found for the changed conception.

One partial explanation of the traditional conception presumably is economics' familiar role as a policy guide,[9] apparently the most important role it has played throughout modern times. When serving in this capacity, analysis is supposed to help policy-makers predict the results of possible decisions instead of telling them what they themselves will do.[10] But, however compelling this reason may be for not predicting advisees' behavior, it clearly cannot *by itself* logically account for a tradition that classifies all government behavior as autonomous.

First, analysis may play another role in addition to its advisory one. "Economic science," like astronomy, seems to command interest in its own right.

Next, economics may serve as an aid to other decision-makers as well as government officials: e.g., corporation and labor-union executives and noncorporate investors.

Finally, even when economics serves as a guide to government, the mainstream economists' traditional conception of their function logically must have some complementary cause or causes. As the preceding section stated, estimates of policies' effects logically call for, instead of ruling out, questions about administrators' behavior. Moreover, except in a completely centralized—and timeless—world economy, some of the questions that policy officials logically must ask concern the effects of *their* actions on *other* policy officials: i.e., those in different countries, in different units within a federal union, and in different branches of government (when the advised branch is not the sole policy-maker), also the officeholders who will serve as their own successors, and perhaps even their own future selves, as they react to future pressures that arise.[11]

Beliefs about expertise are a second part of the explanation of the traditional conception of function. Mainstream economists have looked upon themselves as knowledgeable students of market behavior, but have not, except perhaps in areas of very special expertise, had the same impression of themselves as students of politics or as students of public administration. In part, these beliefs seem to have concerned comparative expertise, i.e., different persons' relative strengths. When analysis has called for fairly specific predictions about government, mainstream economists have usually thought practicing politicians and their "practical" consultants better equipped; and, when it has called for more abstract reasoning, they have usually paid political scientists the same compliment. But thoughts about absolute expertise may have been even more significant. Codes of professional ethics appear to stress the degree of confidence that professional training and experience are thought to justify more than they do different analysts' comparative advantages, and such a code seems to have importantly helped set the limits that mainstream economists have usually assigned their public statements.

Because of what will be said later about causes of recent trends, the relationship between belief about knowledgeability and possession of a special analytical technique merits special attention here. Mainstream economists' faith in their power to analyze market behavior largely consisted of their confidence that marginalist theory was pretty generally applicable and yielded reasonably precise predictions and explanations; i.e., they believed that they did not have to depend very much on a mass of unintegrated generalizations. But—and this is the crucial point—they regarded "marginalism" as a general theory of market behavior, not as a more comprehensive theory of social action. (Or, at least, they so regarded it when they did not look upon it merely as the logic of optimizing choice.) They did not believe that their special possession could be used to explain and predict government behavior.[12]

In a sense, of course, these statements about beliefs are not explanations. What was said above about the single sweeping reason for the mainstream tradition is pertinent here as well. A more fundamental explanation must account for a belief, not merely point to it, and both the Marxist and the historicist streams of thought show that analysts regarding themselves as economists need not share the mainstream beliefs. Indeed, until recently political science has hardly existed in Germany and Austria as a separate discipline. Apart from jurists and historians, the academicians who have most frequently analyzed government have called themselves economists, and have done so because of the predominant nature of their interests.[13]

But to account for the mainstream beliefs would be to review two centuries of intellectual history, a lengthy as well as otherwise formidable task. The only cause that seems to call for special notice here is one that appears not only to help explain the beliefs about expertise but also to serve directly as a major complement to economics' role as a policy guide (i.e., as a complement to that role in helping to account for mainstream economists' traditional conception of their function).

That cause is the nature of the economies which mainstream economics was designed to analyze and which, until recently, it has usually been employed to analyze. True, even in the heyday of (so-called) laissez-faire, government's direct economic roles were more important than mainstream central theory might lead an uninformed reader to believe. A thorough explanation of micro and macro variables would have had to account for public finance, decisions about money, and the banking system, and various other "interventions," as well as business firms' and private householders' responses to market stimuli. By the 1920's, welfare-state, protectionist, and related attitudes had made the central theory even less descriptive, especially in its European homeland. But, except during major wars and other emergencies (e.g., the 1923 struggle over the Ruhr) economic analysis was not dramatically incomplete when it treated governmental policies as autonomous. Public spending was a small fraction of national income and state enterprise an even smaller fraction of productive capacity, and although protectionist measures were often collectively important, they tended to be fairly stable, so that general interdependence theory could largely ignore economically influential governmental responses. Although the economic world which the mainstream economists saw around them did not require that they treat policy decisions as data, it allowed and even invited that practice.

Similarly, the general nature of the bureaucracies in the economies usually studied allowed and even invited the practice of usually assuming that administrators' follow-up actions (to the kinds of policies usually considered) would be obedient and efficient. True, historians of the time can tell interesting tales of scandal and inefficiency at all levels; but, if the bureaucracies had more closely resembled those of some Mercantilist regimes or some contemporary developing countries, economists presumably would not have felt quite as free to ponder so little about the nature and the causes of administrative behavior.

II. RECENT TRENDS

Causes and Types

The foregoing statement about reasons for the mainstream tradition also points to reasons for departures from it. Both changes within economics' environment and changes within the discipline itself have helped to modify economists' basic conception of themselves as analysts of (nongovernmental) market behavior. More specifically:

1. The altered nature of the economies chiefly studied in earlier days,[14] the proliferation of and increased emphasis on Soviet-type economies, and post-1945 emphasis on the development of Asian, and Latin American economies have made conclusions about government behavior much more important (than before) in explanations and predictions of economic affairs.

2. The changed policies noted in 1, plus the nature of proposed policies that recently have seemed to have at least a "minimally reasonable" chance of being adopted, have increased the possible significance of ("not too unlikely") economic programs for political institutions, political practices, and the distribution of political power. Micro- and macroeconomics' traditional dependent variables have, for many observers who consider themselves economists, not seemed *relatively* as important as they formerly did in ("reasonably relevant") policy appraisals.

3. Work with the theory of games, related developments in the theory of small numbers, uncertainty more generally, and spatial competition, and greatly increased emphasis on statistical investiga-

tion have caused an active and influential part of the fraternity to regard themselves primarily as possessors of techniques, rather than as specialized students of a body of subject matter.

Trends for which these causes have been responsible include:[15]

    a. theses about government behavior in the Soviet-type and other types of centrally administered economies:

        (i) generalizations about state enterprises;

        (ii) generalizations about central planners;

    b. theses about government behavior in economically underdeveloped countries:

        (i) conclusions about administration;

        (ii) conclusions about policy-making;

    c. theses about government behavior in predominantly market, relatively advanced economies:

        (i) statistical analyses of public expenditures;

        (ii) theses concerning resources policy;

        (iii) theses about monetary and fiscal authorities not bound by rigid rules;

        (iv) cost-push analyses;

        (v) theories of political countervailing power and cumulative intervention;

    d. analyses of the type indicated by (2) above (in other words, argument concerning the effects of economic programs on political institutions and practices and the distribution of political power);

    e. highly abstract theses about government behavior fairly generally:

        (i) "pure theories" of elections, constitution-making, administrative behavior, and strategy in international affairs (theories quite "economic" in their appearance in that they employ traditional maximization analysis and/or the theory of games);

        (ii) theses (more in the political-science tradition) about partisan mutual adjustment and incremental change.

Relationships between the trends and the causes are perhaps obvious. A few remarks about them may, however, suggest some of the argument to be presented in Part III, which concerns the possible future of economics.

The altered nature of the economies studied is almost certainly a major cause of all the trends. It must chiefly—and directly—account for (a-c), theses about government behavior in centrally administered, in underdeveloped, and in welfare-statish, advanced economies. By intensifying the interests noted in (2) (interests in political fundamentals), it importantly helped give rise to (d), theses about political science's traditional variables. And it certainly gave an added impetus to (e), highly abstract theses about government behavior fairly generally. If today's economies closely resembled those chiefly studied in 1913, very probably *economists* would not have taken nearly as great an interest in general theories of constitutions, elections, legislation, and administration—regardless of advances in maximization theory and in the treatment of uncertainty.

The last cause listed above, economists as possessors of techniques, probably helps to account for more than (e-i), pure theories of government behavior, and (c-i), statistical studies. To the extent that it has helped to instill confidence, weaken inhibitions, and arouse new interests, it must lie behind other trends as well. Moreover, insofar as the *nonstatistical* techniques mentioned in (3) are concerned, a major result of economists' changed conception of themselves has been an increased emphasis on economics as the logic of optimizing choice and thus a decreased emphasis on it as a theory of behavior. Analysts equipped with these techniques have become fairly general advisers where uncertainty and complex allocation problems are involved, and their advice has chiefly concerned the mathematics, or pure logic, of the calculations, rather than theses about how people behave.[16] Another major result has been increased interest in theories of collective decision-making generally —a broader category than government policy-making, and one that is, in various respects, both more inclusive and less inclusive than the overall field of behavior that this paper talks about—government policy-making plus public administration.

Most of the trends, of course, represent types of thinking that are not particularly new. Apart from the highly abstract theses listed under (e), none differs greatly in its subject matter or its mode of reasoning from exceptions that were mentioned, or could have been mentioned, in Part I's comments on the mainstream tradition. For the most part, the term *trend* refers to differences in ambitiousness and frequency rather than in kind. Nor, even in this sense, have the trends gone far enough, or involved a large enough part of the fraternity deeply enough—or been sufficiently similar to each other— to replace mainstream economists' traditional conception of their function with another, equally unified one. Each, however, in its own way represents a noteworthy partial merger of positive economics and positive political theory, and collectively they represent a much higher degree of merger than the exceptions in which mainsteam economists earlier indulged.

The rest of Part II briefly describes and comments on these trends away from the mainstream tradition. (It does not, of course, inquire about the theses' validity. Part II's function is to contrast recent analytical practices with those of mainstream economics, not to evaluate the trends as contributions to knowledge.)

Government Behavior in the Soviet-Type and Other Types of Centrally Administered Economies

As the list of trends indicated, Part I's distinction between administration and policy-making is also quite relevant here. One kind of analysis of government behavior in centrally administered economies has concerned state enterprise (more specifically, their managements in Soviet-type economies); another has concerned top economic officials.

The former has in several respects fairly closely resembled mainstream microeconomics—in its subject matter, its mode of reasoning, its specificity, and its integration. Indeed, it is not too farfetched to say that, just as analyses of consumers', wage-earners', and market farmers' responses in Soviet-type economies have been specialized uses of mainstream theory, so analyses of Soviet-type state enterprises have often been an extension of the familiar reasoning, an ingenious adaptation of the mainstream theory of the business firm to "the firm's" changed environment. The behavior pictured has been consistently optimizing, differential responses to different (positive) directives and (negative) constraints and to varying emphases placed on the success criteria.[17] Both sets of variables, both the autonomous and the dependent, have been either the same as mainstream theory's or sufficiently like them to be fairly easily treated as substitutes or complements. Conclusions about direction of change have been fairly specific, fairly directly testable.

Other similarities also deserve mention. Like the theorists who constructed the mainstream model of "the firm", the analysts who have advanced theses about Soviet-type state enterprise believe that they have been able to take advantage of the principle of large numbers. More specifically, they believe that their theorizings reflect a great mass of empirical evidence and that their generalizations are descriptions of representative behavior. Also, just as mainstream economists have regarded their theories as at least potential, indirect advice to policy-makers in largely market economies, so the analysts of Soviet-type state enterprises have regarded theirs as at least potential, indirect advice to central planners.

Much theorizing about plans also has borrowed heavily from mainstream economics—but mostly in a very different way. Here, what analysts have chiefly done with the familiar reasoning has been to use welfare economics to appraise plans' results, or, in other words, to ask whether planners have enshrined the related principles of "consumer sovereignty" and "allocational efficiency."[18] When planners' *behavior* has been the dependent variable, apparently the micro and macro models' chief function has been to show that certain actions seem designed to "cure imbalances", make allocation "more rational", or satisfy households' wants to a greater extent. Although, "in principle", mainstream economics' central assumption of optimizing can be extended to all studies of "rational" human endeavor, students of central administration (like political scientists over the centuries) have not been able to identify and quantify nearly well enough to attempt as thorough a theory as that of Soviet-type state enterprise. Nor have they been able to make nearly as effective use of the principle of large numbers. For every central planning board in a Soviet-type economy there has been a host of managements subject to its directives, and the history of modern, fairly thorough-going central administration has been short.

But, to repeat, there have been generalizations about plans' and plannings' characteristics, and the preceding paragraph has pointed to a quite important type. When examining the record in order to appraise it, many students of central administration have concluded that planned programs, on the whole, pay little attention to households' preferences and that, indeed, planning procedures are inconsistent with "rational" allocation even in the broader sense of that term. In reaching these conclusions, some analysts have also generalized about more directly observable features of planned programs, i.e., have listed common characteristics. On the whole, such generalizing has been cautious, usually drawing conclusions only about what *has been*, but at least one paper (based chiefly on Nazi experience) has boldly offered theses about central administration's very nature. Top decisions in such economies, said Walter Eucken in 1948, *will have* certain characteristics and will have them for certain reasons. More specifically:

Central administrators will not "graft" scarcity-reflecting prices on to the "controlling mechanism" but will "reserve the direction" of economic activity for themselves; will rely on "standardization and the fixing of norms and types for production"; will prefer maximum scale when new factories are built; will "as a rule" seek a "maximum of investment" and thus cut consumption to the "Subsistence Minimum" required for efficient, energetic work, will fit

distribution "into the production programmes so as to promote maximum output", and will (where such institutions exist) transform cartels, cooperative associations, and labor unions into "instruments of control."

When explaining why central officials will act in these ways, Eucken stressed the fundamental goals of government power and economic growth and the instrumental goals of keeping planning and implementation workably easy.[19]

Even such an analysis as Eucken's, of course, does not offer nearly as complete a theory of central planners' behavior as the analyses of state enterprises offer of managements'. (Comments here concern coverage, not validity.) Nor is the latter as thorough as the mainstream theory of the firm, despite marked similarities to it. An Eucken-like theory of central administration plus the now available theories of state enterprise plus the mainstream theories of consumers', wage-earners', and market farmers' responses do not, collectively, provide nearly as full a story of centrally administered economies as Marshall plus Walras plus Keynes provide of the types of economies that used to be chiefly studied. But, obviously, they provide much fuller coverage than the theories of consumers, wage-earners, and farmers would, unassisted; they concern more of the subjects that an avid seeker of knowledge would like to learn about —and more of the questions that a "sovereign" logically should ask when choosing between alternative systems. Also, as the preceding section stated, Marshall plus Walras plus Keynes do not explain any of today's economies nearly as fully as they do those chiefly studied when the mainstream tradition was formed. Analyses of centrally administered economies are not, *comparatively*, as incomplete as first thoughts about their limitations may seem to indicate.

Government Behavior in Economically Underdeveloped Countries

Much of the analysis that can come under this heading can also come under the preceding one. Much of the literature on government behavior in underdeveloped economies concerns the management of state enterprise and the character of central planning, which are not particularly uncommon in the underdeveloped world and which have often been proposed where they are not present. This section, however, concerns rather different types of reasoning. Analysis of "underdeveloped" administration usually has not been an extension of mainstream theory, neither the theory of an optimizing, calculating household nor the theory of an optimizing, calculating firm. Instead of picturing differential response to differential directives and constraints, it has concerned general qualities of behavior at the administrative level, i.e., the honesty, energy, diligence, and competence that bureaucrats bring to their jobs—and thus has returned to basic questions that early economists often asked but which mainstream economics either ignored or swept under the rug called *ceteris paribus*. Similarly, most analysis of "underdeveloped" policy-making has not concentrated on the same topics as the Von Mises-Hayek-Lange-Lerner-Eucken-et al controversy, but instead has chiefly asked how to increase the quantity and improve the quality of available resources—and in this way it too has returned to one of the central questions of preneoclassical days. On the whole, the literature reads much more like "economic history" than like the theory of value and distribution.

Of the two categories of government behavior, administrators' and policy-makers', the former has, for an obvious reason, received more attention. Although development economics may, like other branches of "the discipline," advise sovereigns about top officials, the parties that it usually addresses are those officials themselves, i.e., the legislators and high-level bureaucrats who choose the contents of development programs. On the whole, warnings have predominated. Students of the developing economies have argued that administration will be significantly faulty in one or more respects.

Elliott G. Berg's paper on tropical Africa provides one of the clearest examples here. The state, Berg argues, "cannot and should not bear the burden that most African socialists would put upon it," chiefly because adequately trained people are lacking and "will not be available for some time," but also because corruption and poor attitudes toward work are "notably troublesome" in the public sector and because "intense" political pressures further reduce efficiency there. Among other regional studies that can be mentioned are Lauchlin Currie's on Latin America and Benjamin Higgins' on Indonesia, the former because of its comment that a national development program should not rely on "a level of administrative competence that is not generally available," the latter because of its harsh judgment that, below an able but small group at the very top, there is "an almost complete absence of administrative training, experience, and ability." More general works that have expressed similar conclusions include (*inter alia*) books by Higgins, P. T. Bauer, Bauer and Basil S. Yamey, and Norman S. Buchanan and Howard S. Ellis. All stress administrative shortcomings, including laxity and corruption, and the last also points to certain "attitudes . . . not well adapted for the planning and execution" of development programs, e.g., "nepotism and ethnic and religious loyalties" and the view of public office "as one of indisputable right rather than of public responsibility."[20]

Some of the writing on administration involves a second level of political theory, and goes beyond the minimum requirements of policy advice by offering explanations for the described behavior. Thus, Berg finds a reason for the Africans' attitude toward work in their former status as subordinates; Currie believes public servants' poor performance partly the result of relatively low salaries; and J. R. Hicks, inquiring why Ceylonese state enterprises have usually fared so badly, attributes the record to a combination of "monopoly," "politics," and an insufficient number of "persons of authority."[21] Generalizations about the nature of administrative behavior have, however, been much commoner than theses about its causes.

Development economists who have in some way theorized about policy decisions include (*inter alia*) Higgins (again on Indonesia), Currie (on Latin America), Hirschman (chiefly on Latin America), Bauer (chiefly on Africa and Asia), Antonin Basch (on development finance), and Harley H. Hinrichs (on tax structure). Among the questions they have considered are obstacles to land reform (Hirschman); indecisiveness in choosing between rivals routes to development (Higgins); reliance on foreign aid and inflationary measures (Currie, Hirschman, Basch); the regional and the urban-rural distribution of benefits and burdens (Hirschman, Bauer); and the significance of an economy's "openness," per capita income, and (governmental) "cultural style" for sources of revenue (Hinrichs).[22]

On the whole, these conclusions about policy-making seem chiefly to reflect an interest in social science per se, or, in other words, a desire to explain for the sake of the satisfaction that knowledge can give. But presumably at least some of the analysts wish their analyses to play an economic advisory role as well, i.e., to point to some of the consequences of various kinds of reliance on state action; and some of the conclusions sound very much like "practical politics" in that they concern the likelihood or unlikelihood of persuading policy-makers to act in certain ways. Hirschman's interests especially appear to be a "practical" political theorist's, both when he generalizes about underdeveloped economies as a type and when he comments on such special cases as Colombia and Chile.

Government Behavior in Predominantly Market, Relatively Advanced Economies

Types of analysis that come under this general heading include statistical studies of public expenditure; theses concerning resources policy; theses about monetary and fiscal authorities not bound by rigid rules; cost-push analyses; and theories of political countervailing power and of cumulative intervention. True, in one sense of the term, none of these can be called a recent trend. None, as *a type of thinking about economic questions,* is either very new or represents a return to an earlier way of thought. Statistical analyses of government spending go back at least to the days of Adolf Wagner; turn-of-the-century writings on "public goods" were precursors of those on resources policy; arguments contra managed currencies were early examples of the next group of analyses, those concerning monetary and fiscal authorities not bound by rigid rules; theses about retaliatory tariffs resemble both the last two types in at least one major respect, i.e., in their being a step toward a more nearly general theory of politico-economic interdependence. But, as is stated above, this paper does not discuss recent departures from the mainstream because their general type of reasoning is particularly new—or recently revived—but because they now comprise a much greater, and a growing, part of the literature turned out by economists who, on the whole, descend more from Marshall and Walras than from the heterodoxies. The term *trend* chiefly refers to ambitiousness and frequency.

STATISTICAL ANALYSES OF GOVERNMENT SPENDING. Among studies of this general sort are those asking about determinants of (1) per capita overall public or national government expenditure in particular countries, (2) per capita state and local expenditure in the United States, and (3) certain kinds of public spending, such as outlays on education. Among examples of (1) are Alan T. Peacock and Jack Wiseman's book on Great Britain, G. Colm and M. Helzner's paper on the United States, and Wilfrid Lewis's paper on the federal sector in national income models;[23] examples of (2) include, *inter alia*, a series of papers in the 1961–1966 *National Tax Journal*;[24] a paper on (3) that might be mentioned is Julius Margolis's on metropolitan finance.[25]

Between 1890 and 1955, say Peacock and Wiseman, the curve of British per capita government expenditure was "a series of plateaus separated by . . . peaks which coincide with the periods of war or preparation for war," and this evidence suggests that, when "societies are not being subjected to unusual pressures," people's ideas of "tolerable burdens of taxation" and "reasonable tax rates" tend also to be rather stable, but that long-lasting change comes with "large-scale social disturbances, such as major wars." These "disturbances," they argue, not only shift revenues to new, higher levels at the time but also create a "displacement effect" which reshapes ideas about "tolerable tax levels." Looking at the United States, Colm and Helzner see much the same story but add the Great Depression to the major wars as a source of long-lived change. Lewis agrees and, incorporating this thesis into a forecasting model, argues that it usually is not "really necessary" to leave as wide a margin for contingencies as is usually found. Despite all talk about spenders and savers, he comments, Congressional elections that alter their relative strengths do not seem to affect total expenditure very much.[26]

"Determining" variables that the *National Tax Journal* authors inserted into their correlations included various income figures, various population figures, certain fiscal data, certain educational data, and a strictly political index (an index of the two-party system). The method of analysis employed was statistical best fit (between certain of these variables and state and local expenditure per capita).

Margolis tied his study to the hypothesis "the greater the number of products offered in the package to the voter, the greater the likelihood of adoption" and found evidence for that reasoning, concluding that "fiscally dependent" departments of education spend more per capita than independent districts and do so because they are functional divisions of a governmental unit. Educational grants from higher-level to lower-level governments, he added, have more commonly occurred where political resistance to locally financed services has been the greatest.[27]

THESES CONCERNING RESOURCES POLICY. Recent analyses of resources policy[28] have, in major respects, been very like analyses of Soviet-type and other central planning. To the extent that they have treated government behavior as a dependent variable, they have chiefly inquired about policy's "efficiency," or, in other words, have asked whether government actions usually have been, and may be expected to be, consistent with the goal of welfare economics. Thus, Margolis, appraising federal irrigation projects, argues that the prices charged are "generally inefficient," and are so because "efficiency," which conflicts with other goals, usually does not govern public-project decisions. No project has ever repaid its cost, he concludes, and in most cases neither farmers nor Congress would accept the degree of price discrimination required for even a potentially self-supporting project to dispense with subsidies. Jack Hirshleifer, James C. De Haven, and Jerome W. Milliman reach similar, more general conclusions with respect to water-supply policies more generally. Unthinking enthusiasm they argue, has caused both policy-planners and legislators to underestimate the costs and overestimate the benefits of developing water resources and, indeed, to lose sight of the principle of optimum use of resources. Moreover, "log-rolling," "pork-barrel" and "patronage" incentives tend to be prevalent in all government decision-making, so that, when the federal government (rather than the states and local units) pays all or a large part of the costs of navigation, prospective beneficiaries have "extremely strong incentives" to push for further government spending of this kind.[29]

THESES ABOUT MONETARY AND FISCAL AUTHORITIES NOT BOUND BY RIGID RULES. Few politico-economic issues have received as much attention in the postwar United States as has the question of "rules versus discretion" in monetary and fiscal spheres.[30] Controversy has been intense, widespread, and prolonged. Insofar as the argument has concerned Federal Reserve behavior, Harry G. Johnson has already provided a succinct summary:

> . . . the real issues are whether the monetary authorities are likely to take appropriate action at the right time, and whether the effects of monetary action on the economy occur soon enough and reliably enough to have a sufficient stabilizing effect.
>
> As to the first question, there is general agreement that the Federal Reserve has committed errors in the timing, extent, and duration of policy changes. Most economists seem inclined to trust the System to improve its performance with experience and the benefit of their criticism. Some, however, are so distrustful of discretionary

authority in principle, or so skeptical of the feasibility of effective stabilization by monetary means, as to advocate that the Federal Reserve should not attempt short-run stabilization. . . .[31]

Johnson's topic, however, kept him from discussing the fiscal aspect of the same general controversy, which he could have summarized in an essentially parallel statement. Also, the pressure of space discouraged spelling out the political reasoning that has led Milton Friedman and other advocates of "rules" to oppose more active stabilization policies.[32]

The overall record, argues Friedman, has been quite bad. Both because of irrelevant or inappropriate objectives and because of limited knowledge, Federal Reserve and fiscal policies have on the whole been net contributors to *in*stability—will continue to have this effect as long as the authorities exercise short-run discretionary powers. When not governed by rigid rules, monetary and fiscal policy often are dominated by other goals incompatible with stability, and, in addition to these goals, inertia and political considerations tend to inhibit ready reversals of policy. Moreover, when policy-makers do attempt short-run stabilization, three types of lags make correct action quite unlikely, namely, those between the need for action and the recognition of that need, the recognition of the need and the actions taken, and the actions taken and their effects. More generally, decision-making experience as a whole shows the folly of trying to consider each case on its own merits. One of the arguments for relying on rules is that, much of the time, decision-makers will examine a limited area only, not try to take into account the cumulative consequences of the whole body of policy.[33]

Economists friendlier to more active stabilization policies have, obviously, at least implicitly rejected much of the Friedman reasoning. As Johnson states, they seem "inclined to trust" the Federal Reserve—and also the fiscal policy-makers—"to improve . . . performance with experience and the benefit of their criticism".[34] But unfortunately (for this paper) the best known "pre-discretion" writings have not analyzed relevant government behavior nearly as explicitly and as thoroughly as have the arguments for "rules." As is often the case, expressions of comparative faith in prevailing practices have not included as detailed explanations as have expressions of distrust.

COST-PUSH ANALYSES. The question here, as in the preceding section, is whether particular stimuli will lead to particular monetary and fiscal actions. But the stimuli are wage boosts and other upward pressures on the supply side, instead of general swings of business activity, and the actions are increases in the volume of money, not "correct" stabilization measures. Indeed, one way of wording the debate is to ask whether monetary and fiscal authorities *act as if* they possess discretionary powers or instead, as in the old literature on the gold standard, *react like* mere automata.

This, of course, is not to argue that the reasoning is usually so explicit that when cost push is the subject, the analysts usually say how government behaves. But the issue is always at least implicit, and some writings have directly asked how stabilization authorities react to cost push. Among the economists who have been thus explicit are J. R. Hicks, G. L. Bach, Abba P. Lerner, K. E. Poole, and William G. Bowen.

Hicks' paper, written after a decade of postwar British experience, virtually reversed the neoclassical theory of money and wages, arguing that monetary (plus fiscal) policy adjusts itself to the prevailing wage level, rather than wage rates to the volume of money. Indeed, Hicks argued, it was not misleading (in 1955) to say that Britain was on a "Labour Standard." Bach, taking a look at the United States just before the 1957 recession, similarly believed that he saw the "sacrosanctity of full employment" and thus argued that "large organizations and power groups" felt free to push wages and prices steadily upward in search of larger shares of total income. No political party, he thought, could "seriously consider inaction when unemployment mounts." Lerner, writing after the phenomenon of inflationary recession, inserted a qualifying parenthesis in his prediction, namely, that the country's full-employment policy might be rather shaky" in its applications, but he too argued that no government "would carry out or even seriously attempt to carry out" a policy of choking cost-push inflation by letting unemployment mount. Poole and Bowen, although representing a theoretical Right (to Hicks' theoretical Far Left), also departed from the mainstream tradition. Poole, after looking at the 1948 and 1953 recessions, reached the negative conclusions that government is not likely to use inflationary finance to combat relatively small, widely distributed unemployment resulting from aggressive wages policies. Bowen, although criticizing Hicks' thesis as "extreme," argued that the authorities' *ability* to control the stock of money does not justify treating that stock "as a completely exogenous or independent variable."[35]

THEORIES OF POLITICAL COUNTERVAILING POWER AND OF CUMULATIVE INTERVENTION. Mention of countervailing power of course brings Galbraith's best-seller to mind. Although its chapter nine, "The Theory of Countervailing Power," chiefly concerns concentrations within the business world, chapter ten, "Countervailing Power and the State," is an essay in political theory, in which the author takes a look at the post-1932 decades and concludes that "the support of countervailing power has become . . . perhaps the major peacetime function of the federal government." Citing the examples of the Wagner Act, the National Bituminous Coal Act, farm legislation, and ("in a considerably more tenuous form") the SEC, he argues that, although political responses to "original power" may not be quick or sure, time lags seem to be growing shorter and domestic political struggle probably will increasingly concern "efforts to develop countervailing power."[36]

Although he apparently does not intend it to be such, Galbraith's thesis can serve as a stepping-stone toward a theory of cumulative intervention—the reason for listing the two together here. Resembling the "conservative" argument that political "favors" "corrupt," it can (via a major shift in emphasis and attitude) be transformed into such a theory as Wilhelm Röpke's, which, denouncing "unhealthy pluralism," sows an unending succession of uses of political power—as groups become more and more accustomed to, and dependent on, government control over income distribution.[37]

A second kind of theorizing that shows cumulative intervention has quite a different emphasis, assigning the key role to market disequilibrium instead of to "corruption" of the electorate. Following the lead that Von Mises gave in the 1920's, these analyses describe a sequence of interventions started by policy-makers' economic naiveté and continued by a combination of that naiveté, the market effects of government policies, and the policy-makers' stubborn refusal to accept the market's verdict. Contributors to this literature, which was fairly extensive during the forties and fifties, include (inter alia) Von Mises himself, Röpke, Walter Eucken, Alfred Müller-Armack, and Milton Friedman.[38] For a decade or more, however, such arguments have been less common, perhaps chiefly because of trends in policies (away from some of the types and degrees of interventionism deplored).

Arguments about Some Political Fundamentals

Just as thought about political countervailing power leads easily to thought about cumulative intervention, so thought about the latter easily leads to ponderings about this section's subject. Apparently, most economists who have argued that intervention leads finally to thorough state control have looked upon their argument as a warning, and a major reason for the warning has been the belief that such control leads to the end of political democracy and civil liberties. Names listed immediately above can be repeated here: Von Mises, Röpke, Eucken, Friedman.[39]

But, despite this connection, theses about this section's general topic differ basically from the cumulative-intervention and other analyses discussed above—which ask only about government actions in the "economic sphere" and which chiefly do so because of those actions' significance for mainstream economics' central variables, i.e., for prices, outputs, inputs, and incomes. This section's theses express an interest in political conditions and happenings per se. As the section on causes stated, they reflect a belief that economics' traditional variables are *relatively* less important than they once were in "reasonably relevant" policy appraisals.

On the whole, the trend that such analyses represent was strongest during World War II and the immediate postwar period, between the years marked, at the beginning, by F. A. Hayek's *The Road to Serfdom* and, at the end, by D. M. Wright's *Capitalism*.[40] But more recent writings also have appeared, including (*inter alia*) Friedman's *Capitalism and Freedom*, which, like the Hayek and Wright volumes, finds central planning and political liberty incompatible; Henry C. Wallich's *The Cost of Freedom*, which criticizes that thesis as too sweeping, too unqualified; and Calvin B. Hoover's *The Economy, Liberty, and the State*, which surveys the record of four decades and concludes that ". . . there seems to be no close . . . correlation between the degree of state intervention and control of the economy and the net limitation upon personal liberty."[41]

Highly Abstract Theses about Government Fairly Generally

Two kinds of analysis come under this general heading: pure theories of government behavior, sometimes called economic theories of government because of their resemblance to familiar mainstream models, and analyses contributed by economists but differing markedly from the pure theories in that their mode or reasoning is more in the political-science tradition.

PURE THEORIES.   As the section on causes stated, these reflect some economists' new conception of themselves as possessors of techniques more than they do the altered nature of the economies chiefly studied. Like the theses about political fundamentals, but unlike the analyses discussed earlier, they reflect an interest in government and politics per se—as is shown by their central topics:

elections, general policy-making, constitution-making, bureaucratic behavior, and strategy in international affairs. Writings that have presented such pure theories include (*inter alia*) Anthony Downs, *An Economic Theory of Democracy*, James M. Buchanan and Gordon Tullock, *The Calculus of Consent*, Mancür Olson, Jr., *The Logic of Collective Action*, Gordon Tullock, *The Politics of Bureaucracy*, Anthony Downs, "A Theory of Bureaucracy," Thomas C. Schelling, *The Strategy of Conflict*, and Kenneth E. Boulding, *Conflict and Defense* and "Toward a Pure Theory of Threat Systems." (As the titles suggest, the listing here roughly follows the order of topics above.)[42]

These theories resemble traditional microeconomics in quite important ways.

First, their analytical procedure is to begin with initial grand assumptions (maximizing, minimizing, minimaxing, etc.), then introduce limiting conditions, and then derive conclusions believed to help explain and predict behavior.

Next, just as utility-maximization and profit-maximization models lead to rather vague predictions about market participants' relevant attitudes and beliefs, so would-be users of the political models run up against this problem of identification. Similarly, the relationships between (on the one side) stated grand assumptions plus limiting conditions and (on the other side) stated *testable* conclusions seem to be parallel within the two bodies of reasoning. Just as the history of micro-economics shows that operational propositions preceded an accurate statement of the necessary conditions and that the pure theory was largely inferred from the operational propositions, rather than the propositions deduced from it, so a look at the testable conclusions in, say, Downs' and Tullock's books (which present more testable conclusions than the other listed writings) suggests such a thesis. The suspicion arises that the propositions were fitted into a theory which they helped bring into being, rather than derived from it, and that perhaps the propositions *cannot* be derived from the assumptions until further (as yet unknown), complementary conditions are stated. In other words, the theories' value seems, wholly or chiefly, to lie in the guidance they give to thought, and perhaps also in the flashes of insight they may inspire, rather than in their ability to provide ready answers.

Finally, both in traditional microeconomics and in the pure theories of government behavior, conclusions about actions and conclusions about "welfare" are closely intertwined.[43] Deductions concerning behavior are accompanied by conclusions about the conditions of an optimum—or, at least, of an improvement. Indeed, as in the case of welfare economics, much of the reasoning does not concern observable behavior at all, but rather shows how changes in the environment will enable political bargainers to achieve preferred positions. This is especially true of Buchanan and Tullock's book, *The Calculus of Consent*, which takes on the job of deducing an "optimum" constitution.

But, to repeat, these pure theories are also unlike mainstream economics in a quite important respect. By analyzing government, they depart from the mainstream tradition—and by displaying an interest in government and politics per se, they depart quite radically. Indeed, a good case can be made for the argument that, despite their "economic" appearance, they represent a greater move away from the mainstream than do most of the trends described above. Thus, although Downs lists 25 "testable propositions" in *An Economic Theory of Democracy*, only two have dependent economic variables, and these propositions are not very concrete, stating only that democratic governments tend to redistribute income from the rich to the poor and tend to favor producers more than consumers in their actions.[44] The other writings listed above are even less informative about economics' traditional topics. True, when dealing with policy-making, the pure theories warn about the political constraints that limit the range of adoptable policies; and when analyzing bureaucracy, they warn about constraints that limit the implementation of policies.[45] But, at the moment, that is nearly all.

But, of course, the pure theories are still quite young.

THESES MORE IN THE POLITICAL-SCIENCE TRADITION. Charles E. Lindblom's writings provide examples here.[46] Legislators, the Yale economist argues, do not and cannot fit specific decisions into a comprehensively conceived, systematically integrated overall program but must instead make "incremental" changes through the give-and-take of "partisan mutual adjustment." Primarily, Lindblom seems to convey a normative message, since statements about abilities and behavior lead to conclusions concerning the relative merits of attempts at "comprehensive overviews" and of deliberate reliance on muddling through via the usual procedures of democratic government.[47] The nonnormative component of his analysis can, however, stand by itself, since he argues that "incremental" policy-making and "partisan mutual adjustment" *will* prevail and since he offers reasons why they will. Nor does his explanation consist solely of the statement that men don't do what they can't. Other parts of it are that conflicts of interest keep democracies from having clearly defined ends (or multidimensional indifference maps), that such conflicts must somehow be resolved, and that different agencies of government serve as the representatives of different interests.[48]

Some of Lindblom's writings concern certain types of legislation (e.g., budgets) and/or replies to certain economists' pleas for more orderly, more systematic policy-making (e.g., Smithies on budgets, Tinbergen on planning procedures); but, as both he and his critics have emphasized, these are merely particular applications of his reasoning.[49] What he offers are elements of a general theory of representative government.

III. THE TRENDS AND THE PAST AND FUTURE OF ECONOMICS

Parts I and II have already presented the paper's main conclusions:

Mainstream economics, the Cambridge-Lausanne-Vienna heritage, treated policy decisions as data and administrative actions either as data or as obedient, efficient follow-ups. The tradition of treating government in this way grew out of a complex mixture of reasons, which together created mainstream economists' conception of themselves as analysts of (nongovernmental) market behavior.

In recent decades there have been major trends away from the mainstream tradition: more specifically, analyses of policy-makers' and administrators' behavior in various types of economies, arguments about some political fundamentals, and pure theories of government. Most of these trends seem mainly attributable to the altered nature of the economies chiefly studied, but another cause has been some economists' conception of themselves as possessors of techniques.

Certain questions remain to be asked, however, questions concerning the trends' relationships to earlier economic thought and their possible significance for the future content of the "discipline."

The Trends and Earlier Thought

If Part II's analyses were chiefly a continuation of earlier, widespread thought within the general area of economics, they would be much less noteworthy phenomena—they would not be recent trends. One of the questions thus concerns their relationship to historicism-institutionalism, an intellectual movement never accepting the mainstream tradition. Certainly the trends share characteristics with that movement, including the belief that market analysis by itself is inadequate, emphasis on the economic role of the state, ambition for a theory of collective action, and (as a consequence thereof) a blurring of boundaries between economics and its fellow social sciences. Generalizations about policy-making sound quite institutionalist indeed; even the statistical studies bring Mitchell and Wagner to mind, not Marshall and Walras.

But, despite these similarities, the trends are not merely, or even largely, a mid-twentieth-century continuation of historicist-institutionalist thought. Instead, they are mostly the products of mainstream citadels, their authors chiefly the intellectual descendants of the Cambridge-Lausanne-Vienna greats, rather than the disciples of

Schmoller, Weber, and Sombart, or of Veblen, Patten, and Commons. Indeed, not only have most of the analysts not shared the historicist-institutionalist distrust of mainstream theory, they have relied heavily on it in much of their analysis of government behavior. Neoclassicism and mathematicism have, on the whole, been greater sources of aid than earlier writings dealing with the non-mainstream topic of collective action.

This last point, of course, should not be overstressed. As Part II indicated, neoclassicism's and mathematicism's aid has been most direct and greatest in the pure theories of government behavior and in analyses of Soviet-type state enterprises; elsewhere their chief contributions probably have been to the theory of cumulative intervention and to the welfare-economics preludes to generalizations about central planning and resources policy. Analytical aid from the mainstream sources has been slight or zero in the cases of some of the trends. But, to repeat, an interesting feature of some movements away from the mainstream tradition has been the extent to which they have utilized mainstream economics.

Two other types of earlier thought that the trends bring to mind are pre-mainstream theorizings about economic development and, of course, certain elements of traditional political science. The former was a long-ago precursor of recent development economics; the latter has been a continuing part of a cousin "discipline," so that no long lag occurred between its appearance in such analyses as, say, Pendleton Herring's and its incorporation in Lindblom's writings. But, even though these predecessors are there for all to see, the term *recent trends* still seems justified; the analyses still seem noteworthy. After all, about a century passed between the development economics of the earlier period and the recent parallel thought, and it was quite a notable event when an economist borrowed from political science in order to theorize better about economic policy.

The Trends and the Future Content of the Discipline

Perhaps the basic question about the future is whether the trends will continue, i.e., whether nonheterodox economists will continue, on a fairly large scale, to analyze government behavior. Both Part I's musings about reasons for the mainstream tradition and Part II's pondering about reasons for departures from it are, of course, relevant here, and together they imply that the trends' continuation is very likely. Political economics will hardly recede unless two improbable conditions are met, i.e., unless the politico-economic environment returns to its former pattern and economists reject the conception of themselves as possessors of techniques. True, there is the possibility that both political economics and market economics will shrivel and programming will take over, or, in other words, that economists will come to think of themselves chiefly as applied mathematicians telling decision-makers how to choose. But, despite the meteoric rise of this side of the profession, it is hard to believe that its triumph will be so thorough. As Part II emphasized, one aspect of interest in techniques has been a desire to use them as aids in theorizing, as well as aids to choice.

An opposite question to whether political economics will recede is whether it will come to be regarded as part of the "discipline's" core, i.e., whether curricula will honor it as an equal partner of market economics and the mathematics of choice. This, too, seems unlikely, since, as Part II showed, the analyses of government lack the integration, elegance, and precision that have been market economics' pride; and although the pure theories of government *may* eventually supply integration and elegance, there is little evidence so far that they will do so, and precision seems even more improbable. The history of political science suggests that most theorems about government must remain at least as vague as the vaguer ones about oligopoly and bargaining.

Another possible outcome, of a very different sort, is migration from economics to political science, or, in other words, analysts of government ceasing to think of themselves primarily as economists and affiliating more and more with the other social science. The record of both historicism and institutionalism shows how this can happen, since quite a few sociologists began their careers as members of those schools. But this too seems improbable—or, at least, *mass* migration does. As the paper has stressed, analysis that treats government actions as data is today more incomplete than it was a few decades ago, so that mass departure of political economists from the discipline would mean that economists would either have to reconcile themselves to such incompleteness or to depend on political scientists to make the analysis less incomplete; and the second of these alternatives would mean that the analysts who left the economics fraternity would have to continue to concentrate on "economically interesting" government behavior—and to train successors to carry on the tradition.

Some branches of political economics may, indeed, migrate. One of the candidates here is analysis of economic systems' effects on political fundamentals. As Part II pointed out, theses about these questions treat the dependent political variables as "terminal," not merely as intermediate; they do not, like most of the other trends, concern "economically interesting" government behavior. Another candidate is pure theory, which also seems chiefly to reflect an interest in government and politics per se and so far has said little that is definite about economic phenomena. A plausible hypothesis is that these two kinds of analysis will come to look less and less like political interests within economics and more and more like economic-policy and other interests within political science, while analyses of Soviet-type economies, "underdeveloped" policy-making, "underdeveloped" administration, budgets, central bankers' behavior, and the like remain governmental areas of economists' endeavors. But, to repeat, *mass* migration of political economics seems quite unlikely.

A kindred, and in some ways more radical, development would be for political economics to become a sort of "discipline" of its own, or, in other words, for its expounders to form their own professional body and publish their own professional journals. Certain moves in this direction already have occurred. But, partly for the same reasons that seem to rule out the above possibilities, this outcome too seems rather improbable. The various branches of political economics have too little in common with each other, and too much in common with policy-minded economics as a whole, for such a union to be "natural." There is too little cohesion holding the various parts together, too much adhesion pulling them apart. Very probably, movements toward particular subdisciplines will continue, but not toward a comprehensive one including all or most political economics.

But, of course, the record of peerings into the future reveals many a bad guess. Perhaps the safest prediction is that economics will continue to be at least as mixed a mixture as it has been in the past, that economists' interests will continue to be wide-ranging, and that the "discipline's" development (like that of other institutions) will conform to the laws of an institutional logic instead of to rules of system or order. This leaves quite a few possible paths for political economics.

NOTES

1. More specific topics that come under the third of these headings are statistical studies of public expenditure, theses about resources policy, theses about monetary and fiscal authorities not bound by rigid rules, cost-push analyses, and theories of political countervailing power and cumulative intervention.

2. Indeed, the warning transmitted by the Latin phrase has amounted to "if no other independent change takes place *and* if the posited independent change affects the dependent micro and/or macro variables *only* through the routes that the theory pictures." (The same seems to be true of *mutatis-mutandis* propositions, which presumably do not claim to take into account all channels of influence, but only those to which the analyses pay attention.)

3. Stanislaw Wellisz, *The Economies of the Soviet Bloc* (New York: McGraw-Hill, 1964), p. 7.

4. Walter A. Morton, "Keynesianism and Inflation," *Journal of Political Economy*, vol. 59 (June 1951), pp. 258–61.

5. As some of the statements below indicate, there is no clear boundary between policy-making and administrative behavior. The general concepts, however, seem to be helpful. This paper does not discuss a third

general category of government behavior, constitution-making, which Buchanan and Tullock stress in *The Calculus of Consent* (Ann Arbor: University of Michigan Press, 1962); nor does it divide policy-making and administration into subcategories that differ significantly from each other for some analytical purposes.

6. Talk about "efficiency," of course, introduces questions about an agency's ability to achieve certain results as well as to act in certain ways and thus moves discussion beyond the strict boundaries of a theory of administrative *behavior*. All economic analysis that expresses conclusions about policies' effects ipso facto includes at least one positive political element, i.e., belief that the governmental agencies involved are able, in the situation analyzed, to achieve these effects. This paper, however, pays little attention to this variety of positive political theory.

7. The danger of tautology is obvious here. But an accurate statement avoiding this danger would be long and complex. Which of the two interpretations to assign the mainstream theory does not seem to be an important question. Their implications for applied economics appear to be the same.

8. The distinction between the two roles does not concern the formal analytical apparatus employed, since *marginalism* may be used in either way, but the precise questions asked and their purposes. Social science (as defined here) consists of (conceivably falsifiable) generalizations about behavior; economics as the logic of choice does not. Of course, to the extent that a would-be optimizer (or his adviser) uses "marginalism" to predict other persons' or groups' behavior, the optimization calculations themselves involve social science—and presumably this is the usual case. But such calculations need not involve social science, since they may not include predictions about others' behavior. Also, when they do include such predictions, these may not have been gained via the "marginalist" route.

9. That is, its role of guiding policy by offering predictions about relevant behavior (not by providing a mathematics of optimizing choice).

10. Logic does not, however, rule out predicting a *range* of policymakers' behavior—if that range is "reasonably" wide. Policy advisers may choose to study only those alternatives they believe to have a "reasonable" chance of being seriously considered (within the time period for which the advice is believed to be relevant and by the advisees to whom it is directed).

11. "Pure logic" also calls for a distinction between the predictions in advice given individual members, or other divisions, of a policy-making body and those in advice given the body as a whole—although various middle principles of political philosophy may, by demanding certain kinds of action from the individual members, make the "pure logic" irrelevant; i.e., the middle principles may forbid parts of a policy-

making body to employ strategies that make this distinction significant.

12. This, of course, is not to say that mainstream economists believed that "marginalist" language could not be used to express a highly abstract "pure theory" of policy-makers' and public administrators' behavior. Merely, they did not believe that such a pure theory would provide much in the way of clues for operationally-minded analysts.

13. Some of the most noted of these have been analysts whose more narrowly economic writings placed them within the Cambridge-Lausanne-Vienna, rather than the Marxist or historicist, tradition. Among the interwar examples that come to mind are Ludwig von Mises and Joseph Schumpeter.

14. The changes referred to here include all the various ways in which the state has assumed a larger and more active role in the economies of Western and Central Europe and the English-speaking countries overseas: i.e., the bigger budgets, the budgets' purposes and the ways in which they are financed, and the scope and nature of state enterprise and of governmental regulatory, promotional, and stabilization measures generally.

15. The boundaries between these categories are of course not clear; much overlap occurs.

16. Obviously, to the extent that the techniques themselves embody explicit or implicit conclusions about behavior (e.g., linear input-output relationships), they are not pure mathematics but include a theoretical component. But the technicians' advice is sought—or offered—because of the mathematical expertise, not because of the quite often dubious theory of behavior involved.

17. See, *inter alia*, Edward Ames, *Soviet Economic Processes* (Homewood, Ill.: Richard D. Irwin, 1965).

18. See, *inter alia*, Abram Bergson, *The Economics of Soviet Planning* (New Haven: Yale University Press, 1964).

19. Walter Eucken, "On the Theory of the Centrally Administered Economy: An Analysis of the German Experiment," *Economica*, n.s., vol. 15 (May and Aug. 1948), pp. 79–100 and 173–93.

20. Elliot G. Berg, "Socialism and Economic Development in Tropical Africa," *Quarterly Journal of Economics*, vol. 68 (Nov. 1964), pp. 549–73; Laughlin Currie, *Accelerating Development* (New York: McGraw-Hill, 1966); Benjamin Higgins, *Indonesia's Economic Stabilization and Development* (New York: Institute of Pacific Relations, 1957), and *Economic Development* (New York: W. W. Norton, 1959); P. T. Bauer, *Economic Analysis and Policy in Underdeveloped Countries* (Durham, N.C.: Duke University Press, 1957); Bauer and Basil S. Yamey, *The Economics of Underdeveloped Countries* (Chicago: University of Chicago Press, 1957); and Norman S. Buchanan and Howard S. Ellis,

Approaches to Economic Development (New York: Twentieth Century Fund, 1955).

21. Berg, p. 570; Currie, p. 195; and J. R. Hicks, *Essays in World Economics* (Oxford: The Clarendon Press, 1959), pp. 207–209.

22. Higgins, pp. 108, 118, 124–25; Currie, p. 52; Hirschman, *Journeys Toward Progress* (New York: Twentieth Century Fund, 1963), pp. 135–38, 222–23, and *The Strategy of Economic Development* (New Haven: Yale University Press, 1958), pp. 18, 190–92; Bauer, pp. 66–67, 82–84; Antonin Basch, *Financing Economic Development* (New York: Macmillan, 1964), pp. vii, 10–11, 93, 98–99; and Harley H. Hinrichs, *A General Theory of Tax Structure Change during Economic Development* (Cambridge: The Law School of Harvard University, 1966).

23. Alan T. Peacock and Jack Wiseman, *The Growth of Public Expenditure in the United Kingdom* (Princeton: Princeton University Press, for the National Bureau of Economic Research, 1961); G. Colm and M. Helzner, "The Structure of Government Revenue and Expenditure in Relation to the Economic Development of the United States" (cited by Peacock and Wiseman, p. xxx, fn. 6) in *L'Importance et la Structure des Recettes et des Depenses Publiques*, International Institute of Public Finance (Brussels 1960); and Wilfred Lewis, "The Federal Sector in National Income Models," *Models of Income Determination*, Studies in Income and Wealth, vol. 28 (Princeton: Princeton University Press, for the National Bureau of Economic Research, 1964).

24. Glenn W. Fisher, "Determinants of State and Local Expenditures: A Preliminary Analysis," *National Tax Journal*, vol. 14 (Dec. 1961), pp. 349–52; Seymour Sacks and Robert Harris, "The Determinants of State and Local Government Expenditure," *National Tax Journal*, vol. 17 (March 1964), pp. 75–85; Ernest Kunow, "Determinants of State and Local Expenditures Reexamined," *National Tax Journal*, vol. 16 (Sept. 1963), pp. 252–55; Glenn W. Fisher, "Interstate Variation in State and Local Government Expenditure," *National Tax Journal*, vol. 17 (March 1964), pp. 57–74; R. W. Bahl and R. J. Saunders, "Determinants of Changes in State and Local Government Expenditures," *National Tax Journal*, vol. 18 (March 1965), pp. 50–57; Elliott R. Morss, "Some Thoughts on the Determinants of State and Local Expenditures," *National Tax Journal*, vol. 19 (March 1966), pp. 95–103; Richard Spangler, "The Effect of Population Growth upon State and Local Government Expenditure," *National Tax Journal*, vol. 16 (June 1963), pp. 193–98.

25. Julius Margolis, "Metropolitan Finance Problems: Territories, Functions, and Growth," in the National Bureau of Economic Research volume, *Public Finances: Needs, Sources, and Utilization* (Princeton: Princeton University Press, 1961), pp. 229–70.

26. Peacock and Wiseman, pp. xxi, xxiv; ibid., pp. xxx–xxxi. (Peacock and Wiseman, quote from pp. 60–61 of the Colm-Helzner paper); and Lewis, pp. 245–47.

27. Margolis, pp. 241, 263, 268–69.

28. More specifically, those varieties of policies of special interest to Resources for the Future: e.g., measures concerning water resources, mineral resources, human resources, and air pollution.

29. Margolis, "Welfare Criteria, Pricing, and Decentralization of a Public Service," *Quarterly Journal of Economics*, vol. 71 (Aug. 1957), pp. 448–63; and Jack Hirshleifer, James C. De Haven, and Jerome W. Milliman, *Water Supply: Economics, Technology, and Policy* (Chicago: University of Chicago Press, 1965), pp. 31, 84–86, 110–11, 151, 229–30.

30. As the section on the mainstream tradition pointed out, much earlier economic analysis considered a similar question, i.e., monetary authorities' behavior under a system of inconvertible paper money.

31. Harry G. Johnson, "Monetary Theory and Policy," *American Economic Review*, vol. 52 (June 1962), p. 368. Reprinted as the first chapter of *Surveys of Economic Theory*, vol. I, *Money, Interest and Welfare*, a joint publication of the American Economic Association and the Royal Economic Society (New York: St. Martin's Press, 1965).

32. For Milton Friedman's views, see "A Monetary and Fiscal Framework for Economic Stability," *American Economic Review*, vol. 38 (June 1948), pp. 245–64, which was reprinted in *Essays in Positive Economics* (Chicago: University of Chicago Press, 1953), pp. 133–56; *A Program for Monetary Stability* (New York: Fordham University Press, 1959); "The Lag in Effect of Monetary Policy," *Journal of Political Economy*, vol. 69 (Oct. 1961), pp. 447–66; *Capitalism and Freedom* (Chicago: University of Chicago Press, 1962), especially chaps. 3 and 5, "The Control of Money" and "Fiscal Policy"; and, with Anna J. Schwartz, *A Monetary History of the United States, 1867–1960* (Princeton: Princeton University Press, 1963).

As Friedman has pointed out, his general line of thought stems from the earlier "Chicago School" (Simons-Mints) policy analysis represented, *inter alia*, by the well-known Henry Simons paper, "Rules versus Authorities in Monetary Policy," originally appearing in the *Journal of Political Economy*, vol. 44 (Feb. 1936), pp. 1–30, and reprinted as chapter 7 in Simons' posthumous book, *Economic Policy for a Free Society* (Chicago: University of Chicago Press, 1948).

33. Friedman, *A Program for Monetary Stability*, pp. 9, 51, 85, 93; *Capitalism and Freedom*, pp. 45, 53, 77; "The Lag in Effect of Monetary Policy," pp. 465–66; and *Essays in Positive Economics*, pp. 145–46.

34. Johnson, p. 368.

35. J. R. Hicks, "Economic Foundations of Wages Policy," *Economic Journal*, vol. 65 (Sept. 1955), pp. 389–91; G. L. Bach, *Inflation: A Study*

in Economics, Ethics, and Politics (Providence, R.I.: Brown University Press, 1958), pp. 40, 46; Abba P. Lerner, "Inflationary Recession and the Regulation of Administered Prices," The Relationship of Prices to Economic Stabilization and Growth: Compendium of Papers Submitted by Panelists Appearing before the Joint Economic Committee, 85th Congress, 2nd Session (Washington, D.C.: U.S. Government Printing Office, 1958); reprinted as chap. 26 in M. G. Mueller, ed., Readings in Macroeconomics (New York: Holt, Rinehart, and Winston, 1966), p. 368; K. E. Poole, "Full Employment, Wage Inflexibility, and Inflation," American Economic Review, vol. 45 (May 1955), pp. 585–86; William G. Bowen, The Wage-Price Issue: A Theoretical Analysis (Princeton: Princeton University Press, 1960), pp. 323–24. Compare Bowen's statement with Morton's (marked by note 3) near the start of the paper. (More specifically, the question is whether monetary authorities' actions should be treated as autonomous or determined. The issue to which Bowen refers is not the same as that which Elmus Wicker discusses later in this volume.)

36. John Kenneth Galbraith, American Capitalism: The Concept of Countervailing Power (Boston: Houghton-Mifflin, 1952), pp. 142, 154.

37. Wilhelm Röpke, A Humane Society (Chicago: Henry Regnery Company, 1960), pp. 144–145.

38. See Von Mises' attack on intervention in Human Action (New Haven: Yale University Press, 1949), pp. 712–857; Röpke, The Social Crisis of Our Time (Chicago: University of Chicago Press, 1950), pp. 159–73–Internationale Ordnung–heute (Zurich: Eugen Rentsch, 1954), pp. 24–35, 136–40, 217–50; Eucken, This Unsuccessful Age (London: William Hodge and Co., 1951), pp. 56–82–Grundsätze der Wirtschaftspolitik (Tübingen: J. C. B. Mohr, 1952), pp. 140–75, 185–99; Alfred Müller-Armack, Wirtschaftslenkung und Marktwirtschaft (Hamburg: Verlag für Wirtschaft und Sozialpolitik, 1948); and Friedman, Capitalism and Freedom, p. 57.

39. The writings also largely overlap: e.g., Human Action, The Social Crisis of Our Times, Grundsätze der Wirtschaftspolitik, Capitalism and Freedom.

40. F. A. Hayek (Chicago: University of Chicago Press, 1944), and Friedman (New York: McGraw-Hill, 1951).

41. Henry C. Wallich (New York: Harper & Row, 1960), see especially p. 51 ff., and Calvin B. Hoover (New York: Twentieth Century Fund, 1959), see especially pp. 346–47.

42. Anthony Downs, An Economic Theory of Democracy (New York: Harper & Row, 1957); James M. Buchanan and Gordon Tullock (Ann Arbor: University of Michigan Press, 1962); Mancur Olson (Cambridge: Harvard University Press, 1965); Tullock (Washington, D.C.:

Public Affairs Press, 1965); Downs, "A Theory of Bureaucracy," *American Economic Review,* vol. 55 (May 1965), pp. 439–46; Thomas Schelling (Cambridge: Harvard University Press, 1960); and Kenneth Boulding, *Conflict and Defense* (New York: Harper & Row, 1962; Harper Torchbooks, 1963), and "Toward a Pure Theory of Threat Systems," *American Economic Review,* vol. 53 (May 1965), pp. 424–34.

43. Analysts who reach conclusions about welfare may not attach moral significance to them.

44. For a summary of the propositions, see his chap. 16, pp. 295–300.

45. See, for instance, chap. 15, "A Comment on Economic Theories of Government," in Downs' *An Economic Theory of Democracy.*

46. See Charles E. Lindblom, "Policy Analysis," *American Economic Review,* vol. 48 (June 1958), pp. 298–312; "Tinbergen on Policy-Making," *The Journal of Political Economy,* vol. 66 (Dec. 1958), pp. 531–38; "The Science of 'Muddling Through'," *Public Administration Review,* vol. 19 (Spring 1959); "Decision-making in Taxation and Expenditures," pp. 295–329 of *Public Finances: Needs, Sources, and Utilization,* National Bureau of Economic Research (Princeton: Princeton University Press, 1961); with David Braybrooke, *A Strategy of Decision: Policy Evaluation as a Social Process* (New York: Free Press, 1963); and *The Intelligence of Democracy: Decision-Making through Mutual Adjustment* (New York: Free Press, 1965).

47. As his review of Tinbergen explicitly states, the core of his argument is a political parallel to Adam Smith's famous defense or coordination via the market. (Lindblom, p. 537). Also, it resembles Von Mises' attack on socialist allocation.

48. See, *inter alia,* Lindblom, "Policy Analysis," pp. 305–309.

49. See Arthur Smithies, "Decision-Making in Taxation and Expenditures," pp. 295–98. The proposals attacked appear in Arthur Smithies, *The Budgetary Process in the United States* (New York: McGraw-Hill, 1955). See "Tinbergen on Policy-Making." The book reviewed is Jan Tinbergen, *Economic Policy: Principles and Design* (Amsterdam: North-Holland Publishing Co., 1956).

2

American Unionism: The Membership Problem

BENJAMIN J. TAYLOR AND FRED WITNEY

A considerable amount of the contemporary literature in the labor field deals with the current decline in union membership. The purpose of this essay is to review and evaluate the literature dealing with this aspect of the American labor movement. Union membership reached its zenith in 1955, when 17,700,000 workers held membership and accounted for 33.2 percent of the nonagricultural labor force. Though total union membership increased to 18,-120,000 by 1960, the percentage figure (a more meaningful index than absolute union membership) declined to 31.4 percent because union membership gains did not keep pace with the increase in the total nonagricultural labor force. By 1964, total union membership declined to 17,187,000, and this represented 29.5 percent of the nonagricultural labor force.[1] By the end of 1967, total union membership increased somewhat but the percentage figure continued to decline.

Contemporary literature offers many explanations for this phenomenon. Some writers emphasize the changing structure of the

Benjamin J. Taylor is Associate Professor of Economics at Arizona State University, and Fred Witney is Professor of Economics at Indiana University.

American labor force as the chief cause for this trend. With the advent of automation, there has been a greater than proportionate increase in employment in the service industries (retail, government, personal services) as compared with the goods-producing industries, manufacturing, and construction. As is well known, the membership strength of organized labor is in the goods-producing industries; unions have been only moderately successful in the service industries. Whereas union membership accounts for half the employees in the former group of industries, only about a sixth of the workers in the latter group are organized. Thus, the labor force has been expanding in areas where unions have been moderately successful and declining proportionately in those areas which have traditionally represented union strength. Interwoven with the growth of the service industries is the numerical superiority of white-collar employees: Only about 2,000,000 are members of unions. Some writers do not believe that organized labor can measure up to the task of organizing the white-collar employees, and therefore predict that union membership will continue to decline.

Other writers explain the decline by noting that union leadership does not exhibit the militancy of former years and that the union movement itself no longer possesses the dynamics and vitality which sparked the great increase of union membership. They claim that these factors account for the contemporary decline and predict that they will serve as obstacles to any significant growth in the future. Within recent years, there has been the flight of the intellectual-liberal personnel from unions. Since union membership has declined during this period of exodus, some authors believe this phenomenon constitutes a cause for union membership decline.

Some contemporary literature explains the decline in terms of union racial policies and practices. It is charged that some unions exclude Negroes from membership and that even where Negroes are not excluded, they refuse to join organizations which systematically discriminate against them. Finally, other writers believe that unions cannot deal effectively with some of the major problems of contemporary society by using their major weapon of collective bargaining, and on this premise it is concluded that unions are unable to attract the unorganized employee.

Impressed with these factors, some writers are pessimistic in regard to the growth of organized labor in future years. For example, Raskin asserts:

> Each day brings compelling reminders that labor's strength is on the downgrade, and that, like the colonial powers of Europe, its leaders may soon be presiding over the dismantling of their . . . empires.[2]

Indeed, many writers have in effect written the obituary of the American labor movement, or, at least, have heard its death rattle.

Before reviewing the current literature dealing with union decline, it would be well to point out that trade union membership has always been sporadic, rocketing upward at times only to subside and then inch to a higher plateau. During the World War I era, union membership swelled from 2,700,000 in 1914 to over 5,000,000 in 1920. During the 1920's, union membership dropped to about 3,500,-000, but reached unprecedented heights in the 1930's and 1940's. Aware of this historical record, one scholar is not overly concerned with the current decline in union membership. In this regard, he notes that the union movement "has been doing what it has been doing three out of the four years since the turn of the century, growing at a slow pace, working hard just to stand still."[3] Indeed, if the future of union membership is viewed from perspective of labor history, there is no reason to conclude that the current membership pattern is the harbinger of the demise of the American labor movement.

CHANGING STRUCTURE OF THE LABOR FORCE— THE WHITE-COLLAR PROBLEM

As stated, the outstanding feature of the change in the composition of the American labor force has been the phenomenal increase in the service industries with the resulting large increase in the number of white-collar employees. In the past, unions have been only moderately successful in the organization of this group. As we view the literature, many writers have stressed that the future of union growth depends largely upon its capacity to attract white-collar employees to union membership. Many of them are pessimistic about the ability of the unions to succeed in this job. Thus:

> . . . given the changing complexion of the work force, the unions must make serious inroads into the white collar sector if they are to achieve a rapid growth rate in the future. Yet it is precisely among the white collar employees that the traditional organizing techniques are unlikely to "take."[4]

As expected, union writers recognize the need to organize the white-collar employee and equally are aware of the necessity to adopt special organizing techniques to meet this challenge. A union official states:

> We must organize the white collars. If we don't, unions will represent a dwindling minority of American workers, and the influence of unions for economic and social progress will gradually fade away. This is more easily said than done. The fact is, we don't know how to organize white collar workers. Many an old time organizer has tried it, with all the skill and dedication at his command, only to come away defeated and shaking his head in genuine puzzlement. The old organizing techniques won't work. This is a job for psychologists, for innovators, for pioneers.[5]

Beyond urging that unions adopt new and special organizing techniques to organize the white collar group, some writers contend that the current structure of organized labor be changed to encourage the unionization of these employees.

> It would seem to me that some structural face lifting will be necessary if the A.F.L.-C.I.O. is to make a new and more vivid appeal to

nonmanual workers. . . . I have in mind something like a special
department or division for white collar problems at or near the top
structure of the labor movement itself.[6]

In our judgment, the future success of organization in the white-
collar field depends largely upon the unions themselves. To argue
that white-collar employees are not organizable ignores the fact that
there are currently over 2,000,000 of them in unions. If unions cater
to the special status and problems of the white-collar worker, adopt
sophisticated and special organizing techniques, and provide them
with meaningful labor agreements, the future in this area may not
be as bleak as some of the writers predict. After all, there was a time
when unions had great difficulty in organizing manual employees.
It would be as incorrect to argue today that white-collar employees
are not subject to organization as it was wrong thirty years ago to
argue that unions could not organize the industrial mass production
workers. Moreover, there is a backlash to automation which could
facilitate the organization of white-collar employees. Though automation has been primarily responsible for the creation of the white-
collar organizational problem, there is some evidence that automation itself creates forces which could be the basis of rapid organization of white-collar employees. Some of the modern technological
advancements have the effect of changing the job content to one of
routine and monotonous character. As a former government official
put it:

> Automation will create a new kind of worker, a skilled white col-
> lar factory hand. He will be a "production" worker and will look
> to unions to represent his interests.[7]

To the extent that automation breaks down the individuality of
white-collar jobs, eliminates or reduces the need for the white-collar
employee to make decisions, and circumscribes the opportunities for
promotion, the white-collar employee can be expected to look at
labor unions as more attractive institutions. Equally, to the extent
that automation causes upheaval in the job situation, including dis-

placement, upgrading and downgrading, transfers and the like, the white-collar employee will be more inclined to seek job security in terms of a collective bargaining contract. In addition, the current widespread organization of school teachers and other government employees is evidence that unions are looking more attractive to white-collar employees.

UNION LEADERSHIP AND DYNAMISM

Much of the current literature holds that union leadership has lost the organizational zeal displayed in the years of great union growth. The corollary charge is that the union movement no longer displays the dynamism needed to reach new heights of size and power. One writer explains the decline in union growth on the following grounds.

> Union officers paid and unpaid, seem to be losing their vigor and sensitivity; idealistic motivation of union activity seems to be on the decline . . . lost their sense of missionary zeal; like most Americans, unionists show little sense of moral urgency in this year 1963; representatives seem to have lost some of the idealistic motivation, which made them so effective in the thirties and forties. Men who were once inspired leaders have at times taken on the hardened cynicism of political ward bosses. Recent recruits to union leadership jobs look at the jobs more as a career rather than a cause.[8]

Another writer argues that the union member has "lost his Messianic fervor to help fellow workers; complacency and self satisfaction has taken its place, and workers look upon the labor movement with boredom."[9]

Thus, it is common these days to write of the union leader, the union member, and the union movement as being without fight, dynamism, dedication, or a sense of urgency—resulting in the decline of union membership. If these charges are true, the future of unionism in the United States is indeed gloomy.

How do these charges stand up in view of the historical and contemporary activities of organized labor? In the first place, the contemporary charges against labor leaders are not new. In fact, the same criticisms were hurled against them prior to the years in which organized labor exhibited its greatest growth. Witness, for example, the 1929 comment of Louis Adamic wherein he severely criticized the existing AFL leadership in terms similar to those used by contemporary writers.

> Most of them are prosperous looking, Babbit-like, middleaged or elderly men, well dressed, carefully barbered, fat cheeked, double and triple chinned, vast bellied. . . . They are solid citizens, go getters, full of upper class respectability, pretensions, and ambitions. They play golf and go to country clubs. What impresses them are such facts as that the son of one of their boys is a junior at Princeton, where one of the Rockefeller boys is a student, and according to reports, on good terms with him.[10]

After this characterization, Adamic criticizes the AFL's lack of interest and inability to organize the mass production industries in essentially the same way as union leadership is condemned today for its lack of success in organization of the white-collar worker. Still, it's history that some of the leaders of the AFL rose to the occasion in future years and sparked the great organizational campaigns in the mass production industries. On this basis, an observer points out that present-day cynicism of labor leaders "may be as misplaced in the 1960's as it was in the late twenties."[11]

If militancy and dynamism are to be measured by strike activity, the record of recent years reveals many important battles waged by unions. Regardless of the merits of the union position in these major strikes, the airline and New York subway and bus strikes of 1966, the recent strikes in the shipping, newspaper, and auto industries, and the long steel strike of 1959–1960 show that unions have not lost their fighting spirit. Indeed, if it had not been for government intervention, the country would have been confronted with nationwide railroad strikes in 1963 and 1967. At times, the writers who picture labor unions and their leaders as relics of the past almost in the same breath argue that something should be done to avert such important strikes. For example, Raskin of the *New York Times*, in the same article in which he advocates important changes in the AFL-CIO structure to avert the impending demise of unions, argues that the Federation should be given more power so that its leaders will have "more voice in the peaceful adjustment" of disputes involving key industries.[12] If unions are in truth over-the-hill, weak, led by inept and self-satisfied leaders, why the excitement over policies to limit the right to strike?

If militancy and dynamism are measured by the number of new additions to the union movement, the evidence again shows that the spirit of organized labor is far from dead. People who point to declining union membership do not recognize that each year the union movement adds several hundred thousand new members. The fact that in recent years more members have been lost than gained should not blot out the fact that unions do organize the unorganized. For example, in fiscal year 1966, the NLRB reports that unions were certified as the legal bargaining representative in 5,059 polls and gained the right to represent 339,407 employees who heretofore were not involved in collective bargaining.[13] Such gains are not won by lazy, inept, and surfeited labor leaders. Indeed, since organization today is much more difficult than thirty years ago, the energy and dedication of contemporary leadership may exceed that displayed during the years of great union growth.

Unions continue to police employee's rights before legal and quasi-legal forums. They are not insensitive to employee's rights in their difficulties with employers, for each year unions file thousands of charges against employers alleging violation of employee and union rights under the Taft-Hartley law. In fiscal year 1965, unions filed 10,931 of such charges with the NLRB.[14] This number represents 236 charges above the 1964 total. In increasing numbers, labor unions have invoked the arbitration process to challenge management decisions under collective bargaining contracts. The Federal

Mediation and Conciliation Service remarks that "the Services' arbitration program flourished over the years" and reports that for fiscal year 1965 the Service submitted 5,453 panels of arbitrators to unions and companies.[15] Indeed, the demand for the arbitration of grievances has increased over the years. Here is objective evidence which tends to refute the proposition that union leadership is callous to workers' rights and interests.

Though the contemporary literature criticizing union leadership is extensive and written by people from many different walks of life, it lacks proof. Moreover, it does not take into consideration the different kind of environment in which labor leaders operate as compared to that of the thirties and forties. During the turbulent days of mass organization, the names of many labor leaders became household words. The reason for this is that the great organizational battles were being waged, many of them involving violence to property and person, and, frequently, killing of strikers and management representatives. Who can forget the Memorial Day Massacre of 1937 in which ten strikers were killed and 90 others sustained injuries (30 from gun fire) and 35 of the police sustained injuries?[16] In a sense, there was a war being waged, and it is from wars that generals make their reputations and obtain national prominence. Happily, these days are largely of the past, and today the organization of new plants is fought on different levels which escape the notoriety of the past era. Few people would want a return to those days so that names of labor leaders could become household words.

The attributes and qualifications of labor leaders today are quite different from those of the thirties and forties. This, however, does not mean that labor leaders have lost their drive and spirit. Rather, their potential is expressed in ways different from those of yesteryear. Indeed, there would be great concern for the union movement if its labor leaders did not respond to changing needs and times. As Professor Lester argues: "the frontier stage in American unions is likely completed. Like all other social institutions, unions tend to pass through stages of development."[17] Consequently, it follows that the labor leader must also respond to these changes. Too many critics measure labor leaders of today by the image of former years when they stood on the picket line with bloodied heads defying company guards. Happily, this kind of fortitude is not needed generally today, and it is quite incorrect to measure union leaders by such an image. In the present development of unions and collective bargaining, the labor leader must contend with an infinite number of complicated problems in his relationship with management. Militancy, dedication, and fervor are perhaps not displayed as dramatically as in the past under these circumstances, but those qualities are there when, for example, the labor leader performs the necessary research and bargaining skill to obtain protection for members of his union from the threat of automation. In short, different times and circumstances require a different kind of leader. This is as true within the union movement as in other great social institutions.

UNION DEMOCRACY AND CORRUPTION

Especially since World War II, unions have been increasingly portrayed to the general public as institutions reeking internally from racketeering and corruption brought on by a lack of internal democratic practices. A number of writers and even some union officials contend that the quality of unions has been weakened and is reflected in a declining membership.

The responsibility for internal union malpractices has overwhelmingly been laid at the doorstep of the membership itself.[18] Some evils of membership indifference that have been reported are (1) that a minimal degree of democracy will ordinarily satisfy members,[19] (2) that members do not desire self-government as long as they get their money's worth for dues,[20] and (3) that a low quality of national officer results from (1) and (2).[21]

Such membership apathy has allegedly generated public hostility toward unions. Professor Slichter pointed to the rising percentage of union losses in NLRB-held elections as evidence of public disillusionment with trade unions.[22]

Other critics explain the downward trend by contending that the membership has little to do with internal union practices. Even if internal safeguards against corruption are imposed, it is argued, they have proved ineffective. The ultimate weapon available to unions to control corruption is the power of expulsion from the AFL-CIO. Jacobs contends that expulsion is ineffective since a union, for instance, the Teamsters, can continue to function successfully outside the parent body.[23]

Labor legislation has also been blamed for the deterioration of unions. One writer charged that labor laws permitted corruption and undemocratic practices in general to persist because such laws permitted compulsory unionism, industry-wide bargaining, and directed strikes.[24]

Most solutions suggested to cure the downward trend in union membership call for greater rank-and-file participation in union affairs. Specifically, higher attendance at membership meetings, larger turnouts for union elections, and more member participation as active candidates in elections are among the suggestions receiving widespread attention.

One writer called for the breaking down of union meetings into smaller groups than a general membership meeting in order to generate greater internal democracy.[25] We contend that this system already exists in the form of feedbacks and reports on union activities within individual work groups. Members will show up in large numbers at meetings when they are against an issue or when an issue vital to their interest arises. The absence of large numbers at meetings could be construed as approval of union policies. This behavior is not different from that in national politics. On the national union level recent rejections of MacDonald of the Steelworkers and Carey of the IUE are examples of displays of democracy when the membership decides to change and examples of international officers who lost contact with the rank-and-file, which they had had through officers at the intermediate level.

Communication channels from the rank-and-file to the lofty heights of the hierarchy are shorter than is realized. Union leaders in the main know what the rank-and-file expect and what level of performance will bring forth retaliation. Here is the secret of long or short tenure in office.

Those who advocate greater membership participation in union affairs as demonstration of internal union democracy appear to ignore realities. Huge membership turnouts could result in chaos, and there is the practical problem of adequate physical facilities to accommodate the crowds. Chaos could result because large attendances might lead to endless debate over nearly every aspect of business.

Racketeering and corruption are not widespread in the labor movement[26] even though the exposures in 1957 by the Senate Select Committee on Improper Practices in the Labor and Management Field delivered a sharp blow to the labor movement as a whole. Union members, as stated, do freely participate in the management of union affairs.[27]

Racketeering or corruption has probably, at one time or another, existed in many unions. In the main, at a given time, most unions probably are as free from corruption and racketeering as are most of America's other institutions. Joel Seidman remarked:

> Perhaps it is too much to expect from the members a higher standard of morality within the union than is shown in social affairs generally and in the nation's political life in particular.[28]

The social history of the United States indicates that government regulation of economic groups has been deemed advisable when scandalous conduct has been revealed.[29] To argue that unions are fading away because government-imposed regulations resulted when unions themselves dealt inadequately with corruption and racketeering of union democracy is tantamount to arguing that, for example, railroads, banks, insurance companies, utilities, fade away since all have, at one time or another, been regulated because of corrupt practices. It seems better to argue as Secretary of Labor Wirtz did in quoting the late Adlai Stevenson, "democracy is not self-executing. We have to make it work."[30] Democracy can not be completely legislated; it must be practiced. Evidence of continued decline due to a lack of public confidence in unions is not reflected in NLRB election polls since 1960. Union victories averaged about 58 percent from 1960–1966 with a 61 percent victory record in fiscal 1966.[31] The election data do not support the predicted demise of unionism.

Labor legislation outlawing compulsory unionism is not necessarily related to the corruption problem. Some of the largest unions, such as the auto and steel workers, have negotiated the union shop, and these unions do not present the problem of corruption or undemocratic practices. It is the same with industry-wide bargaining and widespread strikes. These union practices do not indicate corruption or lack of democracy. They prevail in situations where it appears that industrial democracy and effective unionism are advanced by their use. These devices can not be condemned without first making a thorough examination of the circumstances in which they exist. It is possible that union membership would decline much more rapidly in the absence of these weapons because of the inability of unions to present the desires of the rank-and-file in their absence.

INTELLECTUALS AND UNIONISM

The exodus of intellectuals from the union movement is often used to support the contention that unions are unable to continue as effective institutions in American society.[32] The deliberate suppression of ideas, some contend, is aimed at institutional conformity to maintain leadership status quo.[33] Solomon Barkin argues that the lack of approval of labor policies and programs from intellectuals and liberals "has robbed organized labor of the public endorsement necessary for sustained growth."[34]

A significant amount of distortion has occurred in some writings because of misunderstandings of the historical relationship of intellectuals to unions. Except during the 1930's and 1940's liberals and intellectuals have been allies of unions only upon rare occasions. Those occasions occurred when it was felt general societal improvements could be advanced. Maurice Neufeld[35] argues that prior to the New Deal era, liberals and intellectuals were the impartial observers functioning to point out flaws found in all American institutions. Their alliance with CIO unions during the New Deal era was not a healthy one, since it was based on emotionalism. Observers emotionally involved with organizations are both unable and unwilling to report objectively defects in institutional policies and procedures when they arise. One study holds that most intellectuals were blind believers in unions during the 1930's and 1940's.[36] The minds and eyes of intellectuals were supposedly so fixed upon the prospect of general reform of the total society with unions a vehicle for achieving that aim that they refused to see shortcomings of unions. It was hoped that unions would become "involved in pursuits that were actually outside their realm of primary interest."[37] Strauss argues that academicians set higher standards for unions than for management. Possibly as a result of this excessively high standard, the union movement frequently has had problems with intellectuals and liberals. Cohen observed

> in times of depression workers as well as other groups grope for some solution to the mystery behind the difficulties of society. In such periods, there is an inevitable appearance of crackpot schemes, vague panaceas, and proposals for far-reaching reforms. When something seems to be fundamentally wrong with the economy, as in the case of prolonged depression, proposals for extensive reform have an obvious appeal. Equally appealing are panaceas that promise to end all the trouble by some simple scheme.[38]

During prosperity unions more realistically concentrate on improvements in wages and working conditions.

The cooperative movement in the United States offers an interesting analogy regarding intellectual pursuit of idealistic goals. The philosophy underlying the cooperative movement is that the mass of workers and farmers are exploited by the owners of capital.[39] It regarded the system of free enterprise for profit unsound and set out through a program of consumer education to control the business system. Its radical social goals were to be achieved gradually and voluntarily.

Unions also proceeded with a basic philosophy of reallocating income shares which were deemed inequitable. To be sure, a coterie of intellectuals flocked to the union movement brandishing many of the ideas found to exist in the cooperative movement. During the 1930's most American institutions were undergoing reexamination of traditional practices and policies because of the temporary economic disaster. Once the institutions of society began to emerge successfully toward a more stable economy with altered practices, idea men as such were no longer as essential to those institutions that preferred to conduct their operations within the existing American system. Intellectuals occupied important positions of cooperatives, and that movement failed. It failed because it was foreign to reality.

Intellectuals are more interested in the ideals of movements than in the actual operation of organizations on a day-to-day basis. Their role is not as a part of an organization, but as initiators. Perhaps their contribution to unions was all but exhausted once unions obtained initial successes. Once unions were firmly established, they sought quantitative goals such as better wages and working conditions as contrasted to changes in the relationship of unions to the American system.

Unions have historically had narrow and highly specialized interests and goals. The interests and goals of the union movement are deemed far too limited for the solution of the more universal problems plaguing intellectuals.[40] Unions are interested primarily in job-centered problems.[41] When union leaders closed ranks and solidified their political positions within their organizations during the 1940's, intellectuals became less and less influential and thus a flight of intellectuals from the ranks of organized labor was inevitable by 1950. Indeed, as indicated, intellectuals were forced out of the labor movement by union officers in contrast to the voluntary flight reported by many writers. Intellectuals were not suitable for positions of power as union officers became more deeply entrenched politically in their positions[42] and more involved in improving wages and working conditions.

Unions cannot afford to spend much of their energies in new, untried areas when the pedestrian problems of everyday unionism are so great. There is greater realism attached to a movement that spends significant proportions of its time on such subjects as job security provisions in contracts and attempts to hold off unfavorable legislation. Thus, use of the labor union as a vehicle to try out new ideas has met with great caution. New and more exciting movements, moreover, such as the Peace Corps and Civil Rights have captured the fancy of many intellectuals. These newer institutions seem to offer greater promise for idea experimentation than unions, which seem to the intellectual somewhat moribund in comparison.

UNION RACIAL POLICIES AND PRACTICES

Specific evidence has been gathered to show that the union movement is now in a state of decline partially because of its inability to represent Negroes. Despite the goals of the AFL-CIO, it has been argued that its leaders refuse to discipline affiliated unions for violations of Federation policies. AFL-CIO union officers often defend themselves on the ground that the Federation is made up of independent, self-governing bodies and that they are powerless to intervene. Marshall reported that often Federation officers respond to charges of inaction with regard to racial injustices by stating that it is better to have the discriminating unions remain in the AFL-CIO than to withdraw from it.[43]

Evidence of the responsibilities of the AFL-CIO officers is provided in Article I of the Federation's constitution. It states that the

AFL-CIO "shall consist of such affiliates as shall conform to its constitution and the rules and regulations adopted thereunder." The Negro community in many instances has been provoked by the lack of action undertaken in their favor.

The AFL-CIO also adopted a provision in its first constitution immediately upon merger in 1955. Article II, Section 4, states that one object of the Federation is "to encourage all workers without regard to race, creed, color, national origin or ancestry to share equally in the full benefits of union organization."[44] This Federation objective was reaffirmed in 1963 in a publication declaring that "as a minimum the AFL-CIO endorses the omnibus civil rights bill reported by the House Judiciary Committee. We favor every provision in this bill; our only complaint is that in some respects it does not go far enough."[45]

Some contemporary critics declare that unions cannot satisfactorily execute their stated policies of racial equality because they are committed to a historical practice of racial discrimination.[46] Indeed it is charged that organized labor is "incapable of overcoming its habitual discriminatory practices"[47] because union officials purposely maintain the status quo since an ardent stand for racial equality would result in replacement.[48] This predicted trend for the future may indicate that rapid changes in past racial practices could so antagonize white workers that they would leave in far greater numbers than Negro workers would join. However, this prediction as a generalization cannot be supported. Evidence to the contrary is found in industrial union history, especially since 1935. More recently the craft-type unions have been undergoing some change with respect to racial practices. Thus, it is not at all clear that unions are unable to adjust their racial practices at least as rapidly as those of other institutions.

Some writers argue that the comparatively small number of Negroes in unions is attributable to employer practices. It is contended that some employers use testing devices which either exclude Negroes from employment or relegate them to the most menial and low-paying jobs.[49] This point of view is advanced by those who desire to exonerate unions in the problem of discrimination.[50] On the other hand, there is the argument that unions cannot successfully insist upon discriminatory employment practices when employers insist that "nondiscriminatory policies must and will be executed."[51]

Currently there is the prediction that unions dedicated to equal opportunities in employment and civil rights will join in a labor-Negro alliance. Such an alliance, it is contended, will have important implications for employers who practice discrimination because of the increased political strength brought about by such a combination.[52] The result of this coalition will secure greater justice in the area of industrial relations. Further, such a joint undertaking will tend to make union membership more attractive to Negroes, and this will tend to reverse the downward trend in union membership.

Blame for job discrimination against America's racial minorities cannot be laid totally at the doorstep of either unions or employers. Lloyd Bailer has observed that, historically, union racial policies have fallen into three groups:[53] unions dedicated to full equality for all workers within the framework of seniority and ability; unions accepting racial practices as they found them without efforts to eliminate discriminatory practices; and unions practicing discrimination by virtue of dedicated exclusion of Negroes from membership or secondarily by the use of auxiliary locals. Prior to the formation of the CIO in 1935, Negroes were highly antiunion because of AFL organizational philosophies.[54] Antiunion sentiments of the Negro community were promulgated by Negro leaders such as Booker T. Washington.[55] Since the formation of the CIO, Negroes have encountered varying degrees of hostility and acceptance as reported by Bailer. However, sweeping generalizations indicting the entire labor movement for racial discrimination represent distortions of Negro experiences with labor unions.

Marshall reported a widened schism developed between the

Negro community and the labor movement as a result of the AFL-CIO merger in 1955.[56] Partially the discontent of Negroes over the merger arose because of the more restrictive racial practices of craft-type unions. But Negroes have been dissatisfied from time to time because of the lack of action taken by the former CIO leaders with regard to racial ills within the Federation.[57] Marshall writes, however, that despite these complaints, Negroes will not withdraw from the labor movement, but will continue to fight for equality within the movement, since many Negroes recognize that unions in general are now facing up to existing problems of racial inequities.[58] To attempt to work outside the labor movement could only result in a step backward in the drive for job equality, since such a move could hardly put the Negro in a position where he could deal most effectively with the roots of discriminatory practices and policies. Furthermore, Negroes want to share in the fruits of the American society equally; and this means they desire inclusion within, and not exclusion from, its institutions.

It must be recognized that both unions and employers are guilty of discriminatory employment practices. As a matter of civil rights, each citizen should have an equal chance for employment at all levels.[59]

Recommendations have been advanced for dealing with past discriminatory practices. These often require altering union and employer recruiting practices.[60] Both parties have been challenged to aggressively solicit Negro applicants for jobs and apprenticeship training. Such a program is necessary because of an attitude held by some Negroes that it is futile to take training to qualify for jobs. Only when the Negro community observes that Negroes are being accepted in apprenticeship programs from which they were formerly excluded and only when they observe Negroes advancing into supervisory positions will they respond by pursuing greater skills and education which will enable them to compete equally with other workers for jobs.

Of course the union movement has been guilty of practices that deviate from AFL-CIO stated policies of equality. But "equal opportunity depends upon more than changing some rule."[61] Growth in minority group employment in the future will depend upon factors such as the economic growth of the economy and changed attitudes and behavior of the white majority with respect to racial minorities.[62] The existence of economic growth alone, as some advocate, is not sufficient. But sustained economic growth over time should assist the attitude change by diminishing white workers' feeling that they compete with Negroes for an inadequate number of suitable jobs. Many local and international union officers have already made bids to change membership attitudes and practices regarding racial discrimination.[63]

Certainly, the argument that past racial practices explain the decline in union membership lacks proof. Since union practices are reflections of deep-seated prejudices of the general population, however, gradual policy changes may be more beneficial to membership growth than rapid ones. It is possible that rapid changes in past racial practices would so antagonize white workers that they would leave in far greater numbers than Negro workers would join.

ADEQUACY OF COLLECTIVE BARGAINING

It is charged that the decline of unionism is attributable to the inadequacy of collective bargaining as a vehicle to deal with the problems of modern society. Harold Davey has summarized some of the common criticisms of collective bargaining:[64] Collective bargaining has not dealt properly with contract renegotiation; crisis bargaining is too prevalent in the renegotiation process and senseless strikes result; collective bargaining has proved unable to adapt outmoded contract provisions to new conditions; labor unions infringe on management rights so that the incentive to innovate, to subcontract work, and to relocate outmoded plants is stifled; efficiency of operation is hampered because of union pressures to prohibit changes in seniority requirements or job reevaluation; collective bargaining is so centralized through pattern bargaining that the individual needs of particular labor-management relations cannot be met; and participants in the collective bargaining process are not equipped with enough knowledge to cope with the problems at hand, such as issues arising out of technological change, pension plans, health plans, or supplementary unemployment benefits.

Beneath the facade of all these charges against collective bargaining lies the deeper questions of what is and what should be the basic philosophy of the labor movement. E. E. Witte argues that the starting point for any study of the trade union movement theory should be Selig Perlman's job scarcity theory.[65] Perlman and Commons were convinced that workers had and should have only limited political objectives for their unions. Those objectives should be sought within the existing economic system. Phillip Taft argued that the

> Commons-Perlman view limits itself to the possibilities of working out a "system of harmony" in the shop; it does not go beyond that point to inquire whether there is sufficient "dynamism" in the economy to make possible the steady gain in standards of life and conduct which has characterized the American economy.[66]

Walter Galenson explains the recorded trend in union membership by contending that the American labor ideology and its rejection of socialism as its central theme occurred because of the relatively high American standard of living, the impressive rate of economic growth, and the absence of class consciousness as demonstrated in other nations.[67] William Gomberg remarks:

> Originally labor made its public appeal as the embodiment of the community's social conscience; its purpose was to establish industrial citizenship for a group that had been enfranchised politically but disenfranchised industrially. Having achieved this goal, the labor movement is now reduced to a bargaining, enforcing, police-type function.[68]

Harold Laski's criticism of the Common-Perlman theories tends to dovetail with those summarized by Davey and those concerned with basic labor movement philosophy. Laski argued that Perlman's theory missed the mark because it

> tended to persuade the worker not to look beyond the walls of the factory in which he is engaged, thereby stunting his personality and giving him that consciousness of scarcity and, therefore, pessimism about himself. . . .[69]

It also destroyed "the zest for innovation, the readiness to experiment with new social forms, the unwillingness to accept the position of the underpriviliged as permanent."[70]

It should be readily apparent that the criticisms levied against the collective bargaining process as explanations for the recorded decline in membership are not new. Hoxie observed at an early date that unionism "cannot be judged and treated as a whole" since what is true of one union is not necessarily true of the whole movement.[71]

Reasons for attitudes toward the recorded and predicted downward trend in union membership have been offered by several observers. Allan Weisenfeld reported that strikes in such industries as railroads, city transit systems, newspapers, and airlines have "given rise to a belief in some quarters that collective bargaining has failed and must be replaced by some other system of dispute settlement."[72]

Strikes and Union Decline

The attitude that unions have monopoly power reflected in strikes is used to predict the continued decline of unions. However, as Perlman notes, they do not possess inexhaustible strike funds and if they did would hardly be so "purblind as to persist in digging their own, as well as their industry's grave."[73] Another writer, C. L. Christenson, argues that contrary to much opinion, strikes in certain industries have not been disastrous,[74] and indeed have not resulted in any significant economic loss.

James Stern is of the attitude that dependence upon strikes to obtain favorable bargaining conclusions will decline. The reason for this attitude is the observed continual rise in the ratio of non-bargaining to bargaining unit employees. Thus, increasingly, non-bargaining unit employees will be available to perform the duties of striking bargaining unit employees.[75] Automation, it is argued, will further diminish the threat of crippling strikes. Moreover, as noted by Ross and Hartman, strike activity in the United States has been on the wane since World War II—that is, during the very period when crisis bargaining and resultant strikes allegedly have helped to account for unionism's decline.[76]

The attitude that strikes explain the observed trend in union membership and are therefore the basis for predicting continual decline fails to recognize some important aspects of business behavior. For example, as Christenson points out, firms may stockpile supplies, since they have sufficient advance notice that strikes may occur. Furthermore, they have the ability through overtime to make up lost production after striking employees return to work. Most American industry has operated at less than capacity in recent years. Thus, production losses in one quarter may be successfully made up over the remaining quarters of a given year without any loss of annual production at all.

Innovations and Collective Bargaining

A number of writers conditionally predict that if collective bargaining is going to survive the current downward trend there must be a formulation of new goals and joint study projects involving management and labor representatives and established for the life of the contractual agreements.[77] Barkin and Blum argue that all labor management problems must be studied for the purpose of developing new policies, programs, and institutions if collective bargaining is to survive.[78]

The literature also reveals other attitudes toward the future of unionism. One governmental agency asserts, "bargaining is not only an extremely creative process; it is one with practitioners quick to imitate the successful innovations of others."[79] Davey reported, after a survey of collective bargaining evidence, that the record showed "continued vitality, flexibility, and adaptability."[80]

Harry Seligson calls attention to various innovative breakthroughs in labor-management relations of the very nature called for by some of the most devoted critics of collective bargaining.[81] Some of the breakthroughs reported deserve brief mention. The first dealt with the Progress Sharing Plan between American Motors and the United Auto Workers. A joint committee of labor-management representatives was established in 1961 to discuss "their philosophies, needs, and common responsibilities to the community, education, recreation, housing, and health facilities."[82]

The second breakthrough reported was the establishment of a Long Range Committee by the Kaiser Steel Company and United Steelworkers Union. Of significance was the establishment of a tripartite committee which provided that public members were authorized to play an active and direct part in contract negotiations. The inclusion of public members in contract negotiations is sufficient evidence that the public is recognized as having a stake in contemporary collective bargaining.

The third was the Human Relations Joint Committee established in the basic steel industry in 1960. This committee was authorized to study such subjects as job classification, seniority, and medical care. In 1962, the committee was charged with studying the area of job security and seeking solutions which were to be reported to the union and management well in advance of contract expiration. Solutions are sought to various problems continuously and not just at the time of contract negotiations.

Fourth, the 1960 agreement between the Pacific Maritime Association and the International Longshoremen's and Warehousemen's Union freed employers from practices of the past, allowing them to revise and even eliminate work rules with a few restrictions such as the requirement that unsafe working conditions were not to be imposed upon workers because of a change in work rules. In exchange a trust fund was provided for early retirement along with a no-layoff provision for the fully registered work force. Agreements such as this, through attrition, may diminish the size of the union's membership. Nevertheless they indicate that unions do adapt to change when they are forced to do so by the realities of economic life.

Fifth, the Armour Automation Fund was established by collective bargaining agreement for the purpose of seeking solutions to problems created by technological change. This program included retraining for workers to be displaced.

The sixth breakthrough in collective bargaining was the establishment in 1962 of the American Foundation on Automation and Employment. The purpose of the Foundation was to determine how workers who are displaced by automation may be retrained. A fund was established and is administered jointly by U.S. Industries, the International Association of Machinists, and members from the general public.

The six breakthroughs discussed by Seligson have been mentioned to demonstrate the viability and creativity of collective bargaining. This is not to deny the apparent immaturity of some bargaining relationships. Certainly, there are bargaining relationships in existence where little has been or possibly ever will be accomplished. Observation of these limited cases do not justify indictment of collective bargaining as an institution. Collective bargaining is not a homogeneous process that is universally either progressive or degenerate.

Quite apart from the apparent failures of collective bargaining under certain conditions, it should be stressed that "some problems transcend the bargaining table and cannot be solved there. We should not expect collective bargaining to cope with them."[83] Some problems demand greater involvement of society in general for solutions that can possibly be provided by the collective bargaining process as it is known in the United States. Dunlop contends that critics make no endeavor to describe the structure of the economic system without the presence of unions and that the failure to do so is the greatest weakness of their arguments.[84] To argue, for example, that unions are weak and dying because they have been unable to solve all the problems which face the institution of collective bargaining is to ignore the things that unions do well. We join Wilcox and contend that:

> The philosophy behind a public policy which fosters free collective bargaining is that private action in the market place is more effective than direct government control; that decision making in a democracy should be greatly decentralized because only in that way can the complexities of a modern economy be handled efficiently and quickly with due consideration of local problems.[85]

The labor movement, in general, is rooted in self-interest like other institutions of modern-day society and the drive of each to serve its own end actually serves to strengthen and provide vigor for the entire economy since each seeks solutions to individual problems as they arise. Shister is in harmony with our view when he writes that "union policies and activities reflect changing environmental pressure rather than an inflexible, rigorous 'ideology.' "[86] Union behavior is highly opportunistic and pragmatic and arguments that collective bargaining is inadequate are based upon inadequate conceptions of what the union movement was and now is. As unions are affected by particular problems, they do lift their horizons beyond the shop level and adjust and deal with issues of more widespread concern. But when they do so, they operate through the major political parties which are integral to the total American heritage just like all the other sectors of the American society.

American workers hold membership in all the nation's institutions and as such can more effectively exert pressure for societal changes through them all than would be the case if membership were held in only one. For this reason the labor movement in general will continue to exert its major energies in the bread-and-butter areas of collective bargaining and only incidentally in other realms.

But because major concern is with the day-to-day operations of tra-ditional union problems bearing heavily on job-oriented horizons, it is erroneous to conclude that collective bargaining is inadequate to cope with new conditions facing society. It is just that collective bargaining was never the cure-all institution in the United States for which some reformers had hoped. The American labor movement is uniquely different from its European counterpart, and its con-temporary collective bargaining practices reflect that difference. Thus, the problem-solving of collective bargaining is directed pri-marily at limited objectives as opposed to problem-solving of every situation that arises in the environment.

CONCLUSIONS

A wide variety of explanations have been offered to explain the downward trend in union membership observed since 1955. We are of the opinion that critics go too far in the development of their cases. Critics have based both their explanations of unionism's recent history and their predictions of its future on limited, often quite tenuous data. Moreover, they have ignored alternative expla-nations, even when they fit the data equally well.

This is not to deny that critics offer valid criticisms of particular unions, at particular times, and in particular circumstances. Regard-less of the subject discussed, be it white-collar organization, union racial practices, union leadership and dynamism, democracy and corruption, and the viability of the institution of collective bargain-ing itself, unfavorable evidence can be found. But the evidence that the critics have appealed to has been highly selective in its character and has been ascribed a weight far beyond its value. It cannot sup-port their hostile generalization concerning the total union ex-perience and the prospects for the future. Certainly the union movement faces many crucial problems as indicated above. How successfully it deals with these problems will determine the extent to which it will remain an important institution.

NOTES

1. *Directory of National and International Labor Organizations in the United States*, U.S. Department of Labor, 1964, Bulletin No. 1395. (These figures include Canadian members of unions affiliated with United States organization.)

2. Statement of Abe Raskin of the *New York Times*, "The Crisis in the American Union," *The Annals*, American Academy of Political and Social Science, vol. 350 (Nov. 1963), p. 4.

3. John T. Dunlop, "The Crisis in the American Union Movement," *The Annals*, Americal Academy of Political and Social Science, vol. 350 (Nov. 1963), pp. 5–6.

4. Joseph Shister, "The Outlook for Union Growth," *Annals of the American Academy of Political and Social Science*, vol. 350 (Nov. 1963), p. 59.

5. "White Collar Workers: A Different Breed of Cats," *AFL-CIO News*, Dec. 27, 1958.

6. Everett Kassalow, "Occupational Frontiers of Trade Unionism in the United States," *Proceedings of the Industrial Relations Research Association* (1960), p. 204.

7. Statement of James Carey, former president of the International Union of Electrical Workers in "Organized Labor in the Next Decade," *Business Horizons*, vol. 1, no. 5 (1959), p. 64.

8. George Strauss, "Union Bargaining Strength: Goliath or Paper Tiger," *Annals*, op. cit. (1963), p. 87.

9. Oscar Ornati, "The Current Crisis: A Challenge to Organized Labor," *Antioch Review*, vol. 20 (Spring 1960), p. 2.

10. Louis Adamic, *Dynamite* (New York: Viking Press, 1929), p. 439.

11. William Gomberg, "The Future of Collective Bargaining," *The Nation*, vol. 194, no. 3 (January 20, 1962), p. 59.

12. Raskin, *Annals*, op. cit., p. 45.

13. *Thirty-First Annual Report of the NLRB*, 1966 (Washington, D.C.: U.S. Government Printing Office, 1966, pp. 206–207.

14. *Thirtieth Annual Report of the NLRB*, 1965 (Washington, D.C.: U.S. Government Printing Office, 1966), p. 7.

15. *Federal Mediation and Conciliation Service, 18th Annual Report*, 1965 (Washington, D.C.: U.S. Government Printing Office, 1966), p. 59.

16. La Follette Committee, Report No. 46, Part 2, *The Chicago Memorial Day Incident*.

17. Richard A. Lester, "Unions in the Next Decade," McGill University, Industrial Relations Centre, *Eleventh Annual Conference Proceedings* (Sept. 1959), p. 1.

18. Arthur J. Goldberg, "Rights and Responsibilities of Union Members," in E. Wight Bakke, Clark Kerr, and Charles W. Anrod, eds., *Unions, Management, and the Public* (New York: Harcourt, Brace, 1960), p. 156.

19. John R. Coleman, "The Compulsive Pressures of Democracy in Unionism," in Walter Galenson and Seymour M. Lipset, *Labor and Trade Unionism* (New York: Wiley, 1960), p. 214.

20. Will Herberg, "Bureaucracy and Democracy in Labor Unions," *Antioch Review* (Fall 1943), p. 417.

21. William M. Leiserson, *American Trade Union Democracy* (New York: Columbia University Press, 1959), p. 60.

22. Sumner H. Slichter, "New Goals for Unions," *Atlantic* (Dec. 1958), pp. 55–56.

23. Paul Jacobs, *Old Before its Time: Collective Bargaining at 28* (Santa Barbara, Calif.: Center for the Study of Democratic Institutions, 1963), p. 21.

24. Maurice R. Franks, *What's Wrong with our Labor Unions?* (New York: Bobbs-Merrill, 1963), p. 210.

25. Herberg, op. cit.

26. Neil W. Chamberlain, *Sourcebook on Labor* (New York: McGraw-Hill, 1958), p. 26.

27. Joseph Kovner, "Union Democracy," *Interpreting Union Movement*, Industrial Relations Research Association (Dec. 1952), p. 84.

28. Joel Seidman, "Democracy in Labor Unions," in Joseph Shister, *Readings in Labor Economics and Industrial Relations* (New York: Lippincott, 1956), p. 132.

29. David J. Saposs, "Labor Racketeering: Evolution and Solutions," *Social Research*, vol. 25, no. 3 (Autumn, 1958), pp. 269–70.

30. W. Willard Wirtz, "The Challenge to Free Collective Bargaining," in Mark L. Kahn, ed., *Labor Arbitration and Industrial Change* (Washington, D.C.: Bureau of National Affairs, 1963), p. 309.

31. *Annual Reports of the National Labor Relations Board*, 1960–1966 (Washington, D.C.: United States Government Printing Office).

32. "Eggheads Who Help Run Unions," *Business Week* (Nov. 11, 1961), p. 47. Also see Kermit Eby, *Protests of an Ex-Organization Man* (Boston: Beacon Press, 1961), p. 44.

33. B. J. Widick, *Labor Today: The Triumphs and Failures of Unionism in the United States* (Boston: Houghton Mifflin, 1964), p. 111.

34. Solomon Barking, *The Decline of the Labor Movement* (Santa Barbara, Calif.: Centre for the Study of Democratic Institutions, 1961), p. 28.

35. Maurice F. Neufeld, "The Historical Relationship of Liberals and Intellectuals to Organized Labor in the United States, *Annals of the American Academy of Political and Social Science*, vol. 350 (Nov. 1963), p. 115.

36. Irving Howe and Lewis A. Coser, *The American Communist Party: A Critical History* (Boston: Beacon Press, 1957).

37. George Strauss, "Labor and the Academicians," *Proceedings of the Sixteenth Annual Meeting of Industrial Relations Research Association* (Dec. 1963), p. 10.

38. Sanford Cohen, *Labor in the United States* (Columbus, Ohio: Charles E. Merrill Books, 1960), p. 77.

39. H. Haines Turner, *Case Studies of Consumers' Cooperatives* (New York: Columbia University Press, 1941), pp. 282–83.

40. Jacobs, p. 24.

41. Harold L. Wilensky, *Intellectuals in Labor Unions* (Glencoe, Ill.: The Free Press, 1956).

42. C. Wright Mills, *The New Men of Power* (New York: Harcourt, Brace, 1948).

43. Ray Marshall, "Ethnic and Economic Minorities: Unions' Future or Unrecruitable?" *Annals*, vol. 350 (Nov. 1963), p. 66.

44. *AFL-CIO Constitution*, 1955 (Washington, D.C.: AFL-CIO Publication no. 1, Jan. 1956), p. 3.

45. *Equal Rights for All* (Washington, D.C.: AFL-CIO Publications no. 133, 1963), p. 9.

46. Jacobs, p. 41.

47. Herbert Hill, "Labor Unions and the Negro," *Commentary*, vol. 28, no. 6 (Dec. 1959), p. 488.

48. B. K. Johnpoll, "Negroes and the Labor Movement, An Exchange," *New Politics*, vol. 2, no. 1 (Fall, 1962), p. 150.

49. Harold Mayfield, "What Industry Can Do," *Management Review*, vol. 53, no. 4 (Apr. 1964), p. 8.

50. Harry C. Baker, "A Voluntary Approach to Equal Opportunity," in Herbert R. Northrup and Richard L. Rowan, eds., *The Negro and Employment Opportunity* (Ann Arbor: University of Michigan, Bureau of Industrial Relations, 1965), pp. 119–21.

51. Theodore W. Kheel, *Guide to Fair Employment Practices* (Englewood Cliffs, N.J.: Prentice-Hall, 1964), p. 18.

52. Sam Barone, "The Impact of Recent Developments in Civil Rights on Employees and Unions," paper presented before the Mid-West Economic Association, April 15, 1966, p. 41.

53. Lloyd H. Bailer, "Organized Labor and Racial Minorities," *Annals of the Academy of Political and Social Science* (Mar. 1951), p. 101.

54. Sterling Spero and Abram L. Harris, *The Black Worker* (New York: Columbia University Press, 1931).

55. Booker T. Washington, "The Negro and the Labor Unions," *Atlantic Monthly* (June 1913), p. 756.

56. F. Ray Marshall, "Unions and the Negro Community," *Industrial and Labor Relations Review*, vol. 17, no. 2 (Jan. 1964), p. 187.

57. AFL-CIO, *Executive Council Minutes*, Dec. 5 and 9, 1955, pp. 11–12.

58. Marshall, p. 202.

59. W. Willard Wirtz, *Labor and the Public Interest* (New York: Harper and Row, 1964), in Barone, p. 1.

60. W. S. Price, "The Affirmative Action Concept of Equal Employment Opportunity," *Labor Law Journal*, vol. 16, no. 10 (Oct. 1965), p. 603.

61. Wirtz, *Labor and the Public Interest*, p. 103.

62. See Fred Witney, "In Defense of Free Collective Bargaining," *The Forensic Quarterly*, vol. 39 (1965), p. 361. Also, Introduction by Eli Ginsberg, in Dale L. Heistand, *Economic Growth and Employment Opportunities for Minorities* (New York: Columbia University Press, 1964), p. xiv.

63. William M. Leiserson, *American Trade Union Democracy* (New York: Columbia University Press, 1959), p. 60.

64. Harold W. Davey, "The Continuing Viability of Collective Bargaining," *Labor Law Journal*, vol. 16, no. 2 (Feb. 1965), p. 113.

65. Edwin E. Witte, "Selig Perlman," *Industrial and Labor Relations Review* (Apr. 1960), p. 337.

66. Phillip Taft, "Job-Conscious Unionism: The Commons-Perlman Theory," in Joseph Shister, *Readings in Labor and Industrial Relation* (New York: J. B. Lippincott Co., 1956), p. 84.

67. Walther Galenson, *Why the American Labor Movement is not Socialist*, Reprint no. 168 (Berkeley: University of California Press, Institute of Industrial Relations, 1961), p. 15.

68. Gomberg, p. 58.

69. Harold J. Laski, *Trade Unions in the New Society* (New York: Viking, 1948); pp. 222–223.

70. Ibid.

71. Robert F. Hoxie, *Trade Unionism in the United States* (New York: Appleton, 1919), p. xxiv.

72. Allan Weisenfeld, "Collective Bargaining at the Crossroads," *Labor Law Journal*, vol. 14, no. 6 (June 1963), p. 508.

73. Selig Perlman, "The Basic Philosophy of the American Labor Movement," *Annals* (Mar. 1951), p. 57.

74. C. L. Christenson, "The Theory of the Offset Factor," *American Economic Review*, vol. 43, no. 4, pt. 1 (Sept. 1953), p. 547: Also C. L. Christenson, "The Impact of Labor Disputes upon Coal Consumption," *American Economic Review*, vol. 45, no. 1 (Mar. 1955), p. 79.

75. James L. Stern, "Automation-End or a New Day in Unionism," *Annals*, op. cit. (1963), p. 28.

76. Arthur M. Ross and Paul T. Hartman, *Changing Patterns of Industrial Conflict* (New York: Wiley, 1960).

77. Solomon Barkin, "A New Agenda for Labor," *Fortune* (Nov. 1960), p. 249.

78. Solomon Barkin and Albert A. Blum, "What's to be Done for Labor? The Trade Unionist's Answer," *Labor Law Journal* (Mar. 1964), p. 107.

79. *Federal Mediation and Conciliation Service, Sixteenth Annual Report*, 1963 (Washington, D.C.: United States Government Printing Office, 1964), p. 3.

80. Davey, p. 121.

81. Harry Seligson, "Breakthroughs in Labor-Management Relations," *Labor Law Journal*, vol. 14, no. 6 (June 1963), p. 500.

82. Edward L. Cushman, "The American Motors—UAW Progress Sharing Agreement," *Proceedings of the 14th Annual Meeting, Industrial Relations Research Association* (1961), pp. 315–324.

83. Irving Bernstein, "The Cockeyed World of Paul Jacobs," *American Federationist* (May 1964).

84. John T. Dunlop, *Aspects of Labor Economics* (Princeton: Princeton University Press, 1962), pp. 343–344.

85. Richard C. Wilcock, "Public Policies toward Organized Labor," Reprint Series No. 70 (Champaign, Ill.: University of Illinois Bulletin, 1958), pp. 10–11.

86. Joseph Shister, *Readings in Labor and Industrial Relations* (New York: Lippincott, 1956), p. 80.

3

Economic Externalities and the Justification for Collective Action

H. J. KIESLING

The past two decades have seen the resolution of considerable confusion with respect to the theoretical role played by economic externality in the justification of collective action.[1] Two separate traditions have been involved, one associated with A. C. Pigou and the other with William H. Bowen and Paul A. Samuelson, both of which led to almost the identical confusion having to do with oversubscription of the size of the public sector. Indeed, a close examination of the two traditions reveals that they are tantamount to different ways of saying the same thing.

This paper will briefly trace the two externality traditions, show how they are similar, describe the erroneous reasoning to which they led, and show how the conflict resulting from the erroneous reasoning has been resolved in the past decade.

THE PIGOVIAN TRADITION: DIVERGENCE BETWEEN SOCIAL AND PRIVATE BENEFIT

The most pervasive modern intellectual tradition concerning the justification for collective action associates the need for collective

H. J. Kiesling is Associate Professor of Economics at Indiana University.

action with externalities generated by individual behavior which does not properly account for social interdependencies. While many of the ideas in this tradition were set down by the nineteenth-century economist Sidgwick, the most thorough statement was made by Pigou in his *Economics of Welfare*, first published in 1920.[2] Pigou demonstrated how the value of social product may diverge from the value of private product:

> . . . the essence of the matter is that one person A, in the course of rendering some service, for which payment is made, to a second person B, incidentally also renders services or disservices to other persons (not producers of like services) of such a sort that payment cannot be exacted from the benefited parties of compensation enforced on behalf of the injured parties. [p. 183]

It is the presence of "incidental services or disservices" which provides Pigou with a proper justification for collective action if that action will increase the value of total production, which Pigou termed the social dividend.

> . . . [the] adjustment of institutions to the end of directing self-interest into beneficial channels has been carried out in considerable detail. But even in the most advanced states there are failures and imperfections. We are not here concerned with those deficiencies of organization which sometimes cause higher noneconomic interests to be sacrificed to less important economic interests. Over and above these, there are many instances that prevent a community's resources from being distributed among different uses or occupations in the most effective way. The study involves some difficult analysis. Its purpose is essentially technical. It seeks to bring into clearer light some of the ways in which it now is, or eventually may become, feasible for government to control the play of economic forces in such wise as to promote the economic welfare, and through that the total welfare, of their citizens as a whole. [pp. 129–30]

> If in all industries the values of marginal social and marginal private net product differed to exactly the same extent, the *optimum* distribution of resources would always be attained, and there would be, on these lines, no case for fiscal interference. [p. 225]

> ... [when] investment under competitive conditions is carried to the point at which the value of the marginal private net product of the resources placed there is equal to the central value, the value of the social net product in that industry must diverge from the central value;* and the national dividend is not maximized. [pp. 214–15]

Collective action should somehow insure that the value of marginal social product per unit of cost is the same in all uses throughout the economic system. Collective action should be employed when this adjustment is not carried out by institutions in the private sector, although such adjustment is made less necessary since "much has already been done with institutional adjustments" to attain the desired result.[3]

The proper policy prescription to cope with any discrepancy between marginal social and marginal private product is for the government to impose taxes or give bounties:

> It is plain that divergences between private and social net product of the kinds we have so far been considering cannot, like divergences due to tenancy laws, be mitigated by a modification of the contractual relation between any two contracting parties, because the divergence arises out of a service or disservice rendered to persons other than the contracting parties. It is, however, possible for the State, if it so chooses, to remove the divergence in any field by 'extraordinary encouragements' or 'extraordinary restraints' upon investments in that field. The most obvious forms which these encouragements and restraints may assume are, of course, those of bounties and taxes. [p. 192]

To summarize then, there are two aspects to Professor Pigou's policy prescriptions concerning the divergences between marginal

---

*By central value *is meant the average value of the divergence between social net product and private net product.*

social benefit and marginal private benefit. First, action should be taken if it would increase the national dividend; second, action should be taken to eliminate any divergence between marginal social and marginal private benefits, or if not to eliminate, at least to make the degree of divergence constant in each industry.

A SECOND EXTERNALITY TRADITION: BOWEN AND SAMUELSON

In an important paper published in 1943, Bowen began a tradition in which the nature of the economic commodity itself assumed central prominence. Where Pigou had dealt with marginal benefits, public and private, of production, Bowen was more interested in the degree to which the recipient of the benefits could be made to pay for them in the marketplace. The key problem which requires collective attention obtains when it is technically possible to price commodities so that the recipients of the benefits can be made to pay for them.

> Economic goods are of two types: Individual goods and Social goods. . . . they differ, however, in the character of their demand. Individual goods are characterized by *divisibility*. They can be divided into small units over which particular persons can be given exclusive possession (e.g., carrots, sewing machines, barber services). Such goods are amenable to individual demands into free consumer choice. The amount consumed by any individual can be adjusted to his particular tastes. Social goods, on the other hand, are not divisible into units that can be the unique possessions of individuals. Rather, they tend to become part of the general environment—available to all persons in that environment (e.g., education, protection against foreign enemies, beautification of the landscape, flood control). Consequently, these goods cannot easily be sold to individual consumers and the quantities available to different individuals cannot be adjusted according to their respective tastes. The amount of the good must be set by a single decision applicable jointly to all persons. Social goods, therefore, are subject to collective or political rather than individual demand.[4]

Bowen proceeded to show that the individual demand schedules for such public goods should be added vertically to form the aggregate demand schedule for public goods instead of adding horizontally in the manner done for private commodities. This means that the greater the number of members there are in the body politic, the higher the price for a given quantity of a public good.[5]

In 1954, Samuelson extended the Bowen idea into a theory of collective goods which could be used in a general equilibrium welfare economics framework. As all economists know, if the world contains only goods which have no externalities and if all markets and goods are characterized by the attributes of classical pure competition, then the operation of the market at a *given* distribution of income will bring the economy to a point of optimal efficiency in the use of resources.[6] What Samuelson did was to carry Bowen's discussion to its logical conclusion and to deal analytically with the extreme instance of a good whose benefits are entirely external, i.e., when benefits of a good automatically accrue to every member of the group if the good is to be produced at all.[7] In so doing, Samuelson posited, for the purposes of theoretical reasoning only, two "polar cases" of economic goods.

I explicitly assume two categories of goods, ordinary *private consumption goods* ($X_1, \ldots X_n$) which can be parcelled out among different individuals ($1, 2, \ldots i, \ldots s$) according to the relations $X_j = 3X_j^i$; and *collective consumption goods* ($X_{n+1}, \ldots X_{n+m}$) which all enjoy in common in the sense that each individual's consumption of such a good leads to no subtraction from any other individual consumption of that good, so that $X_{n+j} = X_{n+j}^i$ simultaneously for each and every ith individual and collective consumptive good.[8]

In doing this, Samuelson was able to give a general equilibrium welfare economic solution, or Pareto optimum, for any given distribution of income, or, with the further addition of the Bergson social welfare function, for all possible distributions of income. The mechanism for doing this was to add the marginal utility of all individuals enjoying the collective good and make the ratio of this to the marginal utility of any private good equal to the ratios of the marginal rates of transformation of the two goods.[9]

THE TRADITIONS COMPARED

These two theoretical constructs concerning externality have been used to some extent by a great majority of Western economists in constructing a justification for collective action.[10] One is concerned with social and private benefits; the other, with the efficiency of the price system and the system of private property ownership. But does either theory make any unique contribution to our understanding, or are the theories merely redundant?

Let us reexamine the essentials of both theories. Pigou's has two central concerns. First, collective action should be taken if it would increase the national dividend; second, collective intervention should be considered if it would eliminate any divergence between marginal social benefit and marginal private benefit, and if this cannot be perfectly accomplished, then the collective action should attempt to make the divergence between marginal social and marginal private benefits proportionally the same in each use throughout the economic system. Bowen and Samuelson define two types of good—private, where the marginal private benefit and marginal social benefit are the same, and social, where it is difficult if not impossible to price all the benefits to the recipients. Another way to express this, which has become popular in the literature, is to say that it is not possible to internalize the externality. But consider what it means to internalize externalities. It means simply that all those who enjoy benefits from the economic system pay for them. This is the same thing as saying that the marginal social product is made equal to the marginal private product in all uses in the economic system, which, except for Pigou's constant of proportionality proviso, is the same thing as eliminating divergences between marginal social and marginal private benefits. With the exception of the proportionality proviso, then (and of course this could be an important exception), the two intellectual traditions concerning externality come to the same thing.

The existence of Pigou's constant of proportionality argument means that there are some differences of emphasis between the two traditions, however. Thus, as we shall see below, the Samuelsonian tradition has it that collective intervention should be contemplated whenever an externality exists. This is not true in the Pigouvian system if we are to maintain some constant of proportionality between marginal social benefits and marginal private benefits in all uses, since there will be some externality involved in every use. Because of this difference, it is quite probable that the Samuelsonian tradition is more misleading when it comes to policy prescriptions, although, paradoxically, the Samuelsonian tradition is more correct formally.

CONFUSION CONCERNING THE JUSTIFICATION FOR COLLECTIVE ACTION

Both externality traditions lead to error and confusion with respect to the proper role of the public sector. Indeed, if the two constructs are, for all practical purposes, identical, it would seem only natural that both would lead toward the same error. This is essentially true, although the error derived from the Pigovian tradition was probably caused much more by later readers of Pigou than by the great welfare economist himself. In the case of the Samuelson analysis, the fault for the error falls completely on the shoulders of later readers, since the analysis itself is flawless.

The erroneous reasoning in the Pigovian tradition was demonstrated in an important paper published in 1960 by R. H. Coase. In the development of his ideas, Pigou had used an example of a railway and surrounding woodland where the railway engine set fire to the woodland from time to time with sparks from the engine. Pigou's solution to this dilemma had been to have the government require the railway to pay compensation to the owner of the woodland. Using this example, Coase is able to demonstrate the nature of the difficulty with Pigou's reasoning.

> Pigou clearly thought it was desirable to force the railway to pay compensation and it is easy to see the kind of argument that would have led him to this conclusion. Suppose a railway is considering whether to run an additional train or to increase the speed of an existing train or to install spark-preventing devices on its engines. If the railway were not liable for fire damage, then, when making these decisions, it would not take into account as a cost the increase in damage resulting from the additional train or the faster train or the failure to install spark-preventing devices. This is the source of the divergence between private and social net products. It results in the railway performing acts which will lower the value of total production—and which it would not do if it were liable for the damage. [p. 31]

> How is it that the Pigovian analysis seems to give the wrong answer? The reason is that Pigou does not seem to have noticed that his analysis is dealing with an entirely different question. The analysis as such is correct. But it is quite illegitimate for Pigou to draw the particular conclusion he does. The question at issue is not whether it is desirable to run an additional train or a faster train or to install smoke-preventing devices; the question at issue is whether it is desirable to have a system in which the railway has to compensate those who suffer damage from the fires which it causes or one in which the railway does not have to compensate them. When an economist is comparing alternative social arrangements, the proper procedure is to compare the total social product yielded by these different arrangements. The comparison of private and social products is neither here nor there. [p. 34][11]

The last two sentences provide the key to the proper treatment of economic externality with respect to public intervention. What counts is whether the institutional arrangement being used is the *best alternative*. There is no way to guarantee that this best alternative is one in which social benefits and private benefits will not diverge.[12]

We now turn to the confusion stemming from the second externality tradition, that of the Bowen-Samuelson concept of public
goods. As stated already, Samuelson's analysis, unlike Pigou's, is
much less vulnerable to formal criticism, although this invulnerabil-
ity is achieved at the cost of a much higher level of abstraction. It
was indeed the very abstract nature of Samuelson's model which
gave rise to some vociferous criticism. Thus, Julius Margolis was
quick to ask, in a critical comment on Samuelson's paper, whether
there were such a thing as a pure public good.

> Are there collective consumption goods? Are they the typical
> public services? . . . [Samuelson] claims that collective goods are
> not rationed—that the use of a good by A does not involve any costs
> to B. Clearly this is not the case in such common public services as
> education, hospitals, and highways, where capacity limitations and
> congestion are topics of the daily press. Would it be true of the
> more sovereign functions of justice and police? The crowded calen-
> dar of the courts certainly implies that the use of this function by
> A makes it less available to B. Similarly a complaint to the police
> ties up the officers in a maze of arguments, forms to be completed,
> and hearings to be attended, reducing their availability to others.
> Possibly the only goods which would seem to conform to Samuel-
> son's definition are national defenses and the aged lighthouse illus-
> tration. The lighthouse shines for all ships, when the lanes are not
> crowded; and everyone receives a full share of protection from the
> military machine.[13]

To this criticism Samuelson had a most reasonable answer. An
understanding of polar situations would allow for an understanding
of in-between cases also. The discussion was specifically meant to be
one of pure theory and is therefore necessarily conducted at the
highest level of abstraction.

> Doctrinal history shows that theoretical insight often comes from
> considering strong or extreme cases. The Grand Walrasian model
> of competitive general equilibrium is one such extreme polar case.

We can formulate it so stringently as to leave no economic role for government. What strong polar case shall the student of public expenditure set along side this pure private economy?[14]

But while Samuelson's analysis is formally correct, it is nevertheless true that his level of abstraction did in fact lead to error, but in a direction *opposite* to that thought by Margolis. The confusion coming from the Bowen-Samuelson division of goods into polar cases of purely public and purely private did not come from the assumption that there could be any pure public good (which there can, as Margolis admits) but from the assumption that there could be a purely *private* good. In effect what is assumed is that there is a sharp line to be drawn between purely private goods, with which it is possible to associate no externalities, and all other goods, with which can be associated some degree of externality, ranging from very little to total. This makes it impossible to develop a general theory for the existence of the public sector which is logically consistent. Considered from a standpoint of practical policy formation, it leads to difficulties in developing a guide to questions of how large the public sector should be, because the assumption of the existence of pure *private* goods placed writers in the position of assuming a strict dichotomy between public and private goods, which in turn leads to the position that public intervention is warranted whenever an externality exists. The direction of the error is the same as that in the Pigovian tradition: The size of the public sector is oversubscribed.

RESOLUTION OF CONFUSION: THE 1960'S

Several papers published in the 1960's helped to provide a consistent analytical framework for the treatment of economic externality and its role in the justification of collective action. Of these, I would list three as providing the basic foundations. The first is Coase's paper, which has already been mentioned. Coase sums up his thesis in the very first paragraph of his paper.

This paper is concerned with those actions of business firms which have harmful effects on others. The standard example is that of a factory the smoke from which has harmful effects on those occupying neighbouring properties. The economic analysis of such a situation has usually proceeded in terms of a divergence between the private and social product of the factory, in which economists have largely followed the treatment of Pigou in *The Economics of Welfare*. The conclusions to which this kind of analysis seems to have led most economists is that it would be desirable to make the owner of the factory liable for the damage caused to those injured by the smoke, or alternatively, to place a tax on the equivalent in money terms to the damage it would cause, or finally, to exclude the factory from residential districts. . . .

The traditional approach has tended to obscure the nature of the choice that has to be made. The question is commonly thought of as one in which A inflicts harm on B and what has to be decided is: how should we restrain A? But this is wrong. We are dealing with a problem of a reciprocal nature. To avoid the harm to B would inflict harm on A. The real question that has to be decided is: Should A be allowed to harm B or should B be allowed to harm A? The problem is to avoid the more serious harm. [Coase, pp. 1–2]

Coase's central argument is that there are two sides to every externality, that there are costs involved in removing an externality, and that there is no assurance that such costs would be less than that of the original externality. Coase also cites a great many court cases to support a much more sweeping declaration: that in instances where bargaining can occur between two parties involved in an externality proceeding, such as cattle destroying crops, the social optimum solution to the externality will be reached *regardless* of the beginning institutional framework with respect to legal liability. Thus, in the instance of cattle destroying crops, if the cattleman is liable for damage by his herd, he will take care to arrive at the herd size which is the point of maximum social gain, since he must cover the cost of any damage to the farmer's crops. If the cattleman is not liable, on the other hand, the farmer will offer to compensate the cattleman to a point where the cattleman feels that the compensation is greater than the value forgone by decreasing the size of herd. In both cases, the optimum herd size is reached, although, of course, the distribution of benefits between the cattleman and the farmer is quite different in each case.[15]

Above we have already discussed Coase's criticism of Pigou's propensity to advocate taxes and subsidies in many situations. This can be demonstrated more rigorously with the help of a diagram used by Turvey.[16] Consider a situation in which A's activity causes air pollution such that B is forced to incur a cost as demonstrated in figure 1. The equilibrium production level for A is OJ, and this is achieved so long as the two parties can bargain, regardless of whether A is legally liable for damage or not; for if not, B will offer compensation, since B's marginal loss is greater than A's marginal gain beyond OJ. Now suppose that the state charges A a tax equal to the

FIGURE I

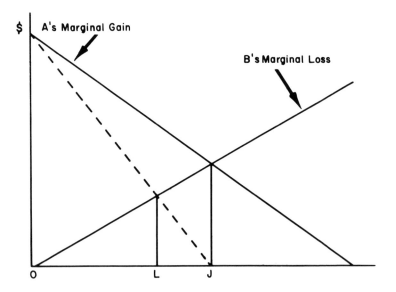

loss he causes B. Subtracting this from his marginal gain schedule gives the dotted line as his marginal net gain. The equilibrium production level for A is OL, which results in less total product. Notice, however, that if the state takes the tax revenue collected from A and *gives it to B*, the total welfare level remains unchanged.

The second paper I wish to discuss is a detailed exploration of the concept of externality by James Buchanan and William Stubblebine.[17] Coase complains in his paper that economists have never determined in any exact sense what it is they mean by externality. Buchanan and Stubblebine repeat this criticism and respond by providing some rigorous definitions of various aspects of economic externality, which by their very nature suggest something concerning the theoretical foundations for collective action. Thus, the general term *externality* (the utility of one individual is to some extent dependent upon an activity controlled by a second individual) is broken down into two categories according to relevance.

> An externality is defined as *potentially relevant* when the activity, to the extent that it is actually performed, generates *any* desire on the part of the externally benefited (damaged) party (A) to modify the behavior of the party in power to take action (B) through trade, persuasion, compromise, agreement, convention, collective action, etc. An externality which, to the extent that it is performed, exerts no such influence is defined as irrelevant [pp. 373–74]

A further distinction of Pareto relevance is made.

> An externality is defined to be Pareto relevant when the extent of the activity may be modified in such a way that the externally affected party, A, can be made better off without the acting party, B, being made worse off. That is to say, "gains from trade" characterize the Pareto relevant externality, trade that takes the form of some change in the activity of B as his part of the bargain. [p. 374]

The important statement that is then made with these distinctions is that "what vanishes in Pareto equilibrium are the Pareto relevant externalities" (p. 375). That is to say, there may still be externalities in existence even at a Pareto optimum. Buchanan and Stubblebine go on to show how this is true with a detailed example involving a fence between two neighbors. The important conclusion from this analysis is obvious. In the words of Buchanan and Stubblebine,

> . . . the observation of external effects, taken alone, cannot provide a basis for judgment concerning the desirability of some modification in an existing state of affairs. There is not a *prima facie* case for intervention in all cases where an externality is observed to exist. The internal benefits from carrying out the activity, net of costs, may be greater than the external damage that is imposed on other parties. [p. 381]

The third important paper in this development was published by Otto Davis and Andrew Whinston in 1962.[18] Buchanan and Stubblebine had, in their paper, made a distinction between externalities on the basis of whether or not they affected costs at the margin. An externality which did not do so was termed an *inframarginal* externality. Davis and Whinston proceed to show how the distinction is a crucial one in the consideration of economic externalities.

Consider two firms, A and B, with the first causing the second some external costs. There are two ways that this can occur. First, A's operations cost B a certain sum of money no matter what the level of B's production. Second, the costs of A's externality vary with the level of B's production. These two types of externality are termed *separable* and *nonseparable* respectively. The difference can be seen most readily by considering B's total cost curve. If A's operation raises the level of the curve but nowhere changes the slope, the externality is separable. If A's operation also changes the slope of B's total cost curve, i.e., if B's marginal cost is in part a function of the level of A's production, then the externality is nonseparable.[19] Having made this distinction, Davis and Whinston are able to prove that in the instance of an inseparable externality there is no way of devising, *even theoretically*, a scheme of collective action which will achieve this social optimum.[20] In game theoretic terms, which Davis and Whinston use in part of their paper, it is not possible for any player (firm) to ascertain his own dominant row.* When externalities are separable, it is possible theoretically to arrive at a collective solution, although in practical terms this requires a great deal of highly sophisticated knowledge.[21] If the separable externalities are reciprocal in nature, i.e., if A's operation causes some external costs or benefits to B and at the same time B's operation causes an external cost or benefit to A, then the situation is much more complicated than in the nonreciprocal case.

POLICY IMPLICATIONS

The theoretical developments discussed above were important to the formulation of economic policy. As Coase demonstrated, the Pigovian analysis indicated that the existence of a divergence between marginal social cost and marginal private cost would suggest a tax upon the offending party and vice versa for benefits. As Coase also points out, this position seems to have been accepted uncritically by most economists from Pigou's day forward. The policy problem which arises in the Bowen-Samuelson framework has to do with the implication that public intervention is warranted whenever an externality exists, which, as discussed above, was due to the acceptance of the theoretical existence of pure private goods.

With the developments in the 1960's, a much more rigorous and general framework has been built for the making of policy recommendations. Two ramifications of the later developments are of special importance. These have to do with the problem of very small externalities and the consideration of multiple alternatives.

The crucial (and embarrassing) question for both traditions discussed above had to do with the question of when an externality was big enough to merit social action. In the Pigovian tradition this

---

*A dominant row *is defined as the policy choice of a player in a game if he will pick the same action no matter what the choice of the other player(s).*

amounts to asking: if we are to use collective action to correct for divergence between marginal-social and marginal-private benefits, *how much* divergence must there be for us to actually start the wheels of the public process turning? Using Pigou's approach, there are two possible answers to this question. If the policy-maker were to try for a strict correspondence between marginal-social and marginal-private benefits (costs) throughout the economy, *any* externality would be enough. But if the policy-maker were content to stop at the point where the relationships between marginal-private and social benefits (costs) are *proportional* throughout the economy, then it would be proper to begin collective action only when the divergence in any one sector was more than that generally true throughout the economy. This would create an empirical problem from the decision-maker which would be almost impossible to solve. In the Bowen-Samuelson tradition the demonstration of externality means that the good is not purely private, which in turn suggests justification for collective action. The policy implication is therefore identical to that of the policy-maker just discussed in the Pigovian tradition who aspires to provide a strict correspondence between marginal-social and marginal-private benefits or costs throughout the economy.[22]

The second important ramification of the later theoretical developments has to do with the consideration of alternatives. Instead of using the central government's taxing and spending power each time an externality comes into view, the new developments teach us to consider as many alternative solutions as our imagination can possibly devise, including changes in the institutional framework. Thus, the institutional framework is no longer accepted as a parameter in the analysis, but instead becomes one of the variables.

It would be useful to close this discussion of policy implications with an illustration taken from the literature. Consider the following from a paper by Alfred Kahn concerning one public service:

The event that first suggested the phenomenon (market failure) to this writer was the disappearance of passenger railroad service from Ithaca, a small and comparatively isolated (since that time even more so!) community in upstate New York. It may be assumed the service was withdrawn because over a long enough period of time the individual decisions travelers made, for each of their projected trips into and out of Ithaca and the other cities served, did not provide the railroads enough total revenue to cover incremental costs (defined over the same period). Considering the comparative comforts and speeds of competing media, those individual decisions were by no means irrational: the railroad was slow and uncomfortable.

What reason, then, was there to question the aggregate effect of those individual choices—withdrawal of the service? The fact is the railroad provided the one reliable means of getting into and out of Ithaca in all kinds of weather; and this insufficiently-exerted option, this inadequately-used alternative was something I for one would have been willing to pay something to have kept alive. This way of looking at the result suggests a simple, though unfortunately subjective and hence not necessarily practical, test of whether the railroad's closing was economically correct: let each traveller or potential traveller have asked himself how much he would have been willing to pledge regularly over some time period, say annually, by purchase of prepaid tickets, to keep rail passenger service in Ithaca. So long as the amount he would have declared (to himself) would have exceeded what he actually paid in that period—and my own introspective experiment shows it would—then to that extent the disappearance of passenger service from Ithaca was an incident of market failure.

This reasoning illustrates well the analytical difficulty of dealing with every externality as if public tax-subsidy intervention and the tendency of neglecting to consider all the alternatives were relevant. Thus, Kahn's proposal involves an externality—option-value—and since this exists to the satisfaction of the writer, a public subsidy is required. No attention is given to the problem of whether the benefit to be derived in so doing would be greater than the social cost. My intuitive assessment of the situation is that it would not. Indeed, there are many such option-values to be found throughout the economy (consumer-surplus is a form of option-value) and the mere existence of an externality in this particular instance may not mean anything at all.

Secondly, only two alternatives are considered: no passenger train and service as before. Intermediate solutions are not entertained. Perhaps the Interstate Commerce Commission might allow the company to run passenger trains on days when there have been blizzards and charge a much higher fare; or trains could be given a small subsidy for running on blizzard days. Both of these solutions and undoubtedly a good many more would be much less expensive to society than running a near-empty passenger train faithfully each day between Ithaca and New York City.

Correct social decisions concerning the allocation of resources between the public and private sectors require that theoretical issues concerning economic externality be clearly understood.[23] This essay has isolated two theoretical traditions with respect to externality concepts and shown how they are essentially identical. Both traditions contained logical pitfalls which could easily trap the unwary into errors leading to the oversubscription of the size of the public sector. Also discussed were a number of papers which contributed substantially to our theoretical understanding of the meaning of economic externality or the making of allocative decisions.

Besides the allocation question, the developments discussed have another important implication for the study of political economy. This is the danger inherent in the widespread practice of assuming the institutional framework constant for the purposes of economic analysis. A proper analysis of the potential benefits of reducing social externalities cannot stop with existing institutional structures; *all* alternatives must be examined. It might be that professional economists are moving toward a more sophisticated latter-day renovation of institutional economics.

NOTES

1. This essay is concerned with the theoretical developments important to the *justification* for collective action in a welfare economics framework. That is to say, assuming an overall goal of maximizing economic well-being, the paper deals with the necessary conditions for intervention broadly defined and not with the necessary and sufficient conditions for the actual provision of public service.

This paper will not deal with issues such as those raised by Mancur Olsen in his important book, *The Logic of Collective Action*, which describes the reasons why collective action does or does not become implemented, assuming that collective action is justified. This paper deals with the necessary conditions; Olsen's theoretical construct, with the working or nonworking of the sufficient conditions.

The author gratefully acknowledges the detailed comments made upon an earlier draft of this paper by Robert Bish, H. Scott Gordon, Henry Oliver, and Vincent Ostrom. Any errors which remain in the manuscript are the sole responsibility of the author.

2. A. C. Pigou, *The Economics of Welfare*, 4th ed. (New York: St. Martin's Press, 1960). Pigou's great teacher, Alfred Marshall, dealt with welfare economic concepts in terms of the partial equilibrium approach of producers' and consumers' surplus. Pigou is generally thought to have introduced (with, to be sure, some influence by writers on the Continent) the general equilibrium idea of dealing with divergences between marginal social and marginal private costs by everywhere equalizing the marginal social products of resources in all industries. A good discussion of the place of both Sidgwick and Pigou in these developments can be seen in Hla Myint, *Theories of Welfare Economics* (New York: Augustus M. Kelley, 1962), pp. 129–32 and chap. 10.

3. Thus, Pigou is essentially optimistic with respect to the general workings of the free market mechanism. He was optimistic also in that he felt desired social changes could be brought about "on the margin" using market money values as a measure of economic welfare. For the purist this analysis already contains two problems. First, social problems may be of such a nature that marginal changes will not accomplish the desired ends. As Myint quotes Professor Hicks as saying, the "total conditions" of the optimum are more important than the marginal conditions (Myint, p. 180). Second, the use of money value of goods to represent subjective value involves an implicit interpersonal comparison of utility. While most pragmatic economists accept this procedure, it would

not be acceptable to the purist, and we get back to the thorny problem of being unable to define exactly what it is we wish to maximize in welfare economics. In point of fact, as Myint demonstrates, it is in the purist sense impossible to evaluate welfare without bringing in ethical judgments or preconceptions concerning the evaluation of commodities and the "proper" distribution of income. But most economists would agree that this difficulty is not of enough importance to require abandoning any attempt at economic analysis where welfare is concerned. As Myint points out, "it is not impossible to find the common denominator among different standards of value and . . . although this important truth is quite trite when explicitly stated, it is frequently forgotten in the abstract discussions of the Ultimate Good" (p. 295).

4. William H. Bowen, "The Interpretation of Voting and the Allocation of Economic Resources," *Quarterly Journal of Economics* (November 1943), p. 27.

The intellectual origin for Bowen's analysis was probably the writings of some of the European masters in the field of public finance in the 1920's and 1930's who were occupied primarily with the problem of the proper distribution of the tax burden according to the benefit principle. Important names in this discussion were Wicksell, Lindahl, and Sax. The former two writers discussed the problem in a framework of developing the proper shares of support of a public good which accrued to everyone. Sax, on the other hand, was a critic of such schemes because he felt that the public goods in question were too indivisible for meaningful analysis. See Richard A. Musgrave, "The Voluntary Exchange Theory of Public Finance," *Quarterly Journal of Economics*, vol. 53 (Feb. 1938), pp. 213–37.

While it was not stressed, the idea of collective goods was not completely absent in the earlier literature. Thus, Pigou quotes Sidgwick's observation "it may easily happen that the benefits of a well placed lighthouse must be largely enjoyed by ships on which no toll could be conveniently levied." Pigou, p. 184. The following passage is also found in *The Economics of Welfare*: ". . . we observe that a further element of divergence between social and private net products, important to economic welfare though not to the actual substance of the national dividend, may emerge in the form of uncompensated or unchanged effects upon the *satisfaction that consumers derive from the consumption of things other than the one directly affected*." (Italics in original; Pigou, p. 191).

5. For example, if there were 100 citizens of country A who each would pay $10 for X units of defense, then the total demand price for X units is $1,000. If there were 200 citizens who felt the same way, the demand would be $2,000, etc.

6. See Francis M. Bator, "The Simple Analytics of Welfare Maxi-

mization," *American Economic Review*, vol. 47 (March 1957), pp. 22–59, and James M. Henderson and Richard E. Quandt, *Micro-Economic Theory* (New York: McGraw-Hill, 1958), Chap. 12.

7. Paul A. Samuelson, "The Pure Theory of Public Expenditure," *Review of Economics and Statistics* (Nov. 1954), pp. 387–89, and "Diagrammatic Exposition of a Theory of Public Expenditure," *Review of Economics and Statistics* (Nov. 1955), pp. 350–56.

8. Samuelson, "Pure Theory of Public Expenditure," p. 387.

9. The analogous solution for private goods only is, of course, that the marginal utility ratio of two goods for each consumer is equal to the marginal technical rate of transformation between the two goods.

10. The following is a passage in one of the more popular undergraduate public finance texts: ". . . the traditional activities of government have been undertaken because the benefits of these activities are social or community in character; that is, they accrue in part or entirely to the members of the community as a group rather than separately to individuals. The activities are thus not divisible into units which can be sold to individuals, and thus, if they are to be provided, they must be rendered by the political organization of society. In more technical terms, marginal social benefits from these activities exceed marginal private benefits; that is, the total gains to society from the services exceed those which accrue directly and separately to individuals." John F. Due, *The Theory of Public Finance*, 2nd ed. (Homewood, Ill.: Richard D. Irwin, 1959).

11. R. H. Coase, "The Problem of Social Cost," *The Journal of Law and Economics*, vol. 3 (Chicago: University of Chicago Press, 1960).

12. But consider the following passage from Professor Coase's paper: ". . . Pigou distinguishes between the case in which a person renders services for which he receives no payment and the case in which a person renders disservices and compensation is not given to the injured parties. Our main attention has, of course, centered on this second case. It is therefore rather astonishing to find, as was pointed out to me by Professor Francesco Forte, that the problem of the smoking chimney–the "stock instance" or "classroom example" of the second case–is used by Pigou as an example of the first case (services rendered without payment) and is never mentioned, at any rate explicitly, in connection with the second case. Pigou points out that factory owners who devote resources to preventing their chimneys from smoking render services for which they receive no payment. The implication, in the light of Pigou's discussion later in the chapter, is that a factory owner with a smokey chimney should be given a bounty to induce him to install smoke-preventing devices. Most modern economists would suggest that the owner of the factory with the smokey chimney should be taxed. It seems a pity that economists (apart from Professor Forte) do not seem to

have noticed this feature of Pigou's treatment since a realization that the problem could be tackled in either of these two ways would probably have led to an explicit recognition of its reciprocal nature." Coase, pp. 34–35. In this passage Coase seems to be implying that it is "most modern economists" who are at fault and not Pigou himself. Coase is able to show, however, that policy prescriptions used by Pigou in many of his examples are erroneous (see Coase, *passim*).

13. Julius Margolis, "A Comment on the Pure Theory of Public Expenditure," *Review of Economics and Statistics*, vol. 27 (Aug. 1955), pp. 347–48.

14. Paul A. Samuelson, "Diagramatic Exposition," p. 350.

15. This does not mean that Coase thinks that questions of income distribution are not important. The point being made is that the two parties, when allowed to bargain, reach a social optimum no matter what the legal framework. This optimum having been reached, it would then be possible for society to redistribute wealth in any way it saw fit.

The limitations of an intellectual exercise such as this one of Coase's should be kept firmly in mind. Thus, the analysis assumed that both parties would bargain rationally in full knowledge of all the relevant facts. In the real world, when the affected parties in an externality situation may be several dozen, or perhaps several million, it is obvious that these assumptions quickly become heroic.

16. Ralph Turvey, "On Divergences between Social Cost and Private Cost," *Economica* (Aug. 1963), pp. 309–13.

17. James M. Buchanan and William Craig Stubblebine, "Externality," *Economica* (Nov. 1962), pp. 371–79.

18. Otto Davis and Andrew Whinston, "Externalities, Welfare and the Theory of Games," *Journal of Political Economy* (June 1962), pp. 341–62.

19. An example of a separable cost function would be $C = A_1 q_1^n + A_2 q_2^n$, where q_1 and q_2 are the levels of output for firms 1 and 2 respectively. The marginal cost function for firm 1 is $n A_1 q_1^{n-1}$ and is therefore a function only of the output of firm 1.

A nonseparable function is, on the other hand, multiplicative, such as $C_1 = A_1 q_1^n + A_2 q_2^n q_1$. Here the marginal cost function is $n A_1 q_1^{n-1} + A_2 q_2^n$ and firm 2's level of production enters into 1's marginal costs.

20. To be exact, this is true only when the nonseparable externalities are reciprocal, i.e., each curve affects the other's marginal cost function. Where the nonseparable externality is not reciprocal, it is conceptually possible for an optimum to be reached with taxes and subsidies but only with extreme difficulty.

21. An example of the proper solution of tax and subsidy policy in the case of a separable externality would be as follows. First, the decision-maker would have to know the relevant cost schedules for both firms and,

using a simultaneous equation approach, solve for optimum social output. Having obtained this, he can compute the proper tax and subsidy for each to be added to each price according to the following:

$$P + t_1 = \frac{\partial C_1(q_1, q_2)}{\partial q_1} \bigg|_{q_1^*}$$

$$P + t_2 = \frac{\partial C_2(q_1, q_2)}{\partial q_2} \bigg|_{q_2^*}$$

Where t is either a tax or a subsidy and q_1^* and q_2^* are the optimum social outputs obtained from the solution to the simultaneous equations. See Davis and Whinston, op. cit.

22. The analytical difficulty shown by this analysis can be better illustrated with an example. Suppose I do not like your gaudy orange-and-black tie. This is an externality since your tie consumption is creating disutility for me. Suppose I convince you that this externality should be internalized. For this, the following procedure would be necessary. You allow every potential viewer of your orange-and-black tie to assemble in one place. You model the tie with every other combination of apparel which you own, and for each combination you elicit a *truthful* response concerning how much it would be worth to them for you not to wear the tie. We then have a lawyer draw up with each person a long contract which shows how many pennies you will pay (or receive from) each person each time they are in a position where they must view the tie. Since the cost of dealing with the externality in this case is greater than the externality itself, it is a nonrelevant externality.

23. In general, economic externalities obtain when actions on the part of an individual or group cause benefits to other members of society for which they are not compensated or costs for which they are not required to pay.

Part 2

RECENT DEVELOPMENTS IN MONETARY
THEORY

4

Is the Money Supply an Exogenous Variable?

ELMUS WICKER

A major transformation is taking place in money supply theory away from the quasi-mechanical models of the textbook to the construction of testable money supply hypotheses useful in predicting the response of the money supply to changes in the stock of reserves, open market rates, and the rediscount rate. This development, I believe, represents the most important innovation in money supply theory since the distinguished contributions to the theory of the money multiplier of Phillips, Rogers, Meade, Angell, and Ficek.[1] When Sir John Hicks called for a "marginal revolution" thirty years ago to rejuvenate the theory of the demand for money, he failed to see at the time one of the most interesting implications of his 1935 suggestion.[2] Why not apply the theory of economic choice to money supply theory as well as to money demand theory? Because knowledge of these recent changes and their implications for the effectiveness of monetary control are not as yet very widely diffused, except perhaps among monetary theorists, a brief review of these developments may serve a useful expository purpose.

A familiar macroeconomic practice has been to treat the money

Elmus Wicker is Professor of Economics at Indiana University.

supply as though it were an exogenous variable completely controlled by the central bank. In its most repetitious form, the statement frequently appears: The central bank can make the money supply what it wants it to be. How this can be done is usually left unspecified. The reasons for this procedure have not always been made clear. It may merely reflect one of the following views: The money supply does not really matter and further specification of the money supply function contributes little to the explanation of the behavior of output, employment, and prices; the money supply matters, but the administration of monetary control is inefficient; the money supply in traditional macroeconomic models is unaffected by changes in such endogenous variables as income and the rate of interest; and the money supply equation is not meant to be a description of how the monetary system does in fact behave but how it should behave. If the central bank behaved ideally, monetary control would be fully effective.

I regard all these as unsatisfactory grounds for viewing the money supply as autonomously determined by the monetary authority. What is ignored are the behavioral relationships relevant to a full description of the money supply process: the public's demand for currency and time deposits; the banks' demand for required reserves and excess reserves; and the banks' borrowing from the central bank. The behavioral relationships incorporate important institutional characteristics into the description of the money supply process; for example, the determinants of commercial bank borrowing from the central bank and the banks' demand for excess reserves. What is required, therefore, is a model of the money supply process which includes not only the stock of unborrowed reserves and reserve requirement ratios (the familiar textbook approach) but also these behavioral relationships as well.

In the first two parts of the paper I construct such a model and review very briefly some estimates of the multiplier and the interest elasticity of the money stock. Attempts to estimate multipliers or elasticities of money supply functions have been made by Ronald

Teigen, Karl Brunner and Allan Meltzer, Stephen Goldfeld, Frank deLeeuw, David Fand, and Thomas Brady.[3] In a recent study David Fand developed a framework for comparing multipliers and money supply elasticities from different econometric models. Although he found that interest rate elasticity exhibited wide variability, depending upon different money supply concepts and model specification, he concluded nevertheless, "the M.S. functions based primarily on financial variables appear to be stable enough to justify further effort toward their refinement and improvement."[4] The results to date remain inconclusive. Enough has been done, however, to cast serious doubt on the advisability of continuing to treat the money supply as though it were independent of the behavior of interest rates.[5]

In the second part of the paper I examine the view of Lyle Gramley and Samuel Chase that the money multiplier equation is not a supply function for deposits.[6] They maintain that the reserve-deposit relationship is in fact an equilibrium solution to a set of equations describing the behavior of the central bank, commercial banks, and the public on the market for reserves. The supply of unborrowed reserves is controlled, it is assumed, by the central bank. The demand for reserves is determined by the preferences of the banks and the public to hold reserves (currency plus deposits of commercial banks at the central bank). Deposit expansion occurs when the commercial banks attempt to rid themselves of an excess supply of reserves. Economists have usually reserved the term *supply function* to mean schedules of quantities offered at alternative prices. Within this context a demand deposit supply function should, according to Gramley and Chase, relate the willingness of banks to supply deposits with the yield on demand deposit balances. The yield on demand deposits is, of course, not an explicit rate since the law specifically prohibits the payment of interest on demand balances.

Gramley and Chase and John Kareken have constructed money supply models which introduce a yield on deposit balances as an important determinant of the banks' willingness to supply deposits.[7]

Traditional money supply theorists have ignored the effect of deposit yields. This oversight might be rationalized if we assume a legal maximum ceiling rate payable on demand deposits of zero. Nevertheless, it is still an interesting theoretical question to raise: How does the explicit introduction of a yield on demand balances affect the willingness of banks to supply deposits?

The final section of the paper indicates the significance and the implications of the new approach for the theory of the money supply and the applied problems of monetary control.

THE MARKET FOR RESERVES: THE TRADITIONAL APPROACH RECAST

By recasting the traditional money multiplier approach within the framework of a market for reserves, we can reveal clearly what the relationship is between deposit expansion and an injection of reserves.[8] For the simplest textbook case the money multiplier shows at what level of deposits commercial banks will be satisfied with holding the actual amount of reserves in existence. At any other deposit level there will be disequilibrium in the market for reserves. The reserve deposit relationship emerges therefore as an equilibrium solution to a set of demand and supply equations describing the behavior of the banking system, including the central bank, on the market for reserves. Suppose that the supply of reserves (R_s) and the reserve requirement ratio (r) are autonomously determined by the central bank. Also assume that currency, time deposits, and excess reserves are all equal to zero. We can represent the banks' demand for required reserves quite simply. Given the legal reserve requirement against demand deposits (r), the demand for required reserves (R_d) is proportional to the level of demand deposits (D):

$$R_d = r \cdot D \qquad (1)$$

Setting the demand for reserves (R_d) equal to the supply (R_s) and solving for demand deposits, we obtain the money multiplier formula:

$$D = R_s/r \qquad (2)$$

Of course, in this oversimplified case it is not quite legitimate to speak of a demand function for required reserves when the reserve requirement (r) is a legal constraint. However, legal considerations alone do not as a matter of fact dictate choice, because commercial banks do have the option of running a reserve deficiency and paying a penalty. Within this abbreviated model of the money supply process, demand deposits appear as an endogenous variable. The exogenous variables are the reserve requirement ratio (r) and the supply of reserves (R_s). The response of deposits to a change in reserves represents an exercise in comparative statics brought about by either a change in r or R_s.

If the money supply process were no more complicated than the quasi-mechanical relationship described by the traditional textbook money multiplier formula, then the money supply could correctly be regarded as autonomously determined by the central bank. The model, however, must be expanded to include the public's preferences for currency and time deposits as well as the banks' demand for excess reserves. Some allowances must also be made for the fact that banks may supplement the amount of reserves by borrowing from the central bank. More realistic models of the money supply process allow for a wider range of choice by banks and the public over both the amount and composition of bank reserves. The public can affect the amount of reserves by altering the ratio of currency to deposits; it can influence the composition of bank reserves between required and excess by increasing the ratio of time deposits to total deposits. Similarly, the banks can change total reserves by borrowing from the central bank; they can change the composition of bank reserves by exercising discretion over the amount of excess reserves they desire to hold.

We can easily extend our money supply model by introducing currency issued by the treasury or the central bank and commercial bank time deposits. The procedure is to assume that currency and time deposits are complements rather than substitutes for demand deposits. But substitution can be introduced later to allow for the effect of interest rate changes on the public's demand for currency and time deposits. Suppose that the public desires to hold some fraction (c) of demand deposits in the form of currency (cD) and an additional fraction (t) in the form of time deposits (tD). When the public desires to hold more currency, the banks experience a decrease in their reserves. The banks obtain currency from the central bank by drawing down their reserve balances. Since the public decides the allocation of its money balances between currency and demand deposits, the banks must stand ready to supply all currency needs of the public by suffering the loss of assets which count as bank reserves. Our demand equation for reserves (R_d) plus currency held by the public (C_p) is now modified to include two additional components besides the banks' demand for required reserves against demand deposits (rD): The public's demand for currency (cD) and the banks' demand for required reserves against time deposits (r'tD) where r' is the legal reserve requirement against time deposits and r' is less than r:

$$R_d + C_p = rD + cD + r'tD \tag{3}$$

Define total reserves (R) as equal to member bank reserves at the Federal Reserve (R_s) plus currency in the vaults of commercial banks (C_B).

$$R = R_s + C_B \tag{4}$$

Let H equal the supply of total reserves (R) plus currency in the hands of the public (C_p):

$$H = R + C_p \tag{5}$$

H is sometimes referred to as high-powered money. Setting the demand equal to the supply and solving for D, we obtain:

$$D = H \cdot 1/r + c + r't \tag{6}$$

The money supply (M) is equal to currency in the hands of the public and demand deposits:

$$M = D + C_p \qquad (7)$$

This slightly more realistic version of the money supply process introduces two elements to complicate the problem of monetary control by the central bank. The public's preferences for both currency and time deposits affect the response of the banking system to a change in either total reserves or reserve requirement ratios. Unless the public's preferences remain relatively stable, monetary control will necessarily be made more difficult. How much more difficult, it is impossible to say without a detailed empirical investigation. No doubt by adjusting the stock of reserves with a relatively short time lag the central bank may confine variations in M within acceptable limits. Nevertheless, it is still misleading to treat M as though its behavior is determined solely by decisions issuing from the central bank without specific reference to the role the public plays in determining the banks' demand for reserves. Since M is not an instrument but a target variable of monetary policy, the money supply process should be fully specified; that is, the relevant behavioral relationships influencing the amount of M cannot be ignored.

We can make a further stride toward greater realism in describing the money supply process by introducing two new variables: the banks' demand for borrowed reserves (R_B) and their demand for excess reserves (R_E). To this point we have assumed that the banks have no demand for excess reserves. Obviously this assumption is unrealistic as a description of U.S. banking practice and must be relaxed. Commercial banks do hold reserves above legal reserve requirements partly as protection against unexpected deposit withdrawals. The amount held will depend on at least two factors: the marginal cost of running a reserve deficiency as measured by the rediscount rate (r_d) and the opportunity cost of holding excess reserves as indicated, for example, by the Treasury bill rate (i):

$$R_E = R(i, r_d) \tag{8}$$

Our demand equation for high-powered money (H_d) now includes a fourth component, the demand for excess reserves:

$$H_d = rD + cD + r'tD + R_E \tag{9}$$

The demand for reserves plus currency outside banks is influenced by two new variables, the rediscount rate and the rate of interest. Either an increase in the rate of interest on Treasury bills or a reduction in the rediscount rate may release surplus reserves and hence lead to an expansion of demand deposits. Thus the stock of deposits that equates the banks' demand and supply of reserves plus currency depends partly upon the interest rate as well as the amount of reserves, reserve requirement ratios, and the rediscount rate.

It is time to relax the assumption that the volume of reserves is determined autonomously by the central bank. Commercial banks can alter the volume of reserves by borrowing from the central bank. We now have two separate components of total reserves: a borrowed (R_B) and an unborrowed (R_U) component:

$$R = R_U + R_B \tag{10}$$

For our purposes let us assume that the central bank has complete control over unborrowed reserves. It uses open-market operations to offset changes in sources and uses of reserves excluding borrowing by member banks. This may not be a reasonable assumption, for some critics maintain that current levels of M and i are important determinants of Open Market Committee decisions concerning the target money stock and the rediscount rate. Banks have an incentive to expand borrowing from the central bank when the marginal cost of borrowing falls short of the opportunity cost of investing funds for short periods; that is, the amount of borrowing increases when the spread between treasury bill rates and the rediscount rate widens. The demand for borrowed reserves is given in equation (10):

$$R_B = R(i - r_d) \tag{11}$$

The volume of borrowing depends positively on the interest rate and negatively on the rediscount rate. Setting the demand for reserves plus currency equal to the supply, we have:

$$C_p + R_U + R_B = rD + cD + r'tD + R_E \qquad (12)$$

From the definition of free reserves (R_F) as excess reserves minus member bank borrowing $(R_E - R_B)$ and rearrangement of terms, we can write the equilibrium condition for demand deposits, as follows:

$$C_p + R_U - R_F(i, r_d) = rD + cD + r'td \qquad (13)$$

Solving for D, we obtain

$$D = C_p + R_U - R_F(i, r_d) \cdot 1/r + c + r't \qquad (14)$$

The response of D to a change in unborrowed reserve, free reserves, interest rates, and the rediscount rate can be obtained by suitable differentiation of equation (14).

Our initial textbook money multiplier formula has been expanded to include the public's preferences for currency (cD) and time deposits (tD) and the banks' demand for free reserves (R_F). The central bank controls the level of unborrowed reserves (R_U), reserve requirement ratios r and r', and the rediscount (r_d). There is one equation to determine two unknowns—demand deposits and the Treasury bill rate. But this situation can be remedied by introducing an additional equation which describes the public's preference for demand deposits as a decreasing function of the interest rate, income and wealth assumed constant:

$$D_D = D(i) \qquad (15)$$

Together then the demand deposit supply equation and the demand equation for demand deposits simultaneously determine the equilibrium level of demand deposits and the interest rate. The money supply process can be extended further by introducing a third endogenous variable, that portion of time deposits which depends upon the rate of interest. We assume that the demand for time deposits varies directly with the rate of interest:

$$D_T = T(i) \qquad (16)$$

Solving equations (14) to (16), we obtain equilibrium solutions for demand deposits, time deposits, and the rate of interest on treasury bills.[9]

We have completed the construction of one approach to the money supply process which, I think, can be labelled correctly the Free Reserves approach. The section which follows describes some recent attempts to test money supply functions and relates one of the tests to the hypothesis set out above.

SOME MONEY SUPPLY FUNCTIONS AND EMPIRICAL TESTS

The money supply hypothesis developed by Ronald Teigen is very similar to the model set out in equations (14) to (16).[10] There are, of course, significant differences of detail, but the fundamental approach is the same. The Teigen money supply hypothesis states that the ratio of the actual money stock to the potential money stock based only upon unborrowed reserves depends upon the return from loans (i) relative to their cost as measured by the rediscount rate (r_d). M* is exogenous and determined by the Federal Reserve:

$$M/M^* = X(r_d, \bar{i}) \qquad (17)$$

The elasticity of the money stock with respect to the rate of interest (i) is made to depend mainly upon the profitability of member bank borrowing from the Federal Reserve $(\bar{i} - r_d)$ where the rediscount rate is a measure of the cost of making loans and (i) is the four to six month commercial paper rate. Teigen claims that excess reserves are determined almost entirely by institutional (noneconomic) factors. Therefore, variations in the demand for free reserves can be attributed to fluctuations in the demand for borrowed reserves. M* in Teigen's formulation is a variant of the term $R_U \cdot 1/r + c + r't$ in equation (14). From quarterly data (1946–1959) he has computed single equation and structural estimates of the interest elasticity of the supply of M. His single equation estimate of interest elasticity was .138 and .195 for the structural estimate from which he inferred that "the interest elasticity of money supply appears to be substantial."[11]

One important implication of introducing a money supply elasticity is that it may tend to increase the size of the Keynesian multiplier. With any given increase in autonomous expenditures, interest rates will rise less and hence will not restrain the income-creating effects of the initial stimulus.

Donald Hester has suggested that it is unreasonable to argue, as Teigen does, that M^* and r_d are exogenous. He states that the Federal Open Market Committee does not set a target M^* or r_d without relation to current M and the rate of interest. During economic expansion Reserve officials pursue a discount rate policy that is passive. Therefore, M/M^* and $(\bar{i} - r_d)$ are likely to be positively correlated.[12] So far no one has made a study of Federal Reserve policy-making that would throw any light on how a target value of M^* is actually derived. In this instance a careful historical analysis using all of the internal records of the Committee might be a useful supplement to econometric model building.

Brunner and Meltzer have also constructed single equation multiplier estimates from quarterly data for two periods: 1949–1958 and 1949–1962. The estimates appear in *An Alternative Approach to the Monetary Mechanism*, which contains a full description of how Brunner and Meltzer view the money supply process.[13] The computed values of the money multiplier lie between 2.5 and 2.7, and the computed elasticity of the money stock with respect to the treasury bill rate is quite small (.012). They used their model to predict the money supply for 16 quarters beyond the period used to obtain the estimates. The average predictive error for the money stock was one-half of 1 percent and for a change in the money stock 10 percent. Although these results are admittedly provisional, they provide reassuring optimism about the fruitfulness of additional empirical research on money supply functions.

But one important problem remains to be faced. Can we legitimately identify the money multiplier formula with a supply function for deposits? Gramley and Chase do not think so. The nature of their objection we examine in the following section.

WHAT IS A MONEY SUPPLY FUNCTION?

Much unnecessary logical confusion has resulted from some recent attempts to identify, mistakenly in the opinion of Gramley and Chase, the money multiplier formula as given in equation (12), for example, with a supply function for deposits.[14] With the exception of Gramley and Chase, most money supply theorists continue to designate money supply equations like equation (12) money supply functions. But Gramley and Chase object to this terminology as seriously misleading. They prefer to reserve the term *supply function* to mean schedules of quantities offered at alternative prices. Within this context a demand deposit supply function should relate the willingness of banks to supply deposits with the yield on deposit balances. The yield on demand deposits, though not an explicit rate, is a measure of the cost to the banks of supplying deposit services to their customers. The flow of deposit services is obviously not supplied at zero cost.

The familiar money multiplier formula, no matter in what guise, is not a supply function in the economists' usually accepted sense of that term. The money multiplier equation does not give us a desired quantity of deposits supplied. It merely shows what the level of deposits must be to equate the demand and supply of reserves. Money supply theorists have ignored the yield on demand deposits mainly because since 1933 in the U.S. the maximum ceiling level payable on demand deposits is zero. Gramley and Chase have insisted, however, that the yield on demand deposits, even although it is implicit, cannot be ignored and that it influences the equilibrium stock of deposits. By holding the rate of return on private securities and time deposits constant, Gramley and Chase make the quantity of demand deposits demanded an increasing function of the rate paid on demand deposits.

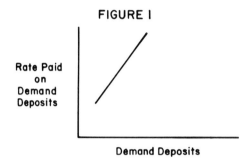

FIGURE I

Rate Paid
on
Demand
Deposits

Demand Deposits

Likewise they construct a demand function for time deposits by holding the rate of return on private securities and demand deposits constant. The demand for time deposits is an increasing function of the rate paid on time deposits (figure 2).

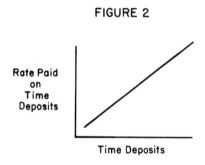

FIGURE 2

Rate Paid
on
Time
Deposits

Time Deposits

Gramley and Chase postulate perfectly elastic supply functions for demand and time deposits. They maintain, "There is little evidence, however, that implicit rates on demand deposits vary appreciably in the short run, and we assume in the argument to follow that r_d [implicit deposit rate] is fixed. [It is also assumed that service charges per check are invariant.]"[15] Given the demand functions, equilibrium levels of both demand and time deposits are determined (figures 3 and 4).

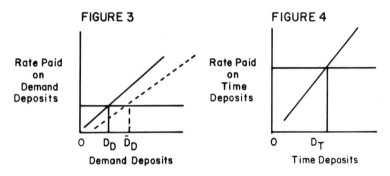

Contrary to the traditional explanation, Gramley and Chase do not regard deposit expansion resulting from an injection of reserves as an increase in the willingness of the banks to supply deposits. According to their interpretation of a money supply function, an increase in surplus reserves will leave the deposit supply function unchanged. Open market operations designed to increase surplus reserves lower the rate of interest on private securities and thus shift the demand function for demand deposits (figure 3) to the right. The equilibrium level of deposits increases from OD to OD̄. Gramley and Chase refer to this process as the "demand pull" theory of deposit expansion. An increase in the willingness of the banks to supply deposits, they maintain, would be reflected in higher rates paid by banks to attract demand and time deposits. Once the bankers set the rates on demand and time deposits, the supply of deposits at those rates is perfectly elastic to the point where all reserves are required to support demand deposits, that is, when time deposits and currency held by the public have been drawn down to zero.[16]

The Gramley-Chase analysis may be clarified if, instead of commercial banks, we apply it to the solution of the problem of determining the amount of savings and loan shares. Given the rate on shares as set by the management of a savings and loan association, the savings and loan association stands ready to satisfy the existing demand for shares. If we assume further that the demand for shares depends positively on the rate paid, then the equilibrium amount of shares created is determined by both demand and supply considerations.

The traditionalist will object to the analogy of the behavior of commercial banks and savings institutions on the grounds that the public cannot influence the amount of demand deposits whereas the public determines the amount of savings and loan shares. He views the money supply as an exogenous variable controlled by the central bank. But we have already indicated how the public's preference for demand and time deposits determines along with the money supply equation the equilibrium level of demand and time deposits and interest rates. The refreshing quality of the Gramley-Chase approach is the emphasis it places on demand considerations as a restraint on deposit expansion.

However, their insistence that the relevant restraint is demand deposits and not legal reserve requirements is inexplicable within the framework of a two equation model. Simultaneous determination of demand deposits and interest rates precludes assigning a more important role to one factor than another.[17] Within the Gramley-Chase model of the money supply process, interest rates and the money supply are endogenous variables and represent a variant of our model as given by equations $(12) - (14)$. What they have added to money supply theory is the explicit introduction of the yield on demand and time deposits and individual bank supply functions which depend upon these yields.

Following Gramley and Chase, John Kareken has derived a more general supply function for demand deposits from microeconomic cost and revenue functions for the individual bank.[18] Kareken interprets traditional money supply theory to include the restriction that the yield on demand deposits is zero. He believes that this restriction precluded traditional money supply theorists from deriving money supply equations of the form suggested by Gramley and Chase. But that is no reason for ignoring the possibility of a market-determined demand deposit rate and appraising its effects.

Gramley and Chase have identified a lacuna in the traditional money supply theory. The significance we attach to it can be determined only by further empirical investigation.

SIGNIFICANCE OF THE FREE RESERVES' APPROACH TO MONEY SUPPLY THEORY

The most significant contribution of the free reserves' approach is that it brings out very clearly how the theory of the money supply fits into the traditional corpus of economic theory. It views the money supply process as an essential aspect of the working of a market—the market for reserves. The output of the commercial banks in the form of deposits is a market phenomenon determined by considerations of both demand and supply. James Tobin effectively put the same point in a different way when he said that Marshall's scissors of supply and demand apply to the output of the banking industry as well as to the output of nonfinancial industries.[19]

Another significant aspect of the new approach is that it provides the theoretical basis for distinguishing between changes in the money supply initiated by the central bank and *induced* changes in the money supply that stem from variations in income and interest rates brought about by a real as distinguished from a monetary disturbance. To treat the money supply as entirely exogenous is to ignore completely the feedback effect of changes in the level of economic activity on the money stock.[20] An induced change in the money supply may occur if short-term open market rates rise relative to the rediscount rate. The effect of such an increase is to reduce the quantity of excess reserves demanded and to generate surplus reserves. Banks eliminate surplus reserves by acquiring earning assets and increasing deposits. Member banks may borrow from the central bank in response to a widening gap between open market rates and the rediscount rate. It is by no means clear how important this mechanism is in explaining the dependence of the money supply on the level of business activity, especially over the cycle. But available evidence on the interest elasticity of the money stock indicates that the interest rate cannot be neglected.

Some of the feedback from interest rates to the money stock could be eliminated by reforming the administration of the discount window. The rediscount rate might be either adjusted automatically to changes in interest rates or altered at the discretion of the monetary authorities to keep the amount of profit-induced borrowing to a minimum. The result would be increased effectiveness of monetary control by a sizable reduction in cyclical variations in the amount of borrowing. One casualty of the proposed change would be the use of the rediscount rate to signal major changes in monetary policy—what Reserve officials usually refer to as announcement effects. No doubt other means could be found to inform the public of monetary policy changes.

There still remains the effect of interest rate changes on the demand for excess reserves. But by eliminating profit-induced borrowing, the interest elasticity of M would be substantially reduced.

One of the important pedagogical by-products of the new approach is that it should lead to a revision of the traditional textbook presentation of the money supply mechanism which inevitably creates the impression among students that the money supply process is more mechanical than behavioral. The theory of the money supply can be integrated with the traditional theory of economic choice. The change is long overdue.

By establishing the fact that the money supply is an endogenous variable, we cannot infer anything about the efficiency of monetary control. Although the central bank is in a position to control the money supply through the effective use of the instruments of monetary management, actual monetary control may be defective because of a lack of understanding on the part of Reserve officials of what determines the money stock. Purely endogenous changes in the money stock can be offset by changes in the monetary base, if and only if the policy-makers understand how the money supply process works. Continuation of the practice of treating the money supply as exogenous only impedes our progress in improving the efficiency of monetary control.

NOTES

1. G. A. Phillips, *Bank Credit* (New York: Macmillan, 1921); J. H. Rogers, "The Absorption of Bank Credit," *Econometrica*, vol. 1 (Jan. 1933); J. E. Meade, "The Amount of Money and the Banking System," *Economic Journal*, vol. 44 (Mar. 1934); J. W. Angell and K. F. Ficek, "The Expansion of Bank Credit," *Journal of Political Economy*, vol. 41, nos. 1 and 2 (Feb. 1933).

2. J. R. Hicks, "A Suggestion for Simplifying the Theory of Money," *Economica*, vol. 2, n.s. (Feb. 1935).

3. R. Teigen, "Demand and Supply Functions for Money in the United States: Some Structural Estimates," *Econometrica*, vol. 32 (Oct. 1964), and "A Structural Approach to the Impact of Monetary Policy," *The Journal of Finance*, vol. 19 (May 1946); K. Brunner and A. Meltzer, "Some Further Investigations of Demand and Supply Functions for Money," *The Journal of Finance*, vol. 19 (May 1964), and *An Alternative Approach to the Monetary Mechanism*, Subcommittee on Domestic Finance, Committee on Banking and Currency, House of Representatives, 88th Congress, 2nd Session, Washington, D.C. (1964); S. Goldfeld, *Commercial Bank Behavior* (Amsterdam: North Holland Publishing Co., 1966); F. deLeeuw, *A Model of Financial Behavior, The Brookings-Quarterly Econometric Model of the U.S.* (Chicago: Rand McNally, 1965); D. Fand and T. Brady, "Free Reserves and the Supply of Deposits," *The National Banking Review*, vol. 4 (June 1967).

4. David Fand, "Some Implications of Money Supply Analysis," *The American Economic Review*, vol. 57 (May 1967), p. 392.

5. See further comment on pages, 114, 119, and 120 about the propriety of treating the money supply as exogenous.

6. L. Gramley and S. Chase, "Time Deposits in Monetary Analysis," *Federal Reserve Bulletin*, vol. 51 (Oct. 1965).

7. See Gramley and Chase, op. cit. Also see John Kareken, "Commercial Banks and the Supply of Money: A Market-Determined Demand Deposit Rate," *Federal Reserve Bulletin*, vol. 53 (Oct. 1967).

8. The new approach to money supply theory in terms of a market for reserves stems from the pioneering work of Gurley and Shaw. It was

elaborated further and integrated into a macroeconomic model by Patinkin in his review of *Money in a Theory of Finance* (Washington, D.C.: Brookings, 1960), and in his article "Financial Intermediaries and Monetary Theory," *The American Economic Review*, vol. 51 (Mar. 1961).

9. The model developed here is essentially the same as the one set out by Warren L. Smith, "Time Deposits, Free Reserves, and Monetary Policy,"*Issues in Banking and Monetary Analysis*, ed. G. Pontecorvo, R. Shay, and A. G. Hart (New York: Holt, Rinehart and Winston, 1967), pp. 81–82. See also William Dewald, "Free Reserves, Total Reserves, and Monetary Control," *Journal of Political Economy*, vol. 71 (Apr. 1963), pp. 142–47, and Ronald L. Teigen, "The Demand For and Supply of Money," *Readings in Money, National Income, and Stabilization Policy*, ed. R. Teigen and W. Smith (Homewood, Ill.: Richard D. Irwin, 1965).

10. Teigen, Ronald, "The Demand for and Supply of Money," *Readings in Money, National Income, and Stabilization Policy*, ed. R. Teigen and W. Smith (Homewood, Ill.: Richard D. Irwin, 1965), pp. 62–63.

11. Ibid., p. 63.

12. Donald D. Hester, Discussion of a paper by Ronald Teigen "A Structural Approach to the Impact of Monetary Policy," *Journal of Finance*, vol. 19 (May 1964), p. 311.

13. Brunner and Meltzer, op. cit.

14. Gramley and Chase, op. cit.

15. Gramley and Chase, p. 1383.

16. Gramley and Chase, p. 1389.

17. W. Dewald, "Money Supply Versus Interest Rates as Proximate Objectives of Monetary Policy," *The National Banking Review*, vol. 3 (June 1966), pp. 511–12.

18. See Gramley and Chase and John Kareken, op. cit.

19. James Tobin, "Commercial Banks as Creators of Money," *Banking and Monetary Studies*, ed. by Deane Carsen (Chicago: Richard D. Irwin, 1963), p. 418.

20. Induced effects of income on the supply of money are recognized by Albert Ando and F. Modigliani, "The Relative Stability of Monetary Velocity and the Investment Multiplier," *The American Economic Review*, vol. 55 (Sept. 1965), pp. 711–13, and by Milton Friedman and David Meiselman in the same volume, "Reply to Ando and Modigliani and to Deprano and Mayer," *The American Economic Review*, vol. 55, (Sept. 1965), pp. 780–81. Part of the feedback, of course, may be through a political channel, but that effect is ignored in this paper.

5

Applications of the Theory of Rational Choice to the Transactions Demand for Cash

EDWARD WHALEN

The Baumol-Tobin approach to the transactions demand for cash can be broadly described as an application of the principles of inventory theory to the transactions demand for cash. William J. Baumol first applied inventory theory to this problem in 1952; four years later, the same principle was developed independently by James Tobin.[1] Although their contribution represents a significant step toward meeting Hicks' long-standing suggestion that the criteria for rational behavior be applied to the demand for money,[2] the implications of their analysis do not appear to be widely appreciated.

This paper attempts to widen the audience beyond a relatively small group of economists interested in monetary theory by presenting a largely nontechnical discussion of the Baumol-Tobin approach. In addition, it presents a simplified version of a more recent model of rational transactions cash balance management which relates optimal cash balance not only to the rate of return on assets but also to the rate of interest charged on borrowed funds.

Edward L. Whalen is Associate Professor of Economics at Indiana University.

THE BAUMOL–TOBIN APPROACH

The Baumol-Tobin approach to the transactions demand for cash is based on the observation that cash balances are similar to stocks of inventories in several essential respects. First of all, cash, like inventories, earns no explicit return, so a firm incurs an opportunity cost when it holds either cash or inventories rather than alternative income-earning assets. Also, the size of a firm's cash holding, like its inventory stocks, can be altered within limits at the discretion of the firm. In the case of inventories, a firm can lower its average inventory by increasing the number and decreasing the size of its orders for replenishment. In the case of money, a firm can lower its average cash balance by engaging in purchases and sales of bonds and other income-earning financial assets which are close substitutes for cash. However, just as a firm incurs a reordering cost each time it replenishes its inventories, it also incurs a brokerage or transfer cost each time it purchases or sells income-earning assets which are alternatives to cash.

Two Costs of Holding Cash Balances

The use of inventory theory to examine the transactions demand for cash, therefore, isolates two costs of holding cash balances: the opportunity cost and the brokerage cost. The opportunity cost can be rigorously defined as the average transactions cash balance times the rate of return on income-earning assets which are close substitutes for cash. If M stands for the average cash balance and r stands for the rate of return on alternative assets, $M \cdot r$ is the opportunity cost of holding cash. The brokerage cost is equal to n, the number of purchases and sales of income-earning assets, times a, the cost of each transaction: $n \cdot a$. About this latter representation, several things should be noted. Since n stands for both purchases and sales of income-earning assets, it is assumed that the brokerage cost of a purchase is the same as the brokerage cost of a sale. In addition, the cost of a purchase or sale is, in this definition, independent of the size of the transaction. In other words, the cost of a purchase of a $1,000 bond is assumed to be the same as the sale of $1,000,000 worth of bonds. Although this may seem to be an extreme assumption, its purpose is mainly to simplify the exposition. When the brokerage cost is constructed to include a consideration of the size of the transaction, the analysis becomes more complicated, but the general conclusions of the simpler model are not invalidated.[3]

The total cost of holding cash balances is defined as the sum of the opportunity cost and the brokerage cost; that is:

$$E = M \cdot r + n \cdot a, \qquad (1)$$

where E represents the total cost of holding cash balances. A firm can reduce its average cash balances—and thus lower its opportunity cost—by engaging in purchases and sales of income-earning assets which are alternatives to cash. When it does so, however, it incurs brokerage costs, and these may become excessive if the firm attempts to reduce its average cash balance too zealously. The objective of a profit-maximizing firm is to hold that cash balance which will minimize the total of these two costs. To determine in general what this optimal cash balance will be is the purpose of the following discussion.

The Pattern of Receipts and Disbursements

In order to determine an expression for optimal average transactions cash balances, the relationship between the number of purchases and sales of income-earning assets, n, and average cash balances, M, must be specified. The relationship between M and n is influenced by the manner in which a firm receives and disburses its cash. The pattern of receipts and disbursements adopted in this presentation is one in which a firm receives a single cash receipt at the beginning of a time period and then spends it at a continuous rate, so that by the end of the period, disbursements are equal to the receipt. To illustrate this pattern of receipts and disbursements, let us say that a firm receives $144 at the beginning of a year and that it then proceeds to spend this amount at the continuous rate of $12

per month, so that by the end of the year its receipt and disbursements are equal.

Table 1

Receipts and Disbursements

Month	Receipts	Disbursements	Transactions Balances
0	144	0	144
1	144	12	132
2	144	24	120
3	144	36	108
4	144	48	96
5	144	60	84
6	144	72	72
7	144	84	60
8	144	96	48
9	144	108	36
10	144	120	24
11	144	132	12
12	144	144	0

This pattern of receipts and disbursements is described in table 1,
which shows receipt and disbursements at the beginning of the
period and at the end of each of the twelve months. At the beginning of the period, the firm has receipts of $144 and disbursements
of zero. With each passing month, disbursements increase by $12,
but receipts remain constant. At the end of the twelfth month, the
firm's total disbursements are equal to $144, the amount of its ini-
tial receipts.

The fourth column of the table introduces a new concept: transactions balances.[4] Transactions balances are those holdings of assets
which are generated by a lack of synchronization between receipts
and disbursements. In the table, they are computed for the beginning of the period and the end of each month by subtracting disbursements at those times from receipts. Since transactions balances
decline in a steady rate from $144 to zero, it is seen that the average

transactions balance for the period is one-half the volume of receipts or disbursements, or $72. A general expression for the average transactions balance, T, is:

$$T = Y/2, \qquad (2)$$

where Y stands for the volume of receipts or disbursements.

FIGURE I

Transactions Balances

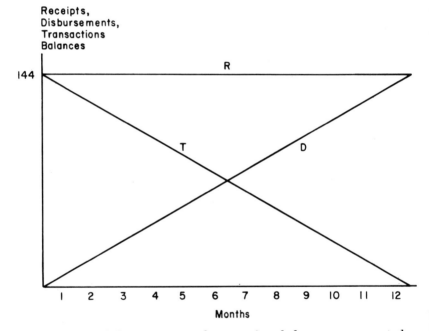

Receipts, disbursements, and transactions balances are presented diagrammatically in figure 1. The vertical axis measures receipts and disbursements at each moment of time, and the horizontal axis measures time. Since the receipt is given at the beginning of the period, it is represented as a horizontal straight line. Disbursements are shown as a diagonal straight line emanating from the origin. The distance between receipts and disbursements at each moment of time is the transaction balance.

Transactions balances are also shown separately in figure 1. In this case, the vertical axis measures transactions balances at each moment of time. The transaction balance at each moment is given by T, the diagonal straight line connecting the point at which T equals \$144 at the beginning of the year to the point at which T equals zero at the end of the year.

Average Cash Balances and the Number of Asset-Switching Transactions

Now it is possible to examine the relationship between the number of purchases and sales of income-earning assets and average cash balances. If the firm engages in no purchases or sales of income-earning assets, the average cash balance is equal to the average transactions balance; that is: $M = T$ when $n = 0$. Since transactions balances decline to zero during the year, it is impossible for the firm to make a bond purchase without making a sale, so n cannot equal 1. If n is equal to 2, the firm is confronted with the problem of buying and selling the appropriate quantity of income-earning assets at the appropriate times so as to maximize its average holdings of these assets. Figure 2 shows that the firm will maximize its average holding of income-earning assets when $n = 2$ if it buys \$72 worth of income-earning assets at the beginning of the period and sells them at the end of six months.[5] The firm then begins the period with a cash balance of \$72, which declines to zero at the end of six months. As a result of its sale of income-earning assets at the end of six months, it begins the second half of the year with a cash balance of \$72, which also declines to zero by the end of this second six-month period. For both of the six-month periods, the average cash balance is \$36, so \$36 is the average cash holding for the entire period; that is: $M = \$36 = 72/2 = T/2$ when $n = 2$. Since the denominator of the fraction $T/2$ is equal to n, it appears that a general expression for average cash balances is:

$$M = T/n \text{ when } n \geqslant 2. \tag{3}$$

FIGURE 2
Transaction Balances When n = 2

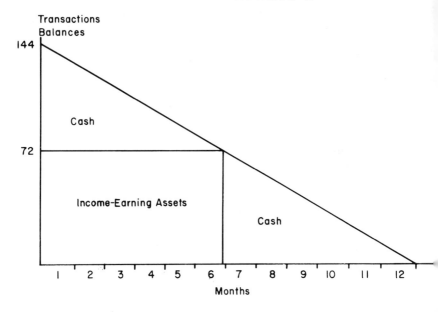

When n is equal to 3, the general expression indicates that average cash balances will be $72/3 or $24. As figure 3 shows, the result given by the general expression is accurate. The firm will maximize its holdings of income-earning assets when at the beginning of the period it buys $96 worth of income-earning assets and sells these in two equal installments of $48 each at the end of the fourth and eighth months. In each of these three four-month periods, the firm begins with a cash balance of $48 which declines steadily to zero, so the average cash balance is $24 for each of the periods and thus for the entire year.

FIGURE 3
Transaction Balances When n = 3

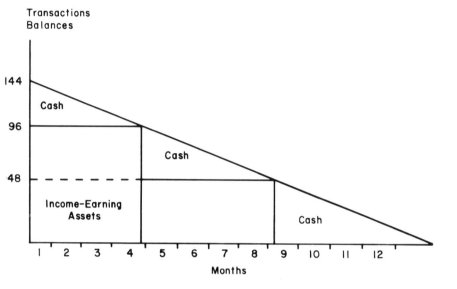

Optimal Average Cash Balances: An Example

Average cash balances for any number of purchases and sales of income-earning assets now can be determined. In table 2, average transactions balances are computed using equation (2), and for each number of purchases and sales of income-earning assets, average cash balances are computed using equation (3). Given an opportunity cost rate, r, and brokerage cost per transaction, a, it is now possible to determine the average cash balance which minimizes the total cost of holding cash. Assuming r is 5 percent and a is $.40, the opportunity cost is determined by multiplying average cash balances by r, and the brokerage cost is determined by multiplying the number of transfer transactions by a. The sum of these two costs is given in the last column of the table, which shows that the optimal cash balance is $24.

Table 2

Optimal Cash Balances When Y = 144

n	Y	T	M	r	M·r	n	a	n·a	E
0	144	72	72.00	.05	3.60	0	.40	0	3.60
2	144	72	36.00	.05	1.80	2	.40	.80	2.60
3	144	72	24.00	.05	1.20	3	.40	1.20	2.40
4	144	72	18.00	.05	.90	4	.40	1.60	2.50
5	144	72	14.40	.05	.72	5	.40	2.00	2.72

Table 3

Optimal Cash Balances When Y = 576

n	Y	T	M	r	M·r	n	a	n·a	E
0	576	288	288.00	.05	14.40	0	.40	0	14.40
2	576	288	144.00	.05	7.20	2	.40	.80	8.00
3	576	288	91.00	.05	4.55	3	.40	1.20	5.75
4	576	288	42.00	.05	3.60	4	.40	1.60	5.20
5	576	288	57.60	.05	2.88	5	.40	2.00	4.88
6	576	288	48.00	.05	2.40	6	.40	2.40	4.80
7	576	288	41.14	.05	2.06	7	.40	2.80	4.86
8	576	288	36.00	.05	1.80	8	.40	3.20	5.00
9	576	288	32.00	.05	1.60	9	.40	3.60	5.20

Let us see what happens if the volume of receipts and disbursements is quadrupled, so that Y is equal to $576, keeping r and a constant. As shown in table 3 the average transactions balance also quadruples so that T is equal to $288. When average cash balances, the opportunity and brokerage costs, and the total cost of holding cash balances are computed, it is seen that the cash balance which will minimize the total cost of holding cash has doubled from $24 to $48. This result indicates that, using this simple model, optimal cash balances will vary with the square root of the volume of receipts or disbursements. A general equation for optimal transactions cash balances will now be established, indicating that this is indeed so.

Optimal Average Cash Balances: A General Equation

It was noted earlier that in order to determine an expression for optimal average cash balances, the relationship between the number of purchases and sales of income-earning assets and average cash balances had to be specified. Equation (3) provides us with the required relationship, and when the equation is solved for n, it becomes: $n = T/M$. When the expression for T found in equation (2) is substituted:

$$n = Y/2M. \tag{4}$$

Substituting into equation (1) this expression for n, the equation for the total cost of holding cash balances becomes: $E = M \cdot r + (Y/2M)a$. Taking the derivative of this equation with respect to M, setting the derivative equal to zero, and solving for M results in the following equation for optimal transactions cash balances:

$$M = \sqrt{Ya/2r}. \tag{5}$$

This equation gives the same result we found earlier by using intuitive methods: Optimal transactions cash balances will vary with the square root of the volume of receipts or disbursements.

Some Implications

Three general conclusions can be derived from the inventory approach to the transactions demand for cash. The first conclusion is that the transactions demand for cash will not vary proportionately with the volume of income or expenditure; instead, it will vary less than in proportion. The second is that the transactions demand for cash is not insensitive to interest rates. These statements are negatively phrased because traditional monetary theory generally has assumed that transactions cash balances vary proportionately with income and are insensitive to the rate of interest.[6] It is true that, given the pattern of receipts and disbursements, average transactions balances are mechanically related to income and are insensitive to interest rates. However, this is not necessarily true of the cash component of transactions balances, which may be altered at a firm's discretion. With the development of sophisticated financial institutions facilitating transfers between cash and income-earning assets, the characteristics properly associated with transactions balances can be used to describe cash balance behavior only with caution.

The third conclusion derived from the inventory approach to the transactions demand for cash is that to the extent that this approach is applicable to general equilibrium analysis, to that extent a fall in the price level—including the price of brokerage services—will tend to stimulate a rise in real income. In other words, the inventory approach incorporates the real balance effect of a fall in prices. A general price reduction will reduce both Y and a. As can be seen from equation (5), the demand for cash will vary in proportion with the fall in prices, creating excess supplies of cash in the money market, which, in turn, may serve to increase aggregate demand.

THE INVESTMENT-BORROWING MODEL

The Baumol-Tobin model requires that income-earning assets purchased at the beginning of a transactions period be sold to meet scheduled disbursements during that period. In other words, according to the model, a cash manager is allowed to engage only in short-term investment. The income-earning assets he buys and sells implicitly are assumed to be highly liquid; if they were illiquid, brokerage costs would preclude the profitability of asset-switching transactions.

In reality, however, short-term investment is not the only alternative available to a cash manager. He may also purchase relatively illiquid income-earning assets and borrow funds during the period to meet scheduled disbursements, since the illiquidity of the assets makes their resale during the transactions period prohibitively expensive. Nevertheless, if the rate of return on illiquid assets is sufficiently high and if interest charges on borrowed funds are sufficiently low, long-term investment in illiquid assets may be preferable to short-term investment in liquid assets. As the following analysis demonstrates, even though the rate of interest charged on borrowed funds may be higher than the rate of return, such a transaction will be profitable if the cash manager selects an appropriate amount to invest in illiquid income-earning assets.

A Cash Manager's Objective

A cash manager will want to select that amount of investment in income-earning assets which will maximize his net return. Net return, in this case, is defined as the difference between the return from an investment and the cost of borrowing. Abstracting from the costs of engaging in investment and borrowing transactions, the return from investment will be explicitly defined as: $A \cdot \rho$, where A is the amount invested in income-earning assets at the beginning of the transactions period and held until the end and ρ is the rate of return on these assets.[7] The cost of borrowing is defined as: $L \cdot i \cdot p$, where L is the amount borrowed, i is the rate of interest charged on borrowed funds, and p is the portion of the transactions period for which the loan is outstanding.

If R is allowed to represent net return, a cash manager's objective now can be restated:

$$R = A \cdot \rho - L \cdot i \cdot p \qquad (6)$$

His problem is to select that level of investment, A, which will maximize net return, R. To determine the optimal level of A, relationships between A and L and A and p must be defined. Establishing these relationships requires an explicit description of the pattern of receipts and disbursements.

The Pattern of Receipts and Disbursements

As before, we will assume that a lump-sum receipt is received at the beginning of the period and that disbursements occur in a steady stream until at the end of the period disbursements are equal to the initial receipts. For the sake of illustration, we will continue assuming that the amount of the receipt is $144, that the transactions period is one year, and that the rate of disbursements is $12 per month.

FIGURE 4
Transactions Balances and a $60 Investment

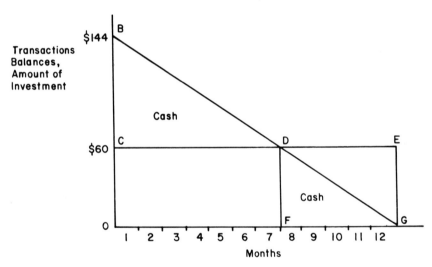

The transactions balances resulting from this assumed pattern of receipts and disbursements are shown in figure 4 as the diagonal line proceeding from $144 at the beginning of the period to $0 at the end of the twelfth month. Figure 4 also shows the effect of an investment of $60. The horizontal line intersecting the vertical axis at $60 represents a cash manager's decision to purchase this amount of income-earning assets and hold them for the entire year. The cash available for meeting disbursements at the beginning of the period thus is reduced to $84, and its subsequent decline is represented by the vertical distance between the transactions and investment lines until the end of the seventh month. At the end of the seventh month, the cash balance is exhausted, and to meet scheduled disbursements for the remainder of the year, $60 must be borrowed at that time. A loan, therefore, is outstanding for the five-month period beginning with the start of the eighth month and ending at the conclusion of the twelfth month.[8]

The areas of the rectangles CEGO and DEFG have an economic interpretation. The area of rectangle CEGO represents the average investment balance for the period, and the area of rectangle DEFG represents the average indebtedness for the period. Similarly, the sum of the areas of triangles BCD and DFG represents the average cash balance held by the cash manager during the year.

Some Investment Alternatives

Of course, selection of $60 as the amount of investment is entirely arbitrary and is used merely as an example. An infinite number of other investment alternatives are available, and table 4 presents the cash and loan balances which result from a sample of seven of the possibilities.

The first pair of columns in the table shows that when no investment takes place, borrowing is not necessary since receipts and disbursements for the period are assumed equal. The cash balance, in this case, corresponds to the transactions balance. The last pair of columns, on the other hand, shows that if $72 is invested, $72 must be borrowed at the end of the sixth month. The cash balance column for the sixth month contains two entries, $0 and $72, indicating that at the end of this month the cash balance retained from the beginning of the period has been completely depleted, and at the moment it reaches zero, the cash manager replenishes his stock

Table 4

AMOUNTS OF MONEY BORROWED AND CASH-ON-HAND

FOR VARIOUS LEVELS OF INVESTMENT

Month	$0 Loan	$0 Cash	$12 Loan	$12 Cash	$24 Loan	$24 Cash	$36 Loan	$36 Cash	$48 Loan	$48 Cash	$60 Loan	$60 Cash	$72 Loan	$72 Cash
0		$144		$132		$120		$108		$96		$84		$72
1		132		120		108		96		84		72		60
2		120		108		96		84		72		60		48
3		108		96		84		72		60		48		36
4		96		84		72		60		48		36		24
5		84		72		60		48		36		24		12
6		72		60		48		36		24		12	$72	0—72
7		60		48		36		24		12	$60	0—60	72	60
8		48		36		24		12	$48	0—48	60	48	72	48
9		36		24		12	$36	0—36	48	36	60	36	72	36
10		24		12	$24	0—24	36	24	48	24	60	24	72	24
11		12	$12	0—12	24	12	36	12	48	12	60	12	72	12
12		0		0		0		0		0		0		0

of cash through borrowing. The columns in between these two extremes show cash and loan balances for levels of investment from $12 to $60, incremented in $12 amounts.

Determining Optimal Investment: Some Examples

Having presented some of the possibilities, attention now turns to determining which of them is optimal; that is, which of the investment levels will maximize a cash manager's net return. To answer this question, the rate of return on income-earning assets and interest charged on borrowed funds must be established. The net return resulting from seven investment alternatives is presented in table 5. For purposes of illustration, a rate of return of 4 percent and of 2 percent on the amount invested and a rate of interest of 6 percent on the amount borrowed were selected.

The amount of return from various amounts of investment is determined as the product of the amount invested and the rate of return and appears in the second and third columns of table 5. The cost of the loan required to meet scheduled disbursements, given these investment levels, is the product of the amount borrowed, the rate of interest on the amount borrowed, and the portion of the period for which the loan is outstanding. It appears in the sixth column of the table. Net return is determined as the difference between the amount of return and the cost of the loan, and it appears in the last two columns. These columns show that when the rate of return is 4 percent and the rate of interest charged is 6 percent, $48 is the amount of investment that will maximize net return. If the rate of return falls from 4 to 2 percent and the rate of interest charged remains at 6 percent, the optimal level of investment will fall to $24. A similar reasoning process shows that an increase in the rate of interest charged, the rate of return being held constant, induces a decline in the optimal level of investment. In other words, the optimal level of long-term investment is positively related to the rate of return and inversely related to the rate of interest charged on borrowed funds.

Table 5

OPTIMAL INVESTMENT

Return from Investment			Cost of Borrowing at 6%			Net Return	
Amount Invested	Amount of Return		Amount Borrowed	Portion of Period	Cost of Loan	At 2%	At 4%
	At 2%	At 4%					
$ 0	$ .00	$ .00	$ 0	0	$ .00	$.00	$.00
12	.24	.48	12	1/12	.06	.18	.42
24	.48	.96	24	1/6	.24	.24	.72
36	.72	1.44	36	1/4	.56	.16	.88
48	.96	1.92	48	1/3	.96	.00	.96
60	1.20	2.40	60	5/12	1.50	−.30	.90
72	1.44	2.88	72	1/2	2.16	−.72	.70

Determining Optimal Investment: A General Equation

Now that the relationships between investment, borrowing, and interest rates have been explored for a particular example, we can return to the equation for net return and attempt to establish a general expression for the optimal investment balance. The equation for net return was defined previously as:

$$R = A \cdot \rho - L \cdot i \cdot p \tag{6}$$

Table 5 shows that, since receipts and disbursements are assumed equal for the period, the amount of a loan is the same as the amount of investment; that is, $A = L$. This table also suggests a relationship between the amount of investment and the portion of the time period for which a loan is outstanding. When, for example, the amount of investment is $12, a loan is contracted for one month or 1/12 of the period. When, say, $36 is invested, the duration of the loan is three months, or 1/4 of the period. Examination of these and other levels of investment show that the portion of the period for which a loan is outstanding, p, can be expressed: $p = A/Y$, where A is the level of investment and Y is the amount of the lump-sum receipt or disbursements.

Substituting these expressions for L and p into equation (6) produces the following statement for net return, expressed in terms of receipts or disbursements, interests rates, and the amount of investment: $R = A \cdot \rho - i \cdot A^2/Y$. The optimal amount of investment is determined by taking the first derivative of R with respect to A, setting the derivative equal to zero, and solving for A. Completion of these operations produces the following statement for the optimal level of investment:

$$A = Y\rho/2i \qquad (7)$$

As a check, we can substitute the values used in our earlier example. If $Y = \$144$, $r = 4$ percent, and $i = 6$ percent: $A = \$144(.04)/2(.06) = \$48$, which agrees with the result in table 5.

Optimal Average Transactions Cash Balances

The optimal amount of investment provides a basis for determining optimal average transactions cash balances. Accomplishing this objective, however, requires that a relationship between the level of investment and average transaction cash balances be established, and this in turn necessitates an exact definition of transactions cash balances.

The average transactions cash balance for the entire transaction period is defined as the sum of the average cash balance held from the beginning of the period to the time a loan is executed plus the average cash balance held from the time a loan is executed to the end of the period. In other words, if M is the average transactions cash balance for the entire period,

$$M = M_1 + M_2, \qquad (8)$$

where M_1 is that portion of the average cash balance held before the loan is executed, and M_2 is that portion of the average cash balance held after the loan is executed.

As already noted, these cash balances are shown in figure 5 as the areas of triangles BCD and DFG. A mathematical statement for average cash balances can be defined by expressing the areas of each of these triangles in terms of Y, the volume of receipts or disbursements, and A, the amount of investment. Triangle BCD is a right triangle with its height equal to BC, the difference between the lump-sum receipt, Y, and amount of investment, A; in other words, the height of triangle BCD is equal to $(Y - A)$. The base of triangle is equal to CD, which is equal to OF; in terms of A and Y, the distance OF can be expressed $1 - A/Y$, which is the portion of the transactions period before a loan is necessary to meet scheduled disbursements. Since the area of a triangle is equal to one-half times the altitude times the base, that part of the average cash balance held before a loan is executed can be expressed: $M_1 = $ Area BCD $= (Y - A)^2/2Y$. The height of right triangle DFG representing M_2 is equal to DF, which is equivalent to the amount of investment, A. Its base, FG, is equal to A/Y, the portion of the period during which a loan is outstanding. Therefore, that part of the average cash balance held after loan negotiation can be expressed: $M_2 = $ Area DFG $= A^2/2Y$. The two components of the average cash balance have now been defined in terms of the volume of receipts or disbursements and the level of investment.

When these two expressions for M_1 and M_2 are substituted into equation (8), the statement for average transactions cash balance becomes: $M = (Y - A)^2/2Y + A^2/2Y$ or $M = (Y^2 - 2AY + 2A^2)/2Y$. This statement merely defines the average transactions cash balance. Optimal average transactions cash balances are determined only when A is at an optimal level. Equation (7) shows that the net return from investment will be maximized when $A = Y_p/2i$. Substituting this expression for A into the preceding equation and simplifying produces the following expression for optimal average transactions cash balances:

$$M = (1 - p/i + p^2/2i^2)Y/2, \tag{9}$$

which shows that optimally average transactions cash balances are related to the volume of receipts or disbursements, the rate of return on income-earning assets, and the rate of interest on borrowed funds. Certain features of this equation deserve special notice.

Some Implications

Unlike the asset-switching model, which indicates that optimally average transactions cash balances will vary with the square root of the volume of receipts or disbursements, equation (9) suggests a linear relationship between optimal transactions cash balances and the volume of receipts or disbursements. In other words, the possibility of cash economization by large-scale transactors is not recognized in the investment-borrowing model.

This difference in the implications of the two approaches is not as substantial as it might at first appear, however. As is shown in the following section, cash-conserving transactions of the asset-switching type can be introduced in the investment-borrowing model. For example, the cash balance held from the beginning of the period to the time of loan negotiation can be reduced by asset-switching transactions between cash and income-earning assets which are close substitutes for cash. Similarly, we assumed that only one loan was negotiated during the entire transactions period. Cash balances held from the time initial cash balances are exhausted to the end of the transactions period can be reduced by negotiating a series of loans. When these possibilities are accounted for in the investment-borrowing model, optimal transactions cash balances are found to increase less than in proportion with the volume of receipts and disbursements.

The unique feature of the investment-borrowing approach is that it explicitly relates optimal average transactions cash balances to not one but two interest rates. Moreover, examination of equation (9) shows that cash balances optimally are independent of the *level* of interest rates and are influenced instead by relative differences between rates of return on assets and rates of interest on borrowed funds. That is to say, if both rates of return on assets and rates of interest on loans vary in proportion, the optimal level of transactions cash balances will not change. The optimal level of transactions cash balances will change only if rates of return vary relative to rates of interest—in other words, only if the *structure* of interest rates changes.

The effect of changes in the structure of interest rates on optimal transactions cash balances can be examined by allowing the rate of return on assets to vary while holding the rate of interest on borrowed funds constant, or vice versa. The effect of changes in the rate of return can most easily be examined by taking the partial derivative of M in equation (9) with respect to ρ; after rearranging terms this operation produces: $\partial M/\partial \rho = -(i - \rho)Y/2i^2$. Similarly, the effect of changes in the rate of interest on borrowed funds can be examined by taking the partial derivative of M with respect to i, which, after rearranging terms, is: $\partial M/\partial i = (i - \rho)\rho Y/2i^3$. Both of these expressions depend on the size of ρ relative to i, and when they are nonzero, their signs will differ.

If the rate of interest on borrowed funds is greater than the rate of return on assets, an increase in the rate of return on assets will decrease the size of optimal transactions cash balances. An increase in the rate of interest on borrowed funds, on the other hand, will increase optimal cash balances. However, if the rate of return on assets is greater than the rate of interest on borrowed funds, an increase in the rate of return on assets will increase the size of optimal transactions cash balances and an increase in the rate of interest on borrowed funds will decrease them.

Therefore, in order to determine an unequivocal statement of the relationship between optimal transactions cash balances and interest rates, the size of the rate of return on assets relative to the rate of interest on borrowed funds must be specified. A plausible assumption appears to be that the rate of interest on borrowed funds is equal to or greater than the rate of return on income-earning assets. If the reverse were true, a profit maximizer presumably would borrow indefinitely since each borrowed dollar would earn more than the cost of servicing the loan. As his indebtedness rose, his credit standing would fall, and the rate of interest on borrowed funds presumably will increase. Diminishing marginal returns suggests that the rate of return on additional investment will fall, so that eventually the two rates will be equated. The investment-borrowing model suggests that this point of equality is not an equilibrium, however; lack of synchronization between receipts and disbursements provides an additional opportunity for further investment and borrowing activity even when the rate of return is less than the rate of interest on borrowed funds.

If the assumption that the rate of interest on borrowed funds is greater than the rate of return on assets which are alternatives to cash is adopted, optimal transactions cash balances will be negatively related to the rate of return and positively associated with the rate of interest on borrowed funds.

A SYNTHESIS OF THE TWO APPROACHES

The Baumol-Tobin approach and the investment-borrowing approach appear to provide significantly different descriptions of optimal cash management behavior. However, each seriously oversimplifies the alternatives available to a rational cash manager. What is needed is a general model which synthesizes these two approaches and recognizes the possibility not only for asset-switching transactions but also for investment and borrowing.

To develop a general model a concept which here will be called net receipts from financial operations must be introduced. Net receipts from financial operations is defined as: return from investment plus return from cash-management prior to loan negotiation minus the cost of debt management after the initial loan negotiation. The objective of a cash manager, in this situation, is to select levels of investment and cash balances before and after the initial loan negotiation which will maximize net return from investment and cash management while simultaneously minimizing the cost of debt management.

In the following presentation, we begin by examining the possibility of reducing transactions cash balances held from the beginning of the period until the initial loan negotiation by engaging in asset-switching transactions. Next, the possibility of reducing cash balances held during the latter part of the period through multiple loan negotiation is developed. Finally, we establish an equation for optimal cash balances in a situation which allows for simultaneous determination of the optimal amount of investment, asset-switching transactions, and loan negotiations.

Cash Management prior to Loan Negotiation

Figure 5 presents a general version of figure 4. The volume of receipts or disbursements is represented by Y, and A stands for the amount of investment. For the sake of mathematical convenience and generality, the duration of the transactions period is considered to be a unit of time and, therefore, extends from o to 1. The point on the horizontal axis indicated by $(Y - A)/Y$ is the moment of the initial loan negotiation. As we indicated earlier, the portion of the transactions period for which a loan is outstanding is A/Y. Hence, the portion of the transactions period which transpires before a loan is negotiated is $1 - A/Y$ or $(Y - A)/Y$.

As in figure 4, the area of triangle BCD represents the average transactions balance from the beginning of the period to the initial loan negotiation. In the absence of asset-switching transactions, the transactions balance corresponds to M_1, that part of the average cash balance held prior to loan negotiation. It is to these balances that the Baumol-Tobin analysis is most directly applicable. However, in this situation, we must employ the dual to the model developed in the first section. In other words, rather than minimizing the cost of transactions cash balance management, we must maximize the return from short-term holdings of income-earning assets which are alternatives to cash. The reason for this modification is that the cost-minimizing model employs the opportunity cost of holding idle cash balances in its construction. This cost cannot be added to

FIGURE 5
Transactions Balances and Investment

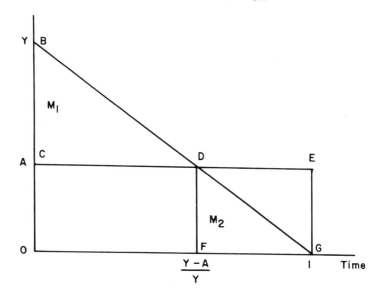

realized returns or actual costs which result from investment or debt management.

Net income from cash management prior to initial loan negotiation can be expressed as the difference between the income received from holding income-earning monetary assets—hereafter referred to as bonds—instead of cash and the cost of engaging in asset-switching financial transactions between cash and bonds. The income received from holding bonds instead of cash is defined as the product of average bond balances, B, times the rate of return on bonds, r. The cost of engaging in asset-switching financial transactions between cash and bonds is defined as the product of the number of purchases and sales of bonds, n, times the broker's cost per transaction, a. The latter definition implicitly assumes, as before, that the cost of purchasing monetary assets is the same as the cost of selling them and that it is independent of the size of a purchase or sale.

If P stands for the profit or net income from transactions balance management, the difference between the income received from holding bonds instead of cash and the cost of engaging in asset-switching financial transactions can be expressed: $P = B \cdot r - n \cdot a$. To make possible an optimal solution, two things must be accomplished: Average bond balances must be expressed in terms of the average transactions cash balance held prior to the initial loan negotiation, and the number of asset-switching transactions must be expressed in terms of this cash balance.

Tobin demonstrates that the sum of the average transactions cash balance and the average bond balance is equal to the average transactions balance.[9] Therefore, the average bond balance can be expressed:

$$B = T - M_1. \tag{10}$$

In this case, however, T is not equal to $Y/2$. It is equal to the area of triangle BCD. In terms of the volume of receipts or disbursements, Y, and the amount of investment, A, the height of this triangle is $Y - A$ and the length of its base is $(Y - A)/Y$. The average transactions balance, therefore, is:

$$T = (Y - A)^2 / 2Y. \tag{11}$$

Hence:

$$B = (Y - A)^2 / 2Y - M_1, \tag{12}$$

which expresses the average bond balance is a form suitable for determining the optimal M_1.

As demonstrated earlier, n, the number of asset-switching transactions, is equal to the average transactions balance divided by the average cash balance, or, for the period prior to the initial loan negotiation: $n = T/M_1$. When the expression for T found in equation (11) is substituted, we have:

$$n = (Y - A)^2/2YM_1. \tag{13}$$

Upon substituting the expressions for B and n in equations (12) and (13), the equation for the profit from transactions balance management becomes:

$$P = [(Y - A)^2/2Y - M_1]r - (Y - A)^2a/2YM_1, \tag{14}$$

which expresses P in terms of the average cash balance held by the cash manager prior to the initial loan negotiation, M_1, and the amount of investment, A.

By engaging in asset-switching transactions between cash and bonds, M_1 can be reduced. Figure 6 presents diagrammatically the situation for a firm engaging in three asset-switching transactions prior to the initial loan negotiation. There is one bond purchase, and this occurs at equally-spaced intervals from the beginning of the period to the initial loan negotiation. The area of polygon BCEFGH represents the average bond balance, and the sum of triangles CDE, EFG, and GHI represents the average cash balance held prior to the initial loan negotiation.

Debt Management after Loan Negotiation

Comparison of figures 5 and 6 shows a difference in loan negotiation as well as in the number of asset-switching transactions. In figure 5, the cash manager borrows A amount at time $(Y - A)/Y$. In figure 6, two loans are negotiated: the first at $(Y - A)/Y$ for $A/2$ amount; the second halfway between the time of initial loan negotiation and the end of the period for the same amount. In figure 5, average indebtedness is shown as the area of rectangle DEFG; in figure 6, average indebtedness is shown as the area of polygon IJKLMN. The area of the polygon is less than that of the rectangle, suggesting that average indebtedness can be reduced by negotiating a series of loans.

The approach to loan negotiation is analogous to the approach to asset-switching transactions. The cost of cash management after loan negotiation is defined as the sum of interest charges on debt

FIGURE 6
Investment with Asset-Switching and Multiple Loan Negotiation

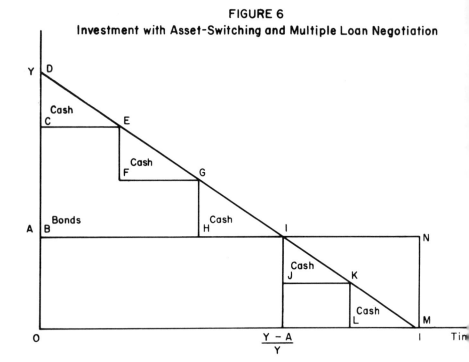

outstanding and the cost of negotiating loans. The objective of this analysis is to determine an equation for the cost of cash management expressed in terms of that part of the cash balance held after the initial loan negotiation, M_2.

Interest charges on debt outstanding is defined as the product of average indebtedness outstanding, L, and the rate of interest charged, i. The cost of negotiating loans is defined as the product of the number of loans negotiated, m, and the cost period loan negotiation, b. If C represents the cost of debt management, the sum of interest charges on debt outstanding and the cost of negotiating loans can be expressed:

$$C = L \cdot i + m \cdot b. \qquad (15)$$

To accomplish our objective, both L and m must be expressed in terms of M_2.

Imagine a situation in which a cash manager negotiates an infinite number of loans. In this case, the average transactions cash balance obtained from borrowed funds will approximate zero, and average debt outstanding will be equal to $A^2/2Y$, shown in figure 5 as the area of triangle DEG and in figure 6 as the area of triangle INM. In figure 5, where one loan is negotiated, average debt outstanding is equal to M_2, shown as the area of triangle DFI, plus $A^2/2Y$, the area of triangle DEG. Similarly, for figure 6, average debt outstanding is equal to M_2, shown here as the areas of triangles IJK and KLM, plus $A^2/2Y$, the area of triangle INM. Thus, we can conclude that average debt outstanding can be determined from:

$$L = [A^2/Y + M_2] \qquad (16)$$

which expresses L in terms of M_2.

Through a process of mathematical reasoning similar to that used for determining the number of asset-switching transactions, it can be demonstrated that, for any given number of loan negotiations, average cash balances obtained from borrowed funds will be minimized when the following relationship holds:[10] $M_2 = A^2/2Ym$. Solving the equation for m,

$$m = A^2/2YM_2, \qquad (17)$$

provides a statement for m expressed in terms of M_2.

Substituting the expressions for L and m found in equations (16) and (17) into equation (15) produces the following equation for the cost of cash management after the initial loan negotiation

$$C = [A^2/2Y + M_2] \cdot i + [A^2/2YM_2] \cdot b. \qquad (18)$$

The cost of cash management after the initial loan negotiation now is expressed in terms of average cash balances held after the initial loan negotiation, M_2, and the amount of investment, A.

Net Receipts from Financial Operations

If we let Π stand for net receipts from financial operations, then by definition: $\Pi = A \cdot \rho + P - C$, where $A \cdot P$ stands for return from investment, P represents the profit from cash management prior to the initial loan negotiation and C is the cost of debt management after the initial loan negotiation. When the expressions for P and C found in equations (14) and (18) are substituted into this equation, net receipts from financial operations becomes:

$$\Pi = A \cdot \rho + [(Y - A)^2/2Y - M_1]r - (Y - A)^2 a/2YM_1 - (A^2/2Y + M_2)i - A^2 b/2YM_2$$

Net receipts from financial operations now is expressed in terms of the variables A, M_1, and M_2.

For Π to be a maximum, the partial derivatives of Π with respect to A, M_1, and M_2 must be zero. Taking the partial derivatives of Π with respect to A, M_1, and M_2 and setting them equal to zero produces the following set of equations:

$$\partial\Pi/\partial A = \rho - (Y - A)r/Y + (Y - A)a/YM_1 - Ai/Y - Ab/YM_2 = 0$$
$$\partial\Pi/\partial M_1 = -r + (Y - A)^2 a/2YM_1^2 = 0$$
$$\partial\Pi/\partial M_2 = -i + A^2 b/2YM_2^2 = 0$$

When these equations are solved for A, M_1, and M_2, we have

$$A = \{[Y(\rho - r) - \sqrt{2Y}(\sqrt{(bi)} - \sqrt{(ar)}]\}/(i - r) \quad (19)$$

$$M_1 = (Y - A)\sqrt{(a/2Yr)} \quad (20)$$

$$M_2 = A\sqrt{(b/2Yi)}. \quad (21)$$

The second-order conditions indicate that when investment and the average cash balances before and after the initial loan negotiation equal these values, net receipts from financial operations will be maximized provided that: $i > r$. In other words, this model requires that the rate of interest charged on borrowed funds be greater than the rate of return on bonds.

The effect on A of changes in the rates of return and interest charges and the costs of engaging in asset-switching transactions and loan negotiation and in the volume of receipts or disbursements is difficult to determine from equation (19). To assist in determining the direction of influence of these variables, the partial derivatives of A with respect to Y, ρ, r, i, a, and b can be taken and are presented below.

$$\partial A/\partial Y = (\rho - r)/2(i-r) + A/2Y$$
$$\partial A/\partial r = -Y[(Y-A)/Y - M_1/(Y-A)]/(i-r)$$
$$\partial A/\partial \rho = Y/(i-r)$$
$$\partial A/\partial i = -Y[M_2/A - A/Y]/(i-r)$$
$$\partial A/\partial a = \sqrt{(Yr/2a)}/(i-r)$$
$$\partial A/\partial b = -\sqrt{(Yi/2b)}/(i-r)$$

This set of equations indicates that the amount of investment will increase when the volume of receipts of disbursements, the rate of return on investments, or the cost of asset-switching transactions increases. It will decrease if the rate of return on bonds, the rate of interest charged on borrowed funds, or the cost of loan negotiation increases.

These conclusions are based on a number of assumed conditions; however, in order for the relationship between investment and the volume of receipts or disbursements to be positive, not only must i > r but also ρ > r. The negative relation between investment and the rate of return on bonds requires that the ratio between the initial cash balance not invested, (Y − A), and the lump sum receipt, Y, be greater than the ratio between the average cash balance held prior to the initial loan negotiation, M_1, and the initial cash balance not invested, (Y − A). Similarly, the negative relation between investment and the rate of interest charged on borrowed funds requires that the ratio between the average cash balance held after the initial loan negotiation, M_2, and the amount invested, A, must be greater than the ratio between the amount invested, A, and the lump-sum receipt, Y. These two requirements impose the rather bizarre condition that $\sqrt{2Y} > \sqrt{a/r} + \sqrt{b/i}$. Since the term on the left-hand side of this equality increases as the volume of receipts or disbursements increases, the likelihood of this condition being met improves with the size of the cash manager's operation. If, for example, a and b were each 100 times greater than r and i, respectively, Y would have to be greater than $200 per transaction period.

Optimal Average Transactions Cash Balances

Equation (8) shows that average transactions cash balances for the entire transactions period are determined as the sum of two components, M_1 and M_2. When the expressions for optimal M_1 and M_2 found in equations (20) and (21) are substituted into this equation, the following statement for average transactions cash balances results:

$$M = (Y - A)\sqrt{(a/2Yr)} + A\sqrt{(b/2Yi)} \qquad (22)$$

where $A = [Y(\rho - r)\sqrt{2Y}(\sqrt{bi} - \sqrt{ar})]/(i - r)$. The optimal average transactions cash balance is now expressed in terms of six variables: Y, ρ, r, i, a and b. To determine the influence of these variables on optimal transactions cash balances, the partial derivatives of M with respect to each of them can be taken and are presented below.

$\partial M/\partial Y = [\sqrt{(a/r)} + (\rho - r)/2(i - r)][\sqrt{(b/i)} - \sqrt{(a/r)}]/2\sqrt{(2Y)}$
$\partial M/\partial r = (\partial A/\partial r)[\sqrt{(b/i)} - \sqrt{(a/r)}]/\sqrt{(2Y)} - [(Y - A)/2Yr]$
$\qquad \sqrt{(Ya/2r)}$
$\partial M/\partial \rho = (\partial A/\partial \rho)[\sqrt{(b/i)} - \sqrt{(a/r)}]/\sqrt{(2Y)}$
$\partial M/\partial i = (\partial A/\partial i)[\sqrt{(b/i)} - \sqrt{(a/r)}]/\sqrt{(2Y)} - (A/2i)\sqrt{(b/2Yi)}$
$\partial M/\partial a = (\partial A/\partial a)[\sqrt{(b/i)} - \sqrt{(a/r)}]/\sqrt{(2Y)} + 1/2(Y - A)$
$\qquad \sqrt{(Y/2ar)}$
$\partial M/\partial b = (\partial A/\partial b)[\sqrt{(b/i)} - \sqrt{(a/r)}]/\sqrt{(2Y)} + (A/2)\sqrt{(1/2Ybi)}$

In order to determine the sign of each of these partial derivatives, the following additional condition must be assumed: $b/i > a/r$. Under this condition and with the information given in the preceding section on the partial derivatives of A with respect to each of the variables, the partial derivatives of M with respect to Y, p, and a are found to be positive, and the partial derivatives of M with respect to b cannot be determined without specifying particular values for the variables.[11]

The assumption $b/i > a/r$ implies that the cost of loan negotiation is greater relative to interest charges than the cost of engaging in asset-switching transactions relative to the rate of return on bonds. A priori, this assumption does not appear implausible. Lenders can ration credit by manipulating the cost of loan negotiation as well as through variation in the rate of interest charged on borrowed funds. In the imperfect markets associated with commercial bank lending, where interest rates are adjusted only occasionally, loan negotiation costs may provide a more convenient and less obvious way of responding to changes in credit conditions. Brokerage costs, on the other hand, presumably will be maintained at minimum levels. Brokers dealing in open-market securities have little incentive to discourage their customers from engaging in asset-switching transactions.

The assumption is capable of being tested empirically, although assigning the effect of particular charges to either b or i in the case of loans or to either a or r in the case of bonds may, in practice, be somewhat arbitrary. For example, to complete a mortgage transaction on a $20,000 loan at 5 percent, a commercial bank may charge $2,000. Should the $2,000 be assigned to b, or should the economic fact that only $18,000 has been obtained from the loan negotiation be recognized and reflected in an interest charge, i, of approximately 5.5 percent?

The general conclusion of the Baumol-Tobin model that transactions cash balances optimally will vary less than in proportion with the volume of receipts or disbursements is preserved in equation (22). The partial derivative of M with respect to Y indicates that transactions cash balances will increase at a decreasing rate as the volume of receipts or disbursements increases.

To ascertain the effect of a change in the *level* of interest rates on optimal transactions cash balances, we can assume that a change in any one of the rates is accompanied by a change of the same amount in the other two. Under this assumption, the partial derivative of M with respect to the level of interest rates is equal to the sum of the partial derivatives of M with respect to r, P, and i, or: $-\sqrt{(Y/2)}$ $[\sqrt{(b/i)} - \sqrt{(\partial/r)}]/(i - r)$. The sign of this derivative is negative, suggesting that optimal transactions cash balances decline as the level of interest rates increase. This finding corresponds as well to the conclusion of the Baumol-Tobin model.

APPLICATIONS AND IMPLICATIONS

Applications of the Demand for Cash Models

The expression for optimal transactions cash balances developed from the Baumol-Tobin approach, equation (5), suggests that a firm's cash balances will vary less than in proportion with changes in its sales. Verification of this description of cash management behavior has been attempted by several investigators, but results so far have not been conclusive.[12]

Two factors may account for the lack of prominence of cash economies in these statistical investigations. First, the Baumol-Tobin approach deals only with optimal behavior or cash balances which are held for transactions purposes. But precautionary and investment motives also provide reasons for holding cash balances, and the presence of these other components of observed cash balances may distort the relationship between a firm's holdings of transactions cash and its sales volume.

A second reason for the apparent absence of statistically detectable cash economies is offered in a recent analytical paper by Brunner and Meltzer.[13] There analysis indicates that relaxing the simplifying assumptions required for a square-root relationship between transactions cash balances and the volume of receipts or disbursements substantially lessens the possibilities for economy. Over wide ranges of variation in the volume of receipts or disbursements, the relationship between transactions cash balances and sales is approximately linear. Since available data do not correspond exactly to their theoretical counterparts and since analytical assumptions frequently are compromised in empirical work, usual regression techniques may not be sufficiently sensitive to detect cash economizing activities.

A synthesis of the investment-borrowing and Baumol-Tobin approaches suggests that the structure as well as the level of interest rates influences demand for cash. Unfortunately, equation (22) is not expressed in a form which lends itself readily to empirical analysis. Equation (9), however, which provides an expression for optimal transactions cash balances developed from the investment-borrowing approach alone, can be adapted for regression analysis with little difficulty.

When both sides of equation (9) are divided by Y, the volume of receipts or disbursements, it becomes $M/Y = 1 - \rho/i + \rho^2/2i^2$. For purposes of regression analysis, this equation can be expressed $y = a + bx + cx^2$, where y is M/Y, the ratio of cash balances divided by the volume of receipts or disbursements, x is ρ/i, the ratio of the rate of return on income-earning assets divided by the rate of interest charged on borrowed funds; a and c are constants greater than zero, and b is a constant less than zero.

Balance sheet and income statement data submitted by firms in connection with payment of their corporate income taxes provide measures of cash balances and the volume of receipts or disbursements for the sixteen-year period from 1946 to 1961. As compiled by the Internal Revenue Service, firms are classified by size of total assets and by the following major industry groups:[14]

1. Agriculture, forestry, and fisheries;
2. Mining;
3. Construction;
4. Manufacturing;
5. Transportation, communication, electric, gas and sanitary services;

6. Wholesale and retail trade; and

7. Services.

To minimize effects arising from differences in scale of operations, only the average cash balances and total compiled receipts of firms whose total assets are between $5 million and $10 million in each of these industry groups were selected. The ratio of cash balances divided by total compiled receipts provides an estimate of y.

A number of interest rate time series are available, and the investment-borrowing model does not provide an a priori reason for selecting any one of them. Accordingly, a number of alternative rates were obtained from the *Federal Reserve Bulletin* for the 16 years from 1946 to 1961 and used to represent x in the regression equation. In most cases, results were similar, and table 6 presents a sample of five equations. For all five equations, the rate of return, ρ, is represented by the time series for the rate of interest on new issues of three-month Treasury bills. The rate of interest charged on borrowed funds, i, is represented by the time series designated in the right-hand column of table 6.

Except for equation (1), the first regression coefficient is negative and the second is positive. These results correspond to the values indicated by the model. The model also suggests that the intercept and first regression coefficient will equal one and that the second regression coefficient will equal one-half. Although estimated values do not approximate closely these predictions, the second regression coefficient is less than the absolute value of the first regression coefficient in four of the five equations. In other words, although estimates of the absolute values have not been predicted successfully, their relative values have been approximated.

Unfortunately, only for the second equation are both regression coefficients statistically significant at the 5 percent level. Although an analysis of variance—not shown in the table—indicates that the equations are statistically significant, their coefficient of determination is quite low, ranging from .053 to .132. That only a small portion of the variation in the dependent variable is explained by any

Table 6

Relationship Between M/Y and ρ/i When ρ Is the Rate of Interest on New Issues of Three-Month Treasury Bills

Equation Number	Intercept Value	Regression Coefficient for ρ/i	Regression Coefficient for $(\rho/i)^2$	Coefficient of Determination	Interest Rate Used for i
1	.096	.157	−.224	.086	Prime Commercial Paper, 4–6 months
2	.655	−1.291*	.723*	.053	Prime Banker's Acceptances
3	.161	−.207	.101	.098	Customer Loans, All
4	.148	−.174	.091	.116	Corporate Bonds, Total
5	.126	−.155*	.106	.132	Dividend Yield

* Significant at the 5 percent level.

of the regression equations is not surprising, however. Synthesis of the Baumol-Tobin and investment-borrowing approaches suggests that the regression equation used in this investigation is a highly simplified, unsophisticated description of optimal cash management behavior. Nevertheless, the results do suggest—albeit not conclusively—that the structure of interest rates plays a measurable role in the demand for cash.

Implications of the Analysis

By combining the Baumol-Tobin and investment-borrowing approach, optimal transactions cash balances have been related explicitly to the volume of receipts or disbursements, rates of return on income-earning assets, a rate of interest on borrowed funds, and the costs of engaging in asset-switching transactions and loan negotiation. The specific form of the relationship depends, of course, on the assumed pattern of receipts and disbursements. If a different pattern of receipts and disbursements had been adopted, equation (22) would be significantly altered. A lump-sum receipt and a steady disbursement stream were assumed, not because this form adequately represents actual income and expenditure flows but for reasons of mathematical simplicity.

As a by-product of this analysis, optimal amounts of investment, A, average indebtedness, L, and bond holdings, B, can also be determined. No claim is made, however, that this model offers a complete and adequate explanation of microeconomic behavior for all of these items which appear in firms' balance sheets. Indeed, even the claim that transactions cash management behavior has been adequately examined is not appropriate!

Nevertheless, the model is suggestive. It suggests, first of all, that, at the margin at least, these asset and liability items are affected by the pattern of receipts and disbursements which confronts an economic unit. Heretofore, the way in which income is received and expenditure is conducted over time has played an insignificant role in analysis. These findings suggest that it may merit greater attention than it has received in the past. Second, cash, bonds, investments, and liabilities are intimately and explicitly related to one another through this approach. Their common connection is the assumed pattern of receipts and disbursements and the profit maximization motive. It seems very likely, therefore, that any set of comprehensive criteria for optimal cash balances will also provide a description for rational management of an economic unit's financial and physical assets, its liabilities, and its net worth.

It often is taken for granted that the demand for money increases when income increases and falls when interest rates rise. The foregoing rather detailed investigation of rational cash management behavior suggests that these relationships are not immutable. They depend on seldom-examined, implicit assumptions regarding the pattern of receipts and disbursements and the relative magnitudes of income, interest rates, and the costs of engaging in financial transactions. Although conditions producing a positive association between cash and income and a negative association between cash and interest rates may be sufficiently pervasive that exceptions to this behavior are unusual, a complete analytical treatment requires that these conditions be described.

Despite its apparent complexity, the immediate relevance of this approach to the transactions demand for cash appears to be for further empirical investigation of the demand for money. A number of recent investigators have related various time series of money stocks to measures of income, wealth, and interest rates.[15] To represent interest rates, a wide variety of time series alternatives are available and have been employed as arguments in regression equations. However, invariably, only one interest rate is used, and this construction neglects the effect of relative changes among interest rates on the demand for money. The preceding analysis suggests that including additional interest rate measures in empirical investigations may enhance their descriptive qualities.

NOTES

1. William J. Baumol, "The Transactions Demand for Cash: An Inventory Theoretic Approach," *Quarterly Journal of Economics*, vol. 66 (Nov. 1952), pp. 545–56, and James Tobin, "The Interest Elasticity of Transactions Demand for Cash," *Review of Economics and Statistics*, vol. 38 (Aug. 1956), pp. 241–47.

2. J. R. Hicks, "A Suggestion for Simplifying the Theory of Money," *Economica*, n.s. vol. 2 (Feb. 1935), pp. 1–19; reprinted in F. A. Lutz and L. W. Mints, eds., *Readings in Monetary Theory* (Homewood, Ill.: Richard D. Irwin, 1951), pp. 13–32.

3. For a discussion of the effect of including costs which vary with the size of the asset-switching transaction, see Tobin, pp. 244–45.

4. For a discussion of transactions balances, see Tobin, pp. 241–42.

5. For a proof that the optimal buying and selling sequence for n transactions is a single purchase at the beginning of the transactions period followed by sales spaced at equal intervals, see Tobin, pp. 246–47.

6. John Maynard Keynes, *The General Theory of Employment, Interest and Money* (New York: Harcourt, Brace & World, 1936), pp. 199–201.

7. The term *investment* is used here in a very general sense. It may refer to the purchase of a financial asset or to the purchase of a physical asset. If a financial asset is purchased, the relevant measure of the rate of return is its yield-to-maturity. If a physical asset is purchased, the relevant measure of return will be that discount rate which makes the future stream of income from the investment equal to its current price. In either case, the asset is assumed to be illiquid. As the subsequent analysis shows, as long as the parameters of the model remain unchanged, a cash manager will have no incentive to sell the asset either in the current transactions period or in any following one.

8. Assuming the same pattern of receipts and disbursements continues in the next period, the loan can be repaid with $60 of the lump-sum receipt. If the cash manager continues to hold the $60 investment, a new loan will have to be negotiated at the end of the seventh month.

9. Tobin, p. 242.

10. In this case, T is equal to M_2, cash balances when only one loan is negotiated at $(Y - A)/Y$. That is: $T = A^2/2Y$.

11. If $b/i < a/r$, the partial derivative of M with respect to b is positive. However, under this condition, the partial derivative of M with respect to p is negative, and the signs of the other partial derivatives cannot be determined unequivocally.

12. Allan H. Meltzer, "Demand for Money: A Cross-Section Study of Business Firms, *Quarterly Journal of Economics*, vol. 77 (Aug. 1963),

pp. 405–22, and Edward L. Whalen, "A Cross-Section Study of Business Demand for Cash," *Journal of Finance*, vol. 20 (Sept. 1963), pp. 423–43.

13. Karl Brunner and Allan H. Meltzer, "Economies of Scale in Cash Balances Reconsidered," *Quarterly Journal of Economics*, vol. 81 (July 1967), pp. 422–36.

14. U.S. Treasury Department, Internal Revenue Service, *Statistics of Income, Corporation Income Tax Returns* (Washington, D.C.: United States Government Printing Office, 1949–1961).

15. For example, see Martin Bronfenbrenner and Thomas Mayer, "Liquidity Functions in the American Economy," *Econometrica*, vol. 28 (Oct. 1960), pp. 810–24; Milton Friedman, "The Demand for Money: Some Theoretical and Empirical Results," *Journal of Political Economy*, vol. 67 (Aug. 1959), pp. 327–51; H. R. Heller, "The Demand for Money: The Evidence from the Short-Run Data," *Quarterly Journal of Economics*, vol. 79 (May 1965), pp. 291–303; Allan H. Meltzer, "The Demand for Money: The Evidence from the Time Series," *Journal of Political Economy*, vol. 71 (June 1963), pp. 219–47; and Ronald L. Teigen, "Demand and Supply Functions for Money in the United States: Some Structural Estimates, *Econometrica*, vol. 32 (Oct. 1964), pp. 276–509.

Part 3

PROBLEMS IN THE ANALYSIS OF
UNDERDEVELOPMENT

6

Trade Policy and Allocative Efficiency
in Underdeveloped Countries

FRANZ GEHRELS

This paper concerns itself with some problems of misallocation of resources commonly found in underdeveloped countries and with the kind of foreign trade policy which can best mitigate these defects of the market system. At the factor level we shall consider the problem of imperfections in the markets for labor and capital. At the goods level we consider the case of monopoly in the manufacturing sector.

As several of the authors mentioned below have pointed out, only intervention in the defective markets themselves, by means of domestic subsidies or taxes, can bring about the marginal equalities which define a Pareto optimum. So, for example, by subsidizing users of labor whose money wage is greater than its opportunity cost, one can in principle eliminate completely this source of misallocation. Graphically, the situation is represented by a lifting of the production-possibility curve to its highest position. A protective tariff for the same factor users cannot bring about such a shift because it does nothing to improve the way in which different sectors

Franz Gehrels is Professor of Economics at Indiana University.

combine the factors of production. One sector will continue to use too much labor in relation to other resources, and another sector will use too little, with the result that their factor rates of transformation will differ.

However, the most effective solutions must often be foregone, because of political and social obstacles. For this reason we are led to consider next-best remedies. These can improve a situation, usually by introducing other market imperfections on top of the one or more already existing, but are inferior to the first-choice remedies. This is the case with foreign-trade tariffs and subsidies, and their equivalents in the economic, if not in the administrative, sense: import and export licenses, quotas, and state trading arrangements. We shall set out to show not only whether a tariff or a subsidy is appropriate for a particular domestic imperfection but also precisely how much should be imposed in terms of certain observable prices.

We have chosen to forego the use of community indifference curves, because this device has special difficulties when used for the kind of society typical of most developing countries. Such societies are anything but homogeneous in way of life, tastes, and income, and their governments generally have little control over distribution of wealth. Many economic changes thus may improve the lot of one group while worsening that of another, even in the long run.

Here, instead, we use a form of argument which is distribution neutral in that its conclusions are not affected by changes in relative shares of national income. Put differently, an economic change is judged the same whether or not the government takes measures to assure that increases of real national income accrue to the whole population. All that concerns us formally is whether it is possible, in moving to a particular position, to make some people better off, after hypothetically compensating any losers, and whether a move *away* from this position again must make some people worse off, even though compensation is allowed for. When the answer to these questions is affirmative, we say that we are at an optimum. This may be a Pareto optimum, in which a number of marginal equalities of transformation and substitution rates are satisfied; or it may be a constrained, or next-best optimum, in which a number of marginal equalities arc simultaneously violated.

All of this is not to say that policy-makers should ignore distributional and other effects of their actions. They may well sometimes choose an alternative which is inferior from the viewpoint of allocative efficiency, because the superior alternatives have undesired political or social by-products. Nevertheless, policy-makers are likely to make better decisions if they can see more clearly the effects of policy on resource utilization, and then modify their decisions to account for other social effects.

Except briefly in the section headed "Modification for Technological Progress and Rate of Saving," the argument does not explicitly consider future production or consumption; therefore, we do not consider the effect on the rate of economic growth of changes in investment or changes in technological progress. Policy-makers might find reason to believe that aggregate investment would be greater in an industrializing society than in an agrarian one with the same real income, or that technology advances more rapidly in manufacturing than in agriculture. Whether or not these views are correct, the kind of optimum we shall find maximizes the value of available goods over a short time horizon. To move away from it by conscious measures means to reduce the supply of present goods out of which the investment and consumption shares must be taken. Awareness that policy can lead to a shrinking of the base from which future income grows might well modify some of the present policies toward sectors which are believed to contribute to faster growth.

Among the noteworthy previous contributions to the discussion of next-best optima in an international-trade setting are those of Fleming, Meade, Lipsey and Lancaster, Bhagwati and Ramaswami, Haberler, Hagen, and Johnson. Deserving special mention, although dealing only with a closed economy, is the paper of Fishlow and David. The present essay sets out to give more precise answers to questions raised in part by these writers.[1]

THE PARETO–OPTIMAL CONDITIONS

For present purposes it is best to take the formulation of Fishlow and David as our point of departure, expanding their version to include the foreign-trade sector. A perfectly competitive economy producing two goods—manufactures and agricultural products—with two factors—labor and capital—would be in full equilibrium under the following conditions:

$$F_{al}/F_{ml} = F_{ak}/F_{mk} = P_m/P_a = \Pi_m/\Pi_a. \tag{1}$$

F_{al} is labor's marginal product in agriculture, F_{ml} the same in manufactures, F_{ak} and F_{mk} are the two marginal products of capital. Finally P_m, P_a, Π_m, and Π_a are the domestic and foreign prices of the two goods.

These conditions are at the same time sufficient for an optimum *if* all marginal products are decreasing, there are no externalities in production or consumption, and foreign prices are independent of domestic demand or supply. In addition, there must be no substitutability between leisure and income through work and no preference for one kind of activity over the other on the part of factor owners.

In order to bring these conditions closer to reality, we make two modifications. One is to take account of the fact that there is substitutability between income and leisure, and the other is to account for the possibility that labor may have a preference for one kind of employment over another. Taking the second of these modifications first, we add the condition that the marginal rate of substitution (mrs) between the two activities matches the ratio of their wages. Wages are here taken to include both contractual and imputed wages as well as remuneration both in money and in kind. This condition gives the alternative equation:

$$1/\mu \cdot F_{al}/P_{ml} = F_{ak}/P_{mk} = P_m/P_a = \Pi_m\Pi_a. \tag{2}$$

The coefficient μ expresses the relative preference between agricultural and industrial activity. It is sometimes held that the agricultural population has a preference for the rural life such that $\mu <$ 1 applies at the margin. One might equally hold that the opposite is true for some underdeveloped countries and cite the large numbers of urban underemployed and unemployed as evidence for this view.[2] Such preferences, of course, apply among occupations within the main activities as well, but these cannot be included in our simplified two-sector model. When caste, taboos, or social pressures take extreme forms, these can be reflected by giving a very large or small value to μ or by substituting an inequality sign for the first equality of (2).

The substitutability between income and leisure can be introduced by means of the following added condition:

$$U_t/U_y = F_{al}P_a = \mu F_{ml}P_m, \qquad (3)$$

where U_t is the marginal utility of leisure and U_y is the marginal utility of income. It is difficult to say to what extent this condition is violated even in an advanced society with nominal full-employment conditions. In an underdeveloped country, quite aside from open unemployment, there is an unknown amount of disguised unemployment.

OPTIMUM WITH IMPERFECT LABOR MARKET

Every real-world economy violates in some degree the conditions above. But our concern here is to consider the kind of distortions present in the underdeveloped countries and to formulate an optimal trade policy, *given the presence of such distortions*. It is not possible to reach the best of all positions, as defined by equations (1) or (2) above; but the constrained optimum reached implies, in general, a different degree of trade restriction from that appropriate for a perfectly competitive and frictionless domestic economy. To anticipate in part the conclusions reached below, the most efficient restriction is not one that equates the domestic transformation rate with the rate of transformation through trade.

In developing an optimal rule we carry further the analysis of

Hagen, who showed that restriction of trade could be justified by the existence of factor-price disparities between sectors. Hagen did not, however, go on to show how much restriction was desirable or what the degree of restriction depended on. Bhagwati and Ramaswami concluded correctly that the presence of domestic factor-market imperfections is a justification for interference in the distorted markets. Interference with foreign trade is an inferior remedy to intervention in the internal markets, if the latter is equally feasible. In contrast to them, we assume that domestic intervention of the desired sort is more difficult to bring about than foreign-trade intervention, and therefore we concentrate our attention on the latter remedy.

We shall give main attention to the consequences of distortions in the labor market, using a qualified version of the situation described by Arthur Lewis.[3] Social and political forces, embodied partly in legislation and union agreements and partly in voluntary action by employers, lead to setting a floor under wages which is above that given by the true supply schedule of labor. To be sure, the true supply schedule may also have a highly elastic portion owing to the need to provide minimal diet and living conditions and the need to assure workers' willingness to work under an industrial discipline. But this by the assumption of the present model is below the institutionally determined wage; unemployment and underemployment could be largely eliminated by reducing the wage, if the social and political situation permitted it. Employees act as if the supply of labor were horizontal for both increases and decreases in demand.

We assume that in general there is substitutability between factors of production. This takes place, however, only when the rentals on factors can adjust. When real wages are inflexible downward, it is not possible to adjust sufficiently the relative returns to capital and management, on the one hand, and labor, on the other, to absorb the full supply of labor. An increase in aggregate demand due to, say, a monetary expansion would not generally lead to more than a temporary absorption of labor because of the rapid upward adjustment of many wages to the price level. Since the removal of such unemployment requires an increase in the supply of complementary resources, our situation would seem to conform to the common usage of the term *structural unemployment*.[4]

We assume that a major part of the redundant labor supply is on the land. Here the presence of family-operated holdings makes it possible to support the excess supply of labor at a level of subsistence which is low but still in excess of its marginal contribution to output. The fact of unequal values of marginal products for labor means that in both equations (2) and (3) at least one of the equalities is violated. It may be, however, that farmers have found an equilibrium between leisure and income within agriculture, because the additional small income from more work would not compensate them for the loss of leisure.

The presence of urban unemployment can be taken account of in the same framework. For the urban unemployed the rate of substitution between income and leisure does not match its real wage in either sector, so that all the equalities in (3) are violated.[5]

The model outlined above may, of course, not be a suitable approximation of conditions in some important underdeveloped regions. For instance, Hia Myint would argue that scarcity of land is an important constraint in countries like India, Ceylon, or Java, but not to other parts of Southeast Asia, or to Africa or much of South America.[6] We should therefore emphasize that the present analysis would need significant modification before being applied to such areas. One might for these areas pay greater attention to the lack of social capital (e.g., transportation, power, irrigation, and flood control) and less to the differential productivities of labor. The latter may still exist but might be eliminated or reduced by improving the allocation of capital. The usefulness of trade policy, compared to a direct attack on the allocation problem, would be considerably less than in the land-scarcity case mainly considered here.

Whether labor's marginal product in agriculture is zero or positive, that of capital is likely to be strongly positive. One need only mention such investment possibilities as flood control, irrigation, communications, storage facilities, implements, and fertilizers. Agricultural output therefore still has strong positive elasticity, even when labor's marginal contribution to output is negligible. Conversely, a transfer of capital to the manufacturing sector must reduce agricultural production.

It is not generally true that the marginal opportunity cost of labor is zero. Even when the loss of output in agriculture from the transfer is zero, there are numerous associated costs. These include not only direct moving cost, but more importantly the urban housing, transportation, schools, health services, and the rest of the public services needed to absorb and make effective the new additions to the urban labor force. These costs generally mean a diversion of scarce resources from alternative uses.

In the case of urban unemployment the foregoing transfer costs may not need to be incurred in the same magnitude in order to draw labor into useful employment. One can, however, argue that much of the same outlay is in practice needed in order to make such labor effective in its new employment. The existence of such unemployment complicates a little the argument below without altering its essentials, as the reader will see.

We now wish to take account of these transfer costs in stating how our economic-efficiency rules are violated. Taking the symbol γ to represent the just-named costs, we write in place of the first equality of equations (2) above: $(\gamma + F_{al})/\mu F_{ml} < F_{ak}/F_{mk}$. Even if labor's marginal product in agriculture were sometimes zero, the existence of transfer costs, γ, means that the left-hand side is still positive.

Urban unemployment can be taken care of with the same inequality where the value of μ is changed to $\mu > 1$, to reflect such labor's preference for urban life if such be the case, and the value of γ might be less than for the labor actually living in rural areas. The fictional F_{al} applying to the urban unemployed would be zero.

In order to facilitate the exposition, we shall intially ignore what happens to the marginal rate of substitution between leisure and income by making the common but unrealistic assumption that the supply of labor is perfectly inelastic with respect to income. We then modify our constrained-optimum tariff, which must intially violate two marginal conditions, to take account of substitutability between leisure and income—in which case three marginal conditions must be violated at once.

FIGURE I

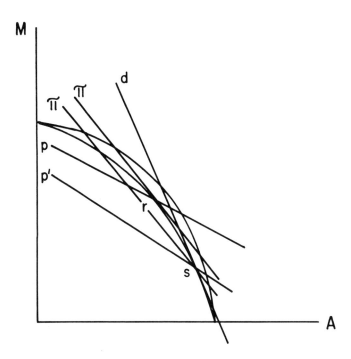

The significance of this condition being violated, and what it implies for trade interference, can best be seen in figure 1. The transformation curve is moved inward by the fact that A is using too much and M is using too little labor. The free mobility of capital cannot erase this because of diminishing returns in agriculture. (This is a disguised way of introducing the third factor, land, which is in limited supply.) If not for this, capital, by moving into A until its rate of return is no higher there than in M, brings about an equalization of returns for labor as well. In that case, production is on the outer transformation curve, but at a point where the price line intersects the transformation curve. This situation reflects the fact that capital's return is higher and labor's is lower than when free mobility of both factors exists.

We might add that a preference by labor for agricultural employment would also affect the shape of the transformation curve, moving it inward toward the origin along the M axis. This reflects the increased opportunity cost of M. In the absence of any market imperfections, the income line would still be tangential to the transformation curve.

Now we wish to find the tariff which is optimal for the situation depicted in figure 1. As a starting point we take that position on the constricted transformation curve which has the same slope as the international terms of trade line, π. Because of the labor-productivity difference in excess of transfer costs, M's money costs overstate its opportunity costs, and so the money-price ratio, P, is less steep than the transformation curve. It might be supposed that r represents the best point one could reach, because the application of a suitable tariff has brought about an equality between the mrt's through production and trade.

This is not the case, however, because consumer's common marginal rate of substitution is equal to P, and not to π. It is not possible to achieve a three-way equality among the two transformation rates and the substitution rate; but one can do better by violating all three equalities than by violating only two.

Let us move a small distance southeast from r by lowering the tariff. Imports of M increase, and domestic production shifts a little from M-output toward more A-output. P becomes steeper while π

keeps the same slope, thus moving the substitution rate closer to the trading transformation rate, but moving the production transformation rate *away* from π. There is improvement on the consumption side because the marginal value in consumption of M is measured by its domestic price P, while its cost in terms of exported A is measured by π.

On the other hand, the first units of domestic M-output displaced by imports have the same cost in terms of A as do the imports, and so there is no loss in value of consumption from this source. As we move farther southeast along the transformation curve, its slope becomes steeper than π, and there is loss because resources are now obtaining M at a higher cost abroad than the opportunity cost of M at home. But this loss is smaller at the margin than is the direct gain to consumers from taking advantage of the difference between P_m and Π_m.

The position S in the figure represents an optimal situation, with the given terms of trade, π, laying halfway between the consumer rate of substitution, P, and the production rate of transformation. We see that the constrained-optimal tariff is less than the one reached at r, where we had ignored the discrepancy between the production marginal rate of transformation and the consumer rate of substitution. It is clear that movements southeastward continue to be profitable until the slope of the transformation curve exceeds π by the same amount as π exceeds in slope the domestic consumer price P. When that position is reached, the marginal loss due to the negative production effect just matches the marginal gain from the consumption effect of additional imports.

It is fairly easy to state the optimal tariff in terms of the relative distortion of costs, T, due to the excess of wages in M over labor's opportunity cost and to the foreign price of imports. At the optimum, foreign price must be halfway between the domestic transformation rate and the consumer substitution rate. That is, $P = (1 + T)d$ and $\pi = (1 + \frac{1}{2}T)d$, so that by substitution $P = (1 + T)\pi / (1 + \frac{1}{2}T)$; d is the technical rate of transformation between M and A. The ad valorem tariff, t, is by definition $P/\pi - 1$, so that we have $t = (1 + T)/(1 + \frac{1}{2}T) - 1 = \frac{1}{2}T/(1 + \frac{1}{2}T)$. Thus the tariff rate is approximately half the relative distortion in price due to the imperfection in the market for labor.

If there were in fact unemployment, urban or otherwise, which could be absorbed in manufacturing without incurring transfer costs, the displaced transformation curve would have a vertical stretch. This would not change the sense of any inequality so far mentioned. It would, however, modify the optimal tariff formula. In particular it would always pay to increase the protection of manufacturing to the extent that its expansion could occur at zero opportunity cost. Doing so means giving up fewer agricultural goods for export and at the same time obtaining the previously imported manufactured goods domestically at no cost. The formula then applies again above the vertical stretch.[7]

We can now modify the formula to account for the case where foreign price is not independent of the tariff rate and quantity imported. Let m be the marginal rate of transformation through trade, where the trading transformation curve is no longer a straight line of constant slope but is convex outward. The relation between m and π, the terms of trade, is $m = E\pi/(E - 1)$, E being the foreign reciprocal-demand elasticity. In the verbal argument above, we replace Π with m everywhere, and the formula is derived much as before: $P = (1 + T)d$, and $m = (1 + \frac{1}{2}T)d$, so that $P = (1 + T)E\pi/(1 + \frac{1}{2}T)(E - 1)$ and $t = [1 + \frac{1}{2}T(E + 1)]/(1 + \frac{1}{2}T)(E - 1)$.

The rule for finding the constrained optimum is thus quite simple in both cases. Where the country suffering from the kind of labor-market distortion described above has no influence on external terms of trade, the best tariff is somewhat less than one-half the relative distortion between the consumer substitution rate and the internal transformation rate. The only parameter to estimate is T. When the external terms of trade are not independent, the formula above applies, and it is necessary to estimate both T and E.

Next we wish to show how the rule is modified when the marginal rate of substitution between leisure and income earned is not equal to the wage earned in manufacturing (but is equal to that earned in agriculture). There is an additional gain not previously included when workers are able to increase income at the expense of leisure through employment in the M-sector. Therefore we move northwest again from s toward r, taking away some consumer gain from imports, but adding some *both* for M-output being cheaper in opportunity cost than its price and for consumers decreasing their leisure to the benefit of their income. But only *some* consumers are failing to equate their mrs between leisure and income with the industrial wage rate—those employed in the agricultural sector and the urban unemployed. Even for those in industry the equating is not precise, but we are unable to say to what degree it is violated. In any event, the fact that the inequality applies only to some consumers makes it impossible to state a precise condition for the optimum.

For the sake of exposition only we shall explore the case where practically all of the labor force is in agriculture and the inequality therefore applies to almost everyone. When the foreign price of M is one-third of the way between domestic opportunity price and consumer price, this condition is met. This is true because the marginal gain from the last unit of imports just matches the sum of marginal losses from a unit reduction of M output and the corresponding amount of additional enforced leisure (which has utility, but less than the income given up).

This result can be stated in the same way as previously:[8] $P = (1 + T)d$ and $\pi = (1 + \frac{1}{3}T)d$, so that $P = (1 + T)\pi/(1 + \frac{1}{3}T)$, $t = (1 + T)/(1 + \frac{1}{3}T) - 1 = \frac{2}{3}T/1 + \frac{1}{3}T$.

MEANING OF THE OPTIMUM

Since we have not assumed any compensation of losers by gainers from the tariff adjustments above and since we have foregone making interpersonal comparisons, it is necessary to clarify our yardstick for judging changes. We shall first state intuitively in what restricted sense our rule is valid and then give a simple proof by mathematical induction.

We can think of any arbitrarily selected consumer's indifference map being placed in an Edgeworth box facing a set of foreign terms-of-trade lines. The equilibrium point of consumption is away from the contract curve because of the initial tariff. Then we place a hypothetical producer of both commodities in a second box facing the same set of foreign terms-of-trade lines. This point is initially on the contract curve because of the tariff, which initially made the domestic mrt equal to the foreign terms-of-trade.

Any reduction of the initial tariff moves us away from the latter contract curve but closer to the former. If we think of a multidimensional contract curve involving all producers, consumers, and the foreign terms of trade, our procedure has moved us on balance closer by moving off the curve in m of the dimensions for the m producers, (vis-à-vis the foreign terms of trade) and closer to the curve in n of the dimensions for the n consumers, also vis-à-vis the external-transformation rate. Since the domestic price distortion, T, is assumed constant, we need not concern ourselves with the n × m contract curves between consumers and producers.

But the foregoing is only an intuitive statement of what happened. We now wish to prove by induction that the optimum found passes two tests: In going to the optimum it was possible for those consumers who gained from the move to compensate any losers and still be better off themselves; and in moving away from the optimum, once it had been reached, it was impossible by any compensation scheme to avoid loss to some members of the community. To start off, we can consolidate all producers into a single unit because of our assumption of no externalities in production. Then we take the case of a single consumer ($n = 1$).

Consider the gradient vector $\Delta f(x) = P$, the elements on the left side of which are proportional to the marginal utilities of the k consumer goods. The vector Δx will represent the change in supplies of the k goods due to a marginal tariff change. The sign of the vector product $P \cdot \Delta x$ then determines whether or not the change brings an improvement. P is taken as the vector of initial prices, but for small changes $P_0 \cdot \Delta x$ positive (or negative) implies the same sign for $P_1 \cdot \Delta x$, because a single consumer must behave consistently (where P_0 and P_1 are prices before and after the change).

Now the simultaneous increase of imports of M and exports of A made $P \cdot \Delta x$ positive because M was valued more highly by our lone consumer than the A sacrificed to purchase the added M. Per additional unit of M imported the gain was proportional to $(P - \pi)$. But every unit imported also caused a decrease in production of M by one unit, and the loss due to this was proportional to $(\pi - d)$, because A was exchanged less favorably for imported M than for home-produced M. The positive $(P - \pi)$ decreased as the tariff diminished by steps while the negative $(\pi - d)$ became larger. Utility was maximized where $(P - \pi) = (\pi - d)$, that is, where π was halfway between p and d. Thus for $n = 1$ it is clearly true that the consumer is best off at the position so defined, because $p \cdot \Delta x \leqq 0$ for any further change of the tariff, either upward or downward.

Now we assume the truth of an equivalent statement for an arbitrary number of consumers, n, and show that it must then be true for $n + 1$. This will suffice to show that we have an optimum for *any* number of consumers we wish to take. The statement for some arbitrary n is that when $(P - \pi) = (\pi - d)$, $P \cdot \Delta x \leqq 0$, and a move away from that position must make at least some consumers worse off. Put the other way around, when $(P - \pi) \neq (\pi - d)$, $P \cdot \Delta x > 0$ for a tariff change which restores the equality, and therefore it is possible to make some people better off while compensating others for their losses.

Assuming the truth of this statement, we add one more consumer. For the $(n + 1)$th consumer we can simply hold constant the ordinal utilities of each of the previous n consumers. The additional value of available goods represented by $P \cdot \Delta x > 0$ when we move toward $(P - \pi) = (\pi - d)$ is then given to him. Conversely, the loss in value of goods represented by $P \cdot \Delta x < 0$ when we move away from the equality can all be taken away from him. Thus if the statement was true for n, it must be true for $n + 1$. This completes the proof.

Our statement that at least some people can be made better off by moving to the equality, and some people must be made worse off by moving away from the equality, is a limited claim. But it is all we are entitled to make and still avoid interpersonal comparisons of utility.[9]

EFFECT OF AN INTEREST-RATE DIFFERENTIAL

It is common in underdeveloped countries for the rural sector to pay higher interest charges than the manufacturing and commercial sectors do. If we assume that this difference is not explained only by the greater risk and administrative costs in lending to small farmers, the effect on the internal transformation curve is similar to that of the wage differential analyzed previously. The important point to notice is that its effect is additive to that of the wage differential: If both factor-market imperfections exist side by side, the transformation curve is moved farther in toward the origin than if only one of them exists. This is true even though relative money costs between A and M are moved closer to their true opportunity costs.[10]

In general the existence of the interest differential reduces the size of the optimal tariff because money cost is adjusted more nearly to opportunity cost. It could become zero, and there is even the unlikely possibility of its becoming negative (that is, a subsidy) when money costs in agriculture over-state opportunity cost because of the excessive rate of interest. This last case, while perhaps of theoretical interest, will not be explored here because of its improbability. Of some practical interest, however, is the possibility that factor-market imperfections may actually imply a low-tariff or even free-trade policy.

COMPARISON WITH IMPERFECTIONS IN COMMODITY MARKETS

The foregoing kinds of situations have of course much in common with imperfections in goods markets. The latter case implies a less-than-optimal position on a given transformation curve for goods, while the former means an inward shift of the transformation curve. But both are cases which can be cured completely only by direct attack, and use of foreign-trade measures is a next-best remedy. Our justification for considering them is the often great, practical difficulty of increasing mobility and removing monopoly positions, either in the supply of goods or in the supply of factors.[11]

Both for comparison and for its own interest, we shall assume the existence of some degree of monopoly on the part of one or a few firms in the manufacturing sector and consider its appropriate foreign trade remedy. There is reason to believe that underdeveloped countries may sometimes have a greater monopoly problem than the developed industrial countries. The smallness of markets, the lack of diversification of production, and the high degree of effective protection (historically through tariffs and exchange rationing) are all reasons why this should have come about.

Let us begin again with the simplest situation—the one in which there are no market defects other than the monopoly in manufacturing and in which the foreign terms of trade are independent. It is then appropriate to start with a zero tariff, as this would be optimal when all domestic markets are perfectly competitive. In which direction should we now move tariff-wise in order to correct for the monopoly situation, it being assumed that any reduction of imports increases the degree of monopoly by raising domestic price relative to cost?

If we increase the tariff from its initial level of zero, domestic output of M increases at the expense of A. M's value to consumers is higher than its opportunity cost, and so any increase of M-output represents an improvement. On the other hand, the reduction of imports worsens the position of consumers—negligibly at first, but by increasing degrees as the gap between cost and domestic price of imports widens. The optimal tariff is then at the point where the marginal loss to consumers from import reduction just matches the marginal gain from additional manufacturing output. The two meet where the consumer price exceeds domestic opportunity cost by the same percentage as it exceeds foreign price. Thus the way to deal with domestic monopoly is to give it protection! This is true even though the degree of monopoly may be increased in the process. We see easily that since $P = (1 + v)d = (1 + v)\pi$, the best tariff is equal to v, the degree of monopoly.

Somewhat paradoxically, the increase of the degree of monopoly with the tariff does not change the formal rule, but it does make the final tariff rate higher. The reason for this is that the marginal value of increases in M output gets larger as V increases with t. Thus it takes a larger decrease of imports to get to the place where the marginal net addition due to the one matches the marginal loss due to the other.

Let us return to the earlier conclusion reached when the money wage exceeded labor's social opportunity cost. We found there that the best tariff is such as to put foreign opportunity cost halfway between domestic cost and consumer price. Does the simultaneous existence of monopoly imply a still higher tariff?

The answer is clearly yes. The fact that M paid too high a wage meant that M-output was too low, and the tariff served to raise it to the point where its increase no longer brought a net gain in value of consumption. The fact that M in addition has a monopoly position means that M-output is too low for an additional reason, and the tariff requires further upward adjustment.

The formula for domestic consumer price p′ would in that case read $p' = (1 + V)p = (1 + V)m(1 + T)/(1 + \frac{1}{2}T) = (1 + V) [(1 + T)/(1 + \frac{1}{2}T)][E/(E - 1)]\pi$, where V is the degree of monopoly, and m is the foreign transformation rate. The tariff which reflects factor market imperfections and domestic monopoly is then

$t' = (1 + V)[(1 + T)/(1 + \frac{1}{2}T)][E/(E - 1)] - 1$. T is again the excess of money cost over opportunity cost due to factor-market distortions, and E is the foreign reciprocal demand elasticity. Since V, the degree of monopoly, is identical with the percentage markup of consumer price over money cost, it is itself a variable.

The difference between this rate and that reflecting only factor-market imperfection is $t' - t = V[(1 + T)/(1 + \frac{1}{2}T)][E/(E - 1)]$. This shows once more that the new rate is higher than the one which is optimal under competitive domestic conditions.[12]

USE OF TARIFF TO FINANCE SUBSIDIES TO FACTOR USERS

The premise so far has been that underdeveloped countries have serious difficulty in finding general domestic revenue sources for the financing of appropriate subsidies to users of overpriced factors of production. If the government has a complete choice of remedies, it can always do best by interfering in factor markets if the source of difficulty lies only there and not in the goods market as well. Now we go partway in this direction by asking whether a tariff whose proceeds are used to subsidize one industry can bring about better results than a tariff whose proceeds are used to replace some domestic source of revenue like the general sales tax or the income tax. One can easily guess that the answer is yes, because anything done to alleviate a factor market imperfection should bring about a higher internal transformation curve. But in addition we wish to see whether the height of the appropriate tariff is changed.

Let us assume that the tariff on imported M is used entirely to pay a subsidy on wages in that sector. Assume further that the optimal tariff as defined previously is inadequate to finance a complete removal of the labor-market imperfection. One can see immediately that the tariff should be higher than before. It should be such that the loss from additional tariff raises balances the gain at the margin from further improvements in the market for factors.

We take as the starting point the position found by applying the rule of the first section. At the optimum position the gain at the margin to consumers from additional imports just matched the loss due to M's opportunity cost being less than its marginal cost through imports. Now every dollar of revenue spent on subsidizing manufacturers in proportion to their payrolls has a favorable effect on the internal transformation curve. There is a gain to be realized here so long as the net cost of labor services is higher to M than to A. Let us measure this gain also in A units at the internal terms of trade, p, prevailing at the initial optimum production point (point s in figure 1). The optimal point is now *northeast* of s where there is a three-way balance among the three imperfections. That is, in raising the tariff from s, we stop at a point where the gain from shifting the transformation curve upward just balances at the margin with the difference between the loss from consumers getting less imports and the gain from the production transformation rate moving closer again to the foreign transformation rate. There is in principle no reason why the optimal tariff could not now move the production point north of r (possibly northeast because it would be on a higher transformation curve). In other words, the tariff could be higher than the one which equates the foreign and domestic mrs.

For completeness we should point out that the principle works in exactly the same fashion when both factor-market distortions—that for labor and that for capital—are present. The appropriate tariff would in general be higher than when only a labor-market distortion of given magnitude is present because subsidies would be paid both to manufacturers who hire labor and to farmers who borrow capital.

As a policy guide, this case does not seem farfetched, in that it provides an automatic source of revenue for the wage subsidy. It does, of course, require policy advisers to estimate the domestic transformation rate *and the shift* of the transformation curve which correspond to a marginal tariff change.

EXTERNALITIES IN PRODUCTION

The comparative simplicity of the foregoing rules may have been due in part to the assumption of no externalities in production or consumption. External economies in production may be important, and in that case the rules must be modified to account for this fact. Generally speaking, if such economies are present in the M-sector alone, a greater concentration of resources in that sector is called for than in their absence.

Because of transportation costs there is a natural tendency for production points to locate together, that is, for their markets to have the same centers. Such concentration minimizes the cost of transportation to consumers, and from suppliers, for any particular producer. Because of it, developed centers of production and commerce tend to have a great advantage over undeveloped localities, and latecomers may never be able to overcome this handicap.

If there were no costs of communication and transportation, it would make little difference whether suppliers of materials and primary factors, and purchasers of outputs, were concentrated in a small area or were scattered widely. Costs for a manufacturer would not be affected by his need to buy equipment, materials, and services at great distances or from nearby sources. Nor would his sales be handicapped by the need to seek markets at great distances abroad or at home.[13]

It is transport costs which are responsible for the existence of market areas: The higher are these costs relative to value of product, the smaller is the market area. As August Lösch has shown so elegantly, the natural tendency of markets is to be hexagonal when the sources of supply are punctiform—because the hexagon is the polygon closest in form to a circle which at the same time fills completely a geographic area.[14] Such areas can, to be sure, be distorted by barriers, natural or man-made, and by communication advantages such as trunk lines and waterways.

If we view all manufactures as a single composite commodity, the consequence of such externalities is a flattening of the transformation curve and an outward movement of the curve at the M-end. Conceivably, a part of the curve could be concave in the outward direction. The rule (and formula) for finding the optimal degree of restriction is not, however, changed greatly. The practical effect of externalities is only in the estimation of T, the coefficient expressing the difference between money cost and opportunity cost of manufactures. T is made greater, and consequently the degree of protection appropriate for an optimum is greater. Also a production point on the concave portion would not be optimal, so that a temporary and large intervention may be necessary to move the production point either northwest or southeast to a convex segment.[15]

MODIFICATION FOR TECHNOLOGICAL PROGRESS AND RATE OF SAVING

There is some reason to believe that a labor-surplus, underdeveloped country might enjoy more rapid technological advance in the manufacturing sector than an economically advanced country. Technology could be imported continually from abroad, so that with a time lag, improvements made in the advanced countries would make their appearance in the less advanced areas. It might be more difficult to do anything similar in agriculture, where tradition weighs heavily and where many improvements tend to displace labor already in surplus.

A related, and equally elusive problem, is the relation of the rate of capital formation to the composition of output. One might argue that business profits are a prime source of current saving and that the greater is the share of manufacturing and related commercial activity in national output, the greater is the rate of saving. If a (discounted) future output were to be included along with current output, then policy-makers would need to consider the effect of differences in saving on the discounted present value of output for different allocations of resources between M and A.

In principle such considerations could easily be taken account of in the calculation. We would compare the discounted streams of M- and A- outputs, where the M- stream was a more rapidly growing one. The formulas stated in the previous section would still apply; but the transformation curve would have different meaning and its slope in the M direction would be steeper. The optimal tariff and the proportion of resources going to the M- sector would be higher than before, if indeed technology and saving work in the way suggested.

CONCLUDING REMARKS

All but one of the foregoing cases tend to reinforce the conclusion that protection may sometimes be a good thing for developing countries. How much protection they add up to in individual cases can be determined only by careful examination. There is reason to suspect, however, that many of these countries have, through a combination of circumstances, reached a degree of trade restriction which cannot be justified by all the arguments put together. Domestic inflation and currency overevaluation have led to the severest exchange restriction. At the same time fiscal convenience has encouraged the use of high import duties along with duties on primary exports, sometimes hidden behind the operation of government marketing boards.[16]

A practical procedure for a government adviser might be to calculate roughly what, if any, protection might be justified by the foregoing arguments. Once this is reached by some combination of import and export duties (which are equivalent in their protective effects), the next step would be to prescribe the right combination of fiscal and monetary measures and currency exchange rate to bring about internal and external equilibrium. This would be a very large order to carry out and could not be done with precision. Its result would likely be a rather different composition and volume of trade from that actually prevailing for the underdeveloped part of the world.

NOTES

1. J. M. Fleming, "On Making the Best of Balance of Payments Restrictions on Imports," *Economic Journal*, vol. 61 (Mar. 1951); J. E. Meade, *Trade and Welfare* (London: Oxford University Press, 1955), Part II, and *The Theory of Customs Unions* (Amsterdam: North Holland Publishing Co., 1955); R. G. Lipsey and K. Lancaster, "The General Theory of Second-Best," *Review of Economic Studies*, vol. 24 (Oct. 1956), pp. 11–32; J. Bhagwati and V. K. Ramaswami, "Domestic Distortions, Tariffs and the Theory of Optimum Subsidy," *Journal of Political Economy*, vol. 71 (Feb. 1963), pp. 44–50; G. Haberler, "Some Problems in the Pure Theory of International Trade," *Economic Journal*, vol. 60 (June 1950), pp. 223–40; E. B. Hagen, "An Economic Justification of Protectionism," *Quarterly Journal of Economics*, vol. 72 (Nov. 1958), pp. 496–514; H. G. Johnson, "Optimal Trade Intervention in the Presence of Domestic Distortions," in *Trade, Growth, and the Balance of Payments*, Essays in Honor of Gottfried Haberler on the Occasion of His Sixty-Ninth Birthday (Chicago: Rand McNally, 1965), pp. 3–34; and G. Fishlow and P. David, "Optimal Resource Allocation in an Imperfect Market Setting," *Journal of Political Economy*, vol. 69 (Dec. 1961), pp. 529–46.

2. The presence of such groups may, of course, not be due so much to rational choice as to past accident. A crop failure may have driven people to the towns who later could not return; others may have gone with false expectations.

3. W. A. Lewis, "Economic Development with Unlimited Supplies of Labor," *The Manchester School* (May 1954), pp. 139–91.

4. For a recent survey of views on unemployment and underemployment in developing economies, as well as some empirical evidence on its magnitude, see the recent article by Stanislaw Wellisz, "Dual Economies, Disguised Unemployment and the Unlimited Supply of Labor," *Economica*, vol. 35 (Feb. 1968), pp. 22–51.

5. At least two writers, Haberler and, following his example, Johnson, have emphasized the distinction between factor immobility and factor-price rigidity. If factors could not transfer out of a sector with a shift in demand (due, for instance, to freeing trade), they could still be retained in employment there if their prices fell sufficiently. But the result would be less desirable than if complete transferability existed together with factor-price flexibility. We have chosen to concentrate attention on institutional rigidities in factor prices, particularly wages, as the main cause of resource misallocation. The Haberler case of immobility can, however, be dealt with in terms of violations of equations (2)

and (3), since it boils down to a case of urban and/or rural unemployment.

6. Hla Myint, *The Economics of the Developing Countries* (London: Hutchinson, 1964).

7. This conclusion is a modification of a conclusion reached by Haberler. Haberler argues that if the choice is between free trade and complete protection, it may be better to have unemployed resources with free trade than to have full employment with no trade. We conclude that restricted trade is better than free trade when it leads to absorption of zero-cost resources and that the degree of restriction should be increased so long as that situation exists.

8. We should perhaps point out that the difficulty of estimating the degree of cost distortion may be considerable. Even if this be the case, formulation of a simple rule makes explicit the information which policy-makers must seek in order to make an intelligent decision. It is better to use an inaccurate estimate of the right parameter than to be guided by faulty considerations.

9. An easier course would have been to assume that the social marginal utility of a dollar was the same for every individual receiving it irrespective of distribution changes. The argument would have proceeded as before, and the social utility function would have been maximized at the same point at which we found our optimum. The alternative course has been followed by Fleming in dealing with balance-of-payments restrictions and by Meade in dealing with customs unions.

Our procedure is related to, but different from, Samuelson's consumption possibilities approach. In the latter, one situation (e.g., some foreign trade) is judged better than another (no trade) if consumers are collectively placed on a higher consumption-possibilities curve. It was necessary for us to make a more complicated statement because in our case consumer prices are *not* proportional to domestic opportunity cost, and therefore it does not follow that a higher range of consumption alternative is always an improvement. Sufficient distortion between opportunity cost and consumer price can actually make the higher consumption curve less desirable than a lower curve.

10. Implicit in this argument are two assumptions which should perhaps be made explicit. One is that capital is not merely a substitute for surplus manpower, as might be the case with some machinery, but rather is a complement to both land and labor. This would presumably be the case with some of the less spectacular forms of investment such as improved seeds, pesticides, livestock, fertilizer, irrigation, etc. It is widely believed that great improvements in acreage yields can still be brought about by these means. The second assumption is that easier or cheaper credit does not merely increase consumption by farmers without contributing to agricultural investment. However, even if there

were some increase of farmers' consumption, the contribution of a fractional investment may still be great enough to raise output by more than consumption (and therefore increase net aggregate saving) while giving a higher marginal return than alternative investments. The present discussion does not, however, consider the effect of alternative allocations on the rate of saving. Rather we are assuming that the aggregate propensity to save is the same no matter how investment is allocated.

11. This section deals with a problem raised by Meade in chapter 14 of *Trade and Welfare*, pp. 226–43, but comes to a different conclusion from his, pp. 234–37. The conclusion is also different, apparently, from Johnson's, p. 23.

12. Johnson explores two other cases of commodity-market imperfection, but does not examine the one discussed here. They are, one, that where M is actually the comparative-advantage sector and monopoly leads it to become the import competitive one instead—here no trade may or may not be better than the wrong specialization; and, two, that where M is the exporter but doesn't export enough because of the monopoly. Here a subsidy is appropriate, and a subsidy on exports is not as good as a subsidy on production. This is as far as Johnson goes. See Johnson, pp. 18–23.

We can go further by showing how much export subsidy is appropriate in his second case. Starting from the free-trade position, we argue in a fashion similar to that in the other case. Remembering that M, and not A, is the export sector, we can see that the first units of additional exports bring more of A at the given foreign terms of trade than do the same units given up if production were shifted a small way toward A. But the export subsidy raises the internal M price above the foreign price and consumers shift their consumption away from M toward A. The marginal production gain meets the marginal consumption loss when domestic opportunity cost of M (d) is as much below the foreign price (π) as the consumer price (p) is above it. So we come to a formula for the export subsidy on M similar to that previously reached for the import duty in the case of factor-market distortions.

13. The extreme case of nontransportability would be some social services—such as education, health care, and maintenance of law and order. It is, however, not obvious that indivisibilities are important enough in these instances to make a strong case for concentration.

14. August Lösch, *The Economics of Location*, trans. W. H. Woglom (New Haven: Yale University Press, 1954).

15. We have not, in the foregoing argument, relied on internal economies of scale, because this has the awkwardness of assuming disequilibrium for some producer of final or intermediate goods unless monopoly is invoked.

16. The deeper causes, as distinguished from these direct and me-

chanical ones, are more difficult to untangle. Henry Oliver has suggested at least three to me.

First, there is often a strong autarchic bias in economic policy due to the desire for national independence and power. Dependence on manufactured imports is reminiscent of the times of colonial rule, besides leading to very real military vulnerability.

Second, domestic business interests often have strong political influence, which they use to obtain favored treatment, both with taxes and subsidies, through foreign-trade policy.

Third, somewhat at cross purposes to the second cause, governments in developing countries use foreign-trade policy as a device to redistribute income. High duties on luxury consumer goods, especially durables, are a simple example. More roundabout is the limitation of such imports with various quantitative controls, together with the use of rationed foreign exchange to import consumer staples.

Some might wish to characterize the attitude of which the third cause is an example by the term *Pigovian* or *Old Welfare*, because interpersonal utility comparisons are explicity made at the outset in policy formulation. By contrast, the point of view taken in the present paper is Paretian in that questions of distribution are postponed from the analysis. In principle the two approaches ought to lead to exactly the same policy decisions; but in practice the order in which particular considerations are taken up may well affect the weight given them. Thus the approach advocated in the present paper might lead to somewhat less weight being given to distribution considerations than the alternative approach would.

7

The Concept of Capital and Its Role
in Economic Growth

GEORGE W. WILSON

The concept of capital and its role in economic growth are two areas of controversy that date back virtually to the birth of the subject of economics. The discussions and controversies concerning them have continued to the present. It would be foolhardy to think that in a short paper much could be contributed to a debate that has attracted the attention of all the world's great economists at one time or another. Yet there may be some utility in a discussion that examines the varying conceptions of capital and assesses their implications. Specifically this paper deals with what may, ungenerously, be called the old view of capital and contrasts this with what, with some generosity, may be deemed the new or emerging view. As will become apparent, the distinction between old and new is not chronological. There are many respectable contemporary economists who retain the old view, and there are some ancient giants in the profession who held at least glimmerings of the new.

George W. Wilson is Professor of Economics, Chairman of the Department of Economics, and Professor of Business Administration in the School of Business at Indiana University.

THE OLD VIEW

Essentially this view defines capital in a rigorously physical sense. Historically the physical conception of capital has included, or even been confined to such diverse items as corn, wage goods, or materials in the process of ripening into consumer goods. This particular set of viewpoints fits neatly into a vision of the productive process that proceeded in stages, so that to feed, house, and clothe workers during time period two required that a bundle of consumption or wage goods be left over from period one. The greater this bundle of leftovers from the past period's production, the greater the number of "productive" workers that could be employed in the current period. The distinction between productive asd unproductive labor from Adam Smith through Veblen (with some exceptions) depended upon whether or not a physical product was left behind.

These views of capital were, consciously or unconsciously, designed partially to account for or justify capitalists' income through their necessity of waiting or abstaining. A stages theory of production, which also assumed that capitalists held all the leftover output, neatly coincided with a justification of their remuneration in terms of deferred consumption. As has been said, "they also serve who only stand and wait." Thus, waiting was not only deemed to be productive, as Eugen V. Böhm-Bawerk later tried to show, but was often construed to involve some alleged sacrifice, although the latter rationale was never especially convincing. The extreme version of the sacrifice interpretation was, of course, scathingly shot down by Karl Marx.

A different interpretation of the productive process—one that envisages a synchronous process where inputs and outputs are in a kind of perpetual stew—makes this notion of delay much trickier to verify, although it can be done.[1]

In any event, when capital later came to be viewed as durable assets, like tools, machinery, and buildings, rather than corn, or consumer goods, the physical nature of capital remained intact: only its ingredients changed.[2]

Indeed durability became the essence of the concept, so that the definition of capital came to be, a durable physical asset lasting for a given number of time periods with some degree of net productivity during the period of durability. The present physical view of capital confines its ingredients to structures, equipment, and, depending on the purpose, inventories. In fact, we have established a national income accounting system such that net investment, defined here as the change in the stock of physical capital, is measured in precisely these terms. Of course, these broad aggregates hide a bewildering variety of assets, and one may legitimately ask for a more microscopic approach—for some of the "organized disaggregation" that Rostow long ago appealed for, rather than the disorganized aggregation that frequently occurs at present. But having locked the physical concept of capital into a statistical system of great value, there is a natural reluctance to abandon the existing notions and measures of capital.[3]

Furthermore, although the national accounting system identifies various components of investment, most macro-static and certainly macro-dynamic analyses assume that capital is homogeneous. It is as if there were a certain capital substance, which, jelly-like, could take on innumerable physical forms and which itself, in the aggregate, inevitably grew, so long as consumption increased more slowly than output.[4] Attempts to render the physical and homogeneous capital concept more realistic take several approaches. One of these recognizes that machines, or whatever form the capital jelly takes, wear out so that machines constructed in period t-n will be less "effective" than those constructed later. This is deemed to occur for two reasons: depreciation and "embodied" technological progress. In both cases, however, the realism so introduced is somewhat fictional, for both depreciation and technological progress are treated as related to time in some predetermined way, so that if d is the rate of depreciation per unit of time and λ the rise in productivity per unit of time, the net change in productivity is simply $\lambda - d$. With such monotonically changing net efficiency, we immediately return to homogeneous capital in the sense that a machine, or plant, manufactured n periods ago, can always be construed in terms of its contemporary efficiency equivalent. All these devices do is provide a mechanistic way of measuring capital in terms of some as yet undefined substance. This attempted realism, does, however, as we note later, alter the significance of capital in economic growth for the simple reason that it changes the measured rate of growth of the capital stock itself. If old machines are always less productive than new ones, either because the new ones are less fully depreciated[5] or because they embody later and hence more productive techniques, or both, then the rate of growth of capital stock will always be higher than if either or both of these assumptions are not made.

In summary, one main strand of capital theory, which we have dubbed the old view, assumes that capital is physical and homogeneous. Whether this commits one to discussion of capital strictly by analogy is another matter. Donald Dewey, for example, argues that it does, but that this makes no difference.[6] On the other hand, Paul A. Samuelson and R. M. Solow, attempting to get away from "neoclassical fairy tales," believe that it is desirable and possible to develop a "complete analysis of a great variety of heterogeneous capital goods and processes through time."[7] Yet their earlier discussion deduced as a by-product the implication that

> even though there is no such thing as a single abstract capital substance that transmutes itself from one machine form to another . . . the rigorous investigation of a heterogeneous capital-goods model shows that over extended periods of time an economic society can in a perfectly straightforward way reconstruct the composition of its diverse capital goods so that there may remain great heuristic value in the simpler . . . models of abstract capital substance.[8]

In a later discussion, it was concluded that under appropriate conditions there was a close similarity between this and the homogeneous neoclassical fairy tale.[9]

These views, which, in effect, support the homogeneity assumption plus some ambiguity regarding the determinacy of development models when it is dropped,[10] and the superior mathematical tractability of the homogeneity assumption probably suffice to explain its persistence. The intuitive appeal and greater ease of measurement when the physical attribute is retained similarly induce acceptance of this assumption as well. It is therefore not surprising that these two assumptions regarding capital continue to predominate in discussions of the role of capital in economic growth.

CAPITAL AND GROWTH

The old view of capital, which persists, not only assumes homogeneous and physical capital, as noted above, but relates economic growth almost solely to changes in capital so defined. I am not suggesting that any particular definition of the nature of capital necessarily commits one to a particular theory of economic growth or to a specific role of capital in the growth process; such a connection, if or when it exists, is tautological. Rather I wish to suggest that capital has traditionally been accorded high priority as a factor in the growth process. Thus for Adam Smith the accumulation of stock was essential to the division of labor, and labor was stimulated in "proportion only as stock is previously more and more accumulated.[11] For J. S. Mill, industry was limited by capital.[12] Similar notions regarding the critical role of capital prevailed in all the mainstream works of classical and neoclassical economics. More recently, models of the Harrod-Domar type relate growth rates almost solely to allegedly fixed capital-output and savings ratios.

On the other hand, mainstream economics has long held that output depends upon land, labor, capital, and entrepreneurship. The fact that it is very tricky to measure land and entrepreneurship is no reason to assume that their productive contribution is zero or that they are insignificant or that they are perfectly substitutable for capital and labor, respectively. Nor does the more recent elimination of these factors of production seem justifiable, at least not for the reasons often given.[13] That is, it is sometimes pointed out that the four factors of production classification was a product of the social structure in England during the formative period of economics as a discipline in which land, labor, and capital were "owned" by relatively distinct social classes. Some economists have even suggested that had a separate social class existed that owned transportation facilities there would have developed a fifth factor of production, namely, transportation.[14] The view that the distinction among productive factors is historical implies that when the social structure changes so does the most relevant factor classification. Thus, in the United States, for example, where social classes were less distinct and where most interest centered upon the dichotomy between owners of property (land and physical assets) and workers, the historical viewpoint would consider a two-factor production function, à la Cobb-Douglas, most appropriate. But the production viewpoint has typically used the factor classification to analyze problems of income distribution. The fact that the analysis frequently got mixed up with questions of social justice does not, ipso facto, impair its validity or usefulness from the point of view of production. There is nothing in the theory of production to warrant the assertion that if land has value or rent equals the marginal product of land, such value needs to accrue to the owner. It is land, not land ownership, that is deemed to be productive, although this distinction was not always steadfastly adhered to.

But even eliminating land and entrepreneurship for a variety of reasons, production theory has long found a Cobb-Douglas (CD) function to be useful and, when suitably constrained, consistent with some major propositions of the theory of the firm. Although such a function assumes homogeneous units of labor and capital, it is clearly more inclusive than a capital-only function. A capital-only production function at best yields only a partial answer to the problem of economic growth and, of course, contributes nothing to the problem of resource allocation or income distribution. Indeed, a capital-only theory à la Harrod-Domar, can be viewed as a special case of the widely used CD or even constant elasticity of substitution functions.

On the other hand, a more inclusive interpretation of capital as nothing more nor less than productive power, which includes everything useful in production, implies that capital is the only factor of production. This capital-only theory in turn suggests that "the output of all things useful in production can be increased by investment":[15] In fact, this is the only way output could be increased under this definition of capital. Thus, a capital-only production function is trivially derived from such a comprehensive view of capital. It is clear, however, that this is not what Harrod-Domar type models imply. Indeed, rooted as they are in the Keynesian framework, they rather obviously restrict investment to the net increase in the stock of physical assets as defined in the national income accounts, which have a much narrower view of capital than that indicated above.

Although there is a logical consistency to the capital-only view of capital—as spelled out by Irving Fisher, Frank Knight, and more recently, Donald Dewey—when such views become intermingled with investment as used in modern macro-theory and national income accounting, they give misleading results. That is, although many people have argued that capital consists of not only machines, buildings, etc., but also nonmaterial resources, such as training and education (i.e., essentially the capital-only argument), there is a tendency to limit subsequent analysis solely to physical goods,[16] and hence rely on contemporary national accounting concepts. This broader view, in short, implies a capital-only theory of production which is carried over almost unconsciously to its contemporary macro-framework where outlays on training and education are not treated as investment. Perhaps this subtle transition explains the early wide acceptance of Harrod-Domar type models of economic growth.

Such capital-only growth models, however, direct attention and policy toward a concerted and one-sided effort designed to raise the

savings ratio to stimulate growth. For a country in which a large proportion of the population is existing at near-subsistence level, such
attempts to curb or even maintain consumption at this low level can
be disastrous. All this, of course, is totally independent of the wholly
inadequate data purporting to measure savings.

But even applied to developed, private enterprise, market economies, this approach is too aggregative and schematic. The composition of the aggregate called *investment* may be just as important
as its magnitude. And there are innumerable factors that could and
do lead to changes in output regardless of any change in the stock of
capital. This is, of course, familiar and there is no point belaboring
misuse of the capital-output ratio or single-factor production functions here.[17] Suffice it to say that many economists have shown increasing signs of rebellion against, or guilt feelings about, such overly
schematic, aggregative, and mechanistic approaches to the problem
of economic growth, especially as far as the underdeveloped countries are concerned. Some (e.g., E. E. Hagen) even question whether
economic growth has much to do with economics at all. This is
partly semantics, for in the long run the distinction between economic and noneconomic factors may be illusory. But more and
more contemporary economists are stressing that political, cultural,
demographic, social, and even personality factors are crucial to economic growth and that whatever happens to the quality or quantity
of capital, unless there are changes, usually unspecified, in these
other factors the prospects for viable economic growth are slim.
Alternatively, economic growth, or the growth in capital stock, is
viewed as causally related to these noneconomic factors and changes
therein. Too many of these discussions, however, end up with a
tautology which stresses a set of noneconomic preconditions which,
inter alia, are alleged to exert pressures to exploit "the impulses to
expansion in the modern sector."[18] Nevertheless, the complexity and
interrelatedness of the innumerable economic and noneconomic factors, as well as the role of feedback mechanisms or even Myrdal's
"cumulative causation" are more and more coming into vogue in

one strand of development literature. This, however, necessarily leads the economist into areas beyond his technical expertise. The role of economic factors as cause or consequence in molding attitudes, political and social systems, and so on, is a pretty tenuous and unstructured aspect of social science research. However important analysis of these relationships or interrelationships might be, they are inevitably fuzzy and extremely difficult to quantify or even test with any degree of empiricism that might have wider application or generality.

At the same time, however, a substantial literature has grown up that examines optimal growth paths under varying conceptions of an aggregate production function with or without technical change (embodied or disembodied) and including labor and capital.[19] The results of this are difficult to evaluate at the moment, but the further expansion and elucidation of simplistic Harrod-Domar type models will certainly improve our knowledge of growth processes. The empirical testing of some of the conclusions, however, awaits further research. In the meantime, especially as far as the underdeveloped countries are concerned, stress on noneconomic constraints to growth continues to preempt the scene largely because the urgency of the problems seems to call for more action and more policy-oriented research rather than further elegance and refinement of economic theory, especially at the macro level. In this regard, the final sentence of Allen's latest summary of macro-theory appropriately concludes, "what remains is to turn the models into econometric form and to try them out with the aid of modern simulation techniques on a computer—and to pass on, in theory and in econometrics, from positive economics to problems of planning and optimalisation."[20]

In my view this further elaboration of and reaction against the theories of economic growth that prevailed around the early to mid 1950's is healthy and desirable. At this point, however, it would be useful to reflect upon the origin and implications of the physical view of capital.

ORIGIN AND IMPLICATIONS OF THE OLD VIEW OF CAPITAL

The old view of capital, which pervades contemporary macro models, was derived originally from a strictly physical conception of production. Indeed, as noted earlier, the long-lived distinction between productive and unproductive labor was based entirely on the perishability of the product. The lineage can be traced back even farther than Adam Smith and extended even beyond Thorstein Veblen. From Aristotle to contemporary Soviet national accounting, production has, with some deviations, referred almost completely to commodities and physical change or transformation of objective materials. This has meant that the service industries, variously defined, have often been regarded as either outright waste and hence something which should be eliminated or as necessary for production (maybe even useful, according to Adam Smith) but not productive in themselves. Even the contemporary theory of the firm implies, when it does not baldly assert, that the cost and demand functions of the firm refer to physical units of production which can be increased or decreased at the firm's discretion by single units. This physical view is partly unconscious and arises primarily because of the problems involved in identifying the output units of service industries.[21] On a more subtle level, what service industries create is capacity to provide a service; whether or not the service is produced depends upon actual use. In an industry producing physical units of output, it is possible to produce independently of actual sales or use of the product and simply stockpile. Of course, in the long run the results would be similar but the ability to distinguish more clearly and intuitively between an act of production and an actual sale when referring to physical units of product tends to orient the analysis of the firm in the direction of physical units in order to differentiate cost and demand functions.

As far as the national accounts are concerned, they are, of course, based upon a concept of production that is simply value added. To this extent there is no necessary implication of physical output. But as far as accumulation is concerned, a strictly physical concept is employed even though some services may "accumulate" or become embodied in people and things. Of course, if services are to "last," they must become embodied in either people or things. The general failure of economists to treat people as assets or a stock of wealth in a nonslave economy analogous to a stock of things further restricts this old view to embodiment in things.[22]

Essentially, the physical concept of production derives from low-level economic stagnation, which means heavy dependence upon agriculture. In these circumstances argiculture becomes a standard by which to judge other forms of economic activity. The reasons for this agricultural orientation seem obvious: Agriculture is natural and somewhat miraculous or mysterious (only God can make a tree, and all that), and it is essential for life.

Thus, the desirability of and necessity for efficient agriculture in premercantilistic times led to an application of the features of agricultural production to other industries, namely, a stages theory of production with emphasis upon physical output. In particular, agriculture is the sector par excellence that appears to offer the greatest physical transformation—the seeds become the crop—and thus seems most productive of a physical surplus.[23]

It is easy to see why this view prevailed in Greek, Roman, and Mediaeval times with their heavy dependency upon agriculture. What is surprising is that after the mercantilistic deviation of identifying the economic surplus with bullion, the physical conception of production was revived by Physiocracy and Adam Smith and, as already noted, persists today with admittedly many exceptions, even though we now define *production* simply as value added, which involves many alternatives to physical transformation.

But if the notion persists, there must be some intuitive appeal, some possible validity to it. This appears to be rooted in the view that what is tangible and durable is real and that society could exist without most service industries. Analytically as noted above, it is also easier to construe output when physical units are involved and in some respects easier to measure. The nature of the product of most service industries raises serious conceptual and empirical problems (e.g., banking, transportation). However we rationalize this, there are important consequences that emerge from a vision of production, investment, or degrees of productiveness stressing physical transformation.

Let me briefly list some, but not all, of the notions that emerge from this vision: A moment's reflection should suffice to indicate how they relate to the physical view:

1. The distinction between productive and unproductive labor—also due, as far as Adam Smith is concerned, to confusion between wealth and income.
2. A hierarchy of occupations based on the extent of physical transformation—indeed the whole notion of degrees of productiveness relates to such a view.
3. Failure to count expenditures of government or outlays for education, health, and so on, as productive.
4. Deemphasis of the role of money.
5. The wages-fund doctrine.
6. The view that the demand for commodities is commodities.

In addition, the homogeneity assumption abstracts from problems of efficient utilization of savings. As J. R. Hicks argues, "if there is just one homogeneous 'capital,' there is nothing to do with our savings but to invest them in this 'capital'; there can be no problem of malinvestment—or of saving going to waste."[24] Much of the contemporary view of government outlays, poverty programs, and so on, held by large segments of the population is rooted in the physical conception of productive activity, although bolstered by ideological fears of big government and alternative explanations of poverty. But many economists seem to hold implicitly to the physical conception of capital as a derivative of the physical notion of production, even though most would deny all of the above-mentioned doctrines that at one time or another held sway.

THE NEW OR EMERGING VIEW OF CAPITAL

The rigorously physical conception of capital has become increasingly suspect during the past decade largely in response to empirical studies indicating that the *quantity* of labor and/or capital accounts for a very small fraction of the increase in total output.[25] Attention then is focused on the *quality* of labor and capital, which in turn implies outlays for education, health, on-the-job training, and so on, on the one hand, and technological change related more or less to research and development expenditures, on the other hand. Furthermore, the disappointing results from even real (i.e., physical) capital injections into the underdeveloped economies has led to a search for other "critical" scarcities such as skills, and entrepreneurial attitudes. Thus, most of the previous capital or capital-mainly analyses have become more and more qualified. But in addition, the concept of capital itself is becoming extended. Investment in human capital, the determination of the contribution to GNP of outlays that do not directly leave behind a physical product, and other activities of this nature imply an enlargement of the capital concept to mean any use of resources that has the effect of enhancing future productivity. This is clearly a useful and in some sense realistic extension. But as the concept is more broadly construed, its measurement becomes even thornier than at present and the meaning becomes grotesquely distorted.

Indeed, if capital is defined to refer to any use of resources that enhances output per some unit of input, we are left with precisely the circularity involved in the old labor theory of value. That is, we cannot determine what is really a capital outlay until we observe its effects, just as the notion of socially necessary labor depended upon whether the products of labor actually sold. The old view of capital, as some *stock* item of man-made productive assets, is clearly a useful, measureable, and intuitive way to view the concept. This does not preclude a calculation of net benefits or rates of return for other types of outlays that may in fact enhance efficiency but which do not, immediately at least, fix themselves in a physical asset (education or research and development, for instance). Indeed, it is essential to make such calculations, tentative as they must be, to prevent an undue allocation of resources toward physical assets. It is therefore useful to construe at least part of educational outlays as investment in man; it is not useful for the reasons mentioned above, to define educational outlays as capital, especially if people are thereby encouraged to aggregate such capitals into a single figure.

However, the magnitude of the residual found in growth models which compare the growth in output or output per head to a weighted average of the growth of inputs of labor and capital has evoked several major responses. On the one hand, it is contended that the magnitude of the residual is an index either of our ignorance of the growth process or of technological change.[26] On the other hand, it is contended that the gap estimates, whether viewed as indexes of ignorance or technological change, are vastly overstated and that they unduly downgrade the importance of the quantity of capital. The latter view argues essentially that labor and capital should not be measured in unweighted homogeneous units; that, over time, the quality of labor and capital has risen sharply, which makes the use of man-hours and value of investment inappropriate as indexes of quantity of these two factors in terms of contemporary "efficiency units." In short, the rate of growth of labor and capital inputs has been much faster when quality considerations have been taken account of, which necessarily reduces the magnitude of the residual and with it, either our ignorance or the extent of technological change. For example, measuring labor input in terms of man-hours actually worked ignores the relationship between shorter hours per day or per week and output per man-hour and neglects the increasing education of the labor force and the changing age-sex composition of the labor force. Thus, between 1929 and 1958 actual man-hours in the U.S. rose by about 14 percent. E. F. Denison's adjustments for the three factors just mentioned yield an increase in man-hours of almost 80 percent, and even this increase does not "reflect changes in attitudes, physical stamina, health, or reliability of the labor force, or intensity of work except insofar as these are related to the change in working hours or education, or to age, sex, and experience."[27]

While there are many problems associated with Denison's computations, it is nevertheless clear that quality adjustments will significantly increase the change in measured labor input and thus sharply reduce the residual.

As far as capital is concerned, it is obvious that few economies exactly replicate existing assets when they wear out. Indeed, in an economy experiencing technical advance or improvements in knowledge, much of this must become embodied in new investment. Thus, as in the case of the labor force, additional capital formation may and probably does involve superior quality for a given real outlay. Growth models with embodied technical change (vintage models) have, accordingly, been developed, although the empirical basis of such estimates has been rather shaky. Essentially, such an approach involves constructing an index of the stock of capital related to the average age of the stock. As noted earlier in this paper, such a weighting system inevitably raises the measured growth of the capital stock above that of a capital stock series not so weighted. In one study, the effect of assuming embodied technological change raises the contribution of capital to the observed increase in output per man to between 50 and 100 percent above estimates assuming disembodied technological change.[28]

These varying conceptions of capital, labor, and technological progress raise important questions about the ability to make a valid distinction between the contribution each makes to economic growth. If we measure capital or labor in terms of present-day efficiency units and adjust each upward in some fashion, then the level of technological change is reduced, as indicated above. As Dewey puts it:

A quantum of knowledge usually has little or no economic payoff until it is "incorporated" or "embodied" in a set of specialized men and machines. One might say that income is increased by the growth of knowledge which makes possible the creation of better men and machines. Alternatively, one might say that income is increased by investment in men and machines who are specialized and make use of the growth of knowledge. One statement is as true as the other; taken together they suggest the logical impossibility of isolating the contribution of investment and technical progress to income growth.[29]

However we choose to view this assertion, the choice of measurement units for labor and capital will determine the relative magnitude of this residual, which is often interpreted as a definition of technological change.

The new view of investment, which expands the concept of capital to include a vast variety of items, some of which leave behind a physical product while others do not, virtually compels a disaggregated view of investment since the meaning to be attached to any single such aggregate is, at the very least, obscure. Thus one useful by-product of the new view, especially in the context of economic planning, is to stress the need for more careful appraisals of rates of return or benefits vis-à-vis costs for specific kinds of outlays that normally would not be subject to such economic calculation. No longer can this approach be limited to major items of physical capital. Indeed, in the new view, the basis for the distinction between consumption and investment, which in the national accounts sense implies that for economic growth the latter must rise relative to the former, would be called into question.

There is, in fact, a growing body of literature on this point that is independent of the inclusion of items such as education in the concept of consumption. Even when consumption is used in the narrow sense of food, clothing, and shelter, it may well be that a rise in consumption has a positive impact upon productivity. All one needs to assume is that an increase in per capita consumption does not alter the composition of consumption so that it is biased toward superfluities or, what is the same thing, that the increment for individuals implies more and/or better quality food, clothing, and shelter such that a positive effect upon health, energy, and vitality results. This is probably reasonable for people already existing at relatively low levels of living so long as the increased income which occasions the growth of per capita consumption is not viewed as transitory. If it is so viewed, then the strictures of the mercantilists regarding the "piping, potting and rioting" that would follow from higher wages was probably not entirely self-serving. Similarly, the backward bending supply curve of labor is based to some extent on the belief that the rise in income cannot be expected to persist. Thus, if the income increase is viewed as permanent, in the aggregate it is probably reasonable to assert that growth in per capita consumption, as well as growth in the capital stock via investment, will raise productivity. Thus growth models relating productivity or growth of income per capita exclusively to investment, and hence savings, may be extremely unrealistic, especially in poor countries where diet deficiency diseases, malnutrition, inadequate sanitation, and other such conditions serve to reduce labor efficiency, raise absenteeism, and, in general, reduce the level of output per unit of input. Indeed, the productivity-enhancing impact of an increment in per capita consumption may be as great as an increase in the capital stock.

Some authors have recently sought to incorporate such considerations into their formal analysis and even compute the efficiency-enhancing attributes of a rise in consumption. For example, Harry T. Oshima, after citing many examples of the impact of nutrition on efficiency, calculates an output elasticity of about two with respect to caloric intake for the average adult Asian male.[30] For the poorer countries the coefficient may be even higher.

Harvey Leibenstein has analyzed underemployment in terms of a production function that shifts positively with real wages. The connection is, of course, between additional caloric intake and health and vitality.[31] A. K. Sen has provided a slightly different rationale by arguing that rising real wages may induce more effort because the marginal disutility of work becomes less when people are better fed, at least up to a point.[32]

Regardless of the form of the rationale, it is clear from these analyses that real output is expected to increase with real wages so long as these are spent in a manner that raises nutritional levels. Such considerations are being belatedly incorporated into models of economic development; their prior exclusion is explained by the fact that the models were formulated in advanced economies, where standards of consumption were already so high that the productivity-enhancing impact of additional consumption was negligible or even negative. In addition, we have tended to treat rising per capita consumption as the *goal* of development; "the end of production is consumption," as Adam Smith put it long ago. It is, therefore, not surprising that the goal has been viewed as distinct from the means of achieving it, so that the analysis has neglected the instrumental aspects of consumption. In fact, *abstaining* from consumption has been viewed as the major way to achieve its ultimate increase.

But in poor countries, as already noted, consumption may be far more than a mere using up of resources. Note that this is true even when consumption is confined to food, clothing, and shelter, exclusive of education, health outlays, etc., where the connection with efficiency is more obvious.

What all this implies is that the patterns of resource allocation, especially in underdeveloped countries, may have been distorted by failure to analyze the instrumental value of consumption. That is, food production, for example, can be raised by allocating resources directly to agriculture or by creating capital equipment and *later* applying this to agriculture in anticipation of an even greater long-run gain due to short-run abstinence. However, calculations of the superior efficiency of more roundabout methods of production do not reckon with the efficiency impact of improved nutritional levels.

It may be that, using a given technology, direct application of more resources to food production may yield a larger net gain than applying a superior technology at a later date would. The balance has in the past been tipped in favor of waiting, savings, abstention from consumption, and so on, mainly because there has been a general denial that the elasticity of output with respect to consumption is greater than zero.

Thus the new or broader view of capital, which runs in terms of any use of resources that enhances productivity, would induce or require a more careful calculation of rates of return and stimulate a more rational allocation of public as well as private expenditures than the old view. In the final analysis, Solow may be right in thinking that "the central concept in capital theory *should* be the *rate of return on investment*," although he appears to be using the old physical concept of investment.[33] Furthermore, the new view calls into question the distinction between consumption and investment.

From a historical point of view, if the reaction against the narrow, or old, view of capital is successful and forces more careful calculation of rates of return from various kinds of outlays not previously defined as capital, we may be back to the notion of degrees of productiveness that Malthus long ago toyed with but abandoned.[34]

There are problems aplenty in this to be sure. What will be required is a more careful and rigorous development and application of benefit-cost or rate of return analysis. This in turn will require more and more economists to ensure proper techniques and make reasonable estimates of public and private costs and gains. Thus those who have argued that in an affluent society economists would become superfluous have erred seriously. But finally, as J. Bonner and D. S. Lees argue, it is important to identify and measure "those uses of gross output that maintain the level of economic performance, those that raise the level of economic performance, and those that do neither."[35] The simplistic identification of net investment in physical and homogeneous terms as *the* main or only factor raising the level of economic performance can no longer be accepted.

NOTES

1. W. J. Baumol, "Waiting and the Period of Production," *Quarterly of Economics*, vol. 73 (Aug. 1959), pp. 361–72.

2. However, the changed nature of the ingredients sounded the death knell of the wages-fund doctrine in two major senses. It destroyed the neat single-period production-function notion rooted in the annual agricultural cycle, for the simple reason that buildings and machines not only had construction periods that often exceeded the periodicity of agriculture but had varying degrees of durability and efficiency over time. In short, the neat periodicity implicit in the the earlier versions of the wages fund became extremely fuzzy when capital came to be construed in terms other than agricultural wage goods. But perhaps most important, the changed view of the nature of capital from consumer goods to nonconsumables demolished any notion that capital itself was in any meaningful sense a wages fund.

3. There is, however, some embarrassment in the Keynesian employment (or better, output) theory when one attempts to measure and more fully define *investment*, since the measured concept includes such disparate items as government-fixed capital formation, new residential construction, new nonresidential construction, and new machinery and equipment, as well as several forms of inventory change. Each of these has, of course, many subcomponents. The Keynesian explanation of the equilibrium volume of investment obviously does not apply to each of these except under a most tortured extension of the marginal efficiency of capital, which itself depends upon a host of determining variables seldom explicitly spelled out. In general, *investment*, in the Keynesian model, really refers to producers' durable machinery and equipment—which does not usually constitute even one-half of public and private capital formation. Thus, the contemporary version of the old, physical view fits rather poorly into the kind of static macro-theory usually presented.

For a more complete discussion of the output theory, see my article "The Relationship Between Output and Employment," *Review of Economics and Statistics*, vol. 62 (Feb. 1960), pp. 37–44.

4. Donald Dewey, *Modern Capital Theory* (New York: Columbia University Press, 1965), pp. 2–11, and J. R. Hicks, *Capital and Growth* (Oxford: Oxford University Press, 1965), p. 35.

5. There are differences of opinion here with various economists arguing that machines wear out suddenly. Of course, in the aggregate, it is still possible to talk about sequential depreciation if the age structure of

capital assets is evenly spread out and technological obsolescence occurs in a continuous fashion.

6. Dewey, p. 9.

7. Paul A. Samuelson and R. M. Solow, "A Complete Capital Model Involving Heterogeneous Capital Goods," *Quarterly Journal of Economics*, vol. 70 (Nov. 1956), pp. 537–62.

8. Ibid., pp. 537–38.

9. Paul A. Samuelson and R. M. Solow, "Parable and Realism in Capital Theory: The Surrogate Production Function," *Review of Economic Studies*, vol. 29 (June 1962), p. 201. A somewhat similar conclusion is reached by M. Bruno, "Optimal Accumulation in Discrete Capital Models," in Karl Shell, ed., *Essays on the Theory of Optimal Economic Growth* (Cambridge, Mass.: M.I.T. Press, 1967), p. 211.

10. Paul A. Samuelson, "Indeterminacy of Development in a Heterogeneous-Capital Model with Constant Saving Propensity," in Shell, chap. 12.

11. Smith, *The Wealth of Nations*, Modern Library (New York: Random House, 1957), p. 260.

12. Mill, *Principles of Political Economy*, Ashley (London: Longmans, Green, 1926), chap. 5, sec. 1.

13. See, for example, D. S. Watson, *Price Theory and Its Uses* (Boston: Houghton Mifflin, 1963), pp. 389–90.

14. Walter Isard, *Location and Space Economy* (New York: Wiley, 1956).

15. Dewey, p. 25. For a discussion and defense of this view, see ibid., pp. 23–30.

16. See, for example, Joan Robinson, *The Accumulation of Capital* (London: Macmillan and Co., 1956), pp. 34, 64.

17. For a detailed critique, see G. Myrdal, *Asian Drama* (New York: Twentieth Century Fund, 1968), appen. 3, pp. 1941–2005, and George W. Wilson et al., *Canada: An Appraisal of Its Needs and Resources* (New York: Twentieth Century Fund, 1965), appen. to chap. 7, pp. 324–28.

18. W. W. Rostow, *The Stages of Economic Growth* (New York: Cambridge University Press, 1960), p. 39.

19. The latest phase of this literature is well illustrated in Shell, op. cit.

20. R. G. D. Allen, *Macro-Economic Theory* (New York: St. Martin's Press, 1967), p. 409.

21. Even when the theory of the firm is applied to banking, there is an occasional and doubtless unconscious slipping back to the viewpoint that the product is physical. For example, D. A. Alhadeff in analyzing banks as multiproduct firms asserts that Chamberlin "shifted the emphasis in defining a product away from its purely *technical* or *physical*

characteristics and towards its substitutability in the minds of consumers." "Monopolistic Competition and Banking Markets" in *Monopolistic Competition Theory: Studies in Impact*, R. E. Kuenne, ed., (New York: Wiley & Sons, 1967), p. 361.

22. This underlies much of the distinction in the social accounts between consumption and investment, a point that is discussed later in this paper.

23. No wonder then that agriculture is extolled. Xenophon, for example, complains that the vulgar arts "utterly ruin the bodies of workers and managers alike, compelling men . . . to led sedentary lives and huddle indoors. . . . Then as men's bodies become enervated, so their souls grow sicklier. And these vulgar crafts involve complete absence of leisure and hinder men from social and civic life." But when he refers to agriculture, the tone is vastly different: "When husbandry flourishes all the other arts are in good fettle: but whenever the land is compelled to lie waste, the other arts of landmen and mariners alike well-might perish," Agriculture then, is imbued with virtue; all other menial tasks are not. A similar attitude prevailed in Roman economic thought. In short, physical transformation becomes the criterion of worthy economic activity—i.e., one must physically change the materials before the activity is deemed worthy of recompense. This view was most explicitly stated by writers in the Middle Ages. For example: Chrysostom argued that "whoever buys a thing in order to make a profit in selling it, whole and unchanged, is the trader who is cast out of God's temple." In reply, Aquinas says that the words of Chrysostom "are to be understood as applying to trade insofar as gain is its ultimate end: and this seems to be the case chiefly when a man sells a thing at a higher price *without making any change in it*; for if he charges a higher price for a thing that has been improved, he seems to receive a reward for his efforts."

Again Gratian argues, "Whosoever buys a thing, not that he may sell it *whole and unchanged*, but that it may be a material for fashioning something, he is no merchant. But the man who buys it in order that he may gain by selling it *unchanged* and as he bought it, that man is of the buyers and sellers who are cast forth from God's temple." For references see my *Classics of Economic Theory* (Bloomington: Indiana University Press, 1964), pp. 14, 15.

24. J. R. Hicks, *Capital and Growth* (Oxford: Oxford University Press, 1965), p. 35.

25. See, for example, M. Abramovitz, *Resource and Output Trends in the United States Since 1870* (New York: National Bureau of Economic Research, 1956); Robert Solow, "Technical Change and the Aggregate Production Function," *Review of Economics and Statistics* (Aug. 1957); Solomon Fabricant, *Basic Facts on Productivity Change*, National Bureau of Economic Research, New York: 1959; and John W.

Kendrick, "Productivity Trends: Capital and Labor," *Review of Economics and Statistics* (Aug. 1956). There are many other references. For a review of the issues involved, see Lester Lave, *Technological Change: Its Conception and Measurement* (Englewood Cliffs, N.J.: Prentice-Hall, 1966), esp. chap. 9; Marvin Frankel, "The Production Function in Allocation and Growth: A Synthesis," *American Economic Review*, vol. 52 (Dec. 1962), pp. 995–1022; E. S. Phelps, "The New View of Investment: A Neoclassical Analysis," *Quarterly Journal of Economics* (Nov. 1962).

26. The first view regarding ignorance is stressed by Abramovitz, op. cit., while the latter is stressed by Solow, op. cit., and Massell, "Capital Formation and Technological Change in United States Manufacturing," *Review of Economics and Statistics* (1960), pp. 182–88.

27. E. F. Denison, *The Sources of Economic Growth in the United States and the Alternatives Before Us*, Supplementary Paper No. 13 (New York: Committee for Economic Development, 1962), p. 84.

28. Robert Solow, "Investment and Technical Change," in *Mathematical Models in the Social Sciences*, ed. K. Arrow, S. Karlin, and P. Supper (Stanford: Stanford University Press, 1960).

29. Dewey, pp. 143–44.

30. Oshima, "Food Consumption, Nutrition and Economic Development in Asian Countries," Nov. 1966, Honolulu, Hawaii, pp. 15–16. The evidence cited is taken from FAO *Nutrition and Working Efficiency*, Rome 1962.

31. Harvey Leibenstein, "The Theory of Underemployment in Backward Economies," *The Journal of Political Economy* (April 1957), esp. pp. 94–99. See also Oshima's comment, "Underemployment in Backward Economies: An Empirical Comment," *The Journal of Political Economy* (June 1958).

32. A. K. Sen, "Peasants and Dualism with or without Surplus Labor," *The Journal of Political Economy* (Oct. 1966), esp. pp. 430–31.

33. Robert M. Solow, *Capital Theory and the Rate of Return* (Amsterdam: North Holland Publishing Co., 1963), p. 16.

34. "All paid labour might be called productive of value; but productive in different degrees, according as the value of their results might exceed the value paid. . . . Upon this principle the labours on manufacturers [are] the next [most productive], and mere personal services [are] the least [productive]. . . . This mode of considering the subject would establish a *scale* of productiveness, instead of dividing labour into two kinds . . . the unproductive labourers of Adam Smith would, upon this system, be placed in the lowest scale of productiveness.

"The great objection to this system is, that it makes the *payment* for labour, instead of the quantities of the product, the criterion of productiveness. . . . Yet if we once desert matter, we must adopt this criterion, or every human exertion to avoid pain and obtain pleasure is productive labour. . . . And if we *do* adopt this criterion, the very same kind of labour will be productive, or not, according as it is paid for, or not.

"Susceptibility of accumulation is essential to our usual conceptions of wealth." *Principles of Political Economy,* 1819, chap. 1, sec. 2.

35. Bonner and Lees, "Consumption and Investment," *The Journal of Political Economy,* Feb. 1963), p. 75.

Part 4

KARL MARX REVISITED AND THE WORKINGS
OF CENTRALLY ADMINISTERED
ECONOMIES

8

On Rereading Marx's "Capital"

SCOTT GORDON

1867–1967

"A spectre is haunting Europe—the spectre of Communism." Thus wrote Karl Marx and Friedrich Engels in the opening sentence of the *Communist Manifesto*, which they composed as a statement for the League of the Just in 1847. As an appraisal of the state of European politics at the time, it turned out to be in error. The revolutionary actions of the following year, which Marx and Engels viewed as being the opening of the great upheaval that would consume capitalism, fizzled out. Marx fled once more across the Channel, to spend his life in placid and satisfied mid-Victorian England, working in the British Museum by day, scribbling endlessly away at night, manufacturing the spectral Lorelei that was in fact to do what the Manifesto had prophesied.

If the same opening sentence were written today it would be an understatement, for Communism is the established ideology of half the world and haunts the other half. "Marxian Socialism," wrote J. M. Keynes in the 1920's, "must always remain a portent to the

Scott Gordon is Professor of Economics at Indiana University.

historians of Opinion—how a doctrine so illogical and so dull can have exercised so powerful and enduring an influence over the minds of men, and, through them, the events of history."[1] It is even more of a "portent" to the historian of opinion today than when Keynes wrote, and it would still be so whether or not one regards it as illogical or dull. Even if it were both completely rational and vividly exciting, it would still be a remarkable phenomenon, for Communism has, already, penetrated farther than any other ideology in human history. It is still an open question whether it will match the great religious ideologies in depth and endurance, but it has already bested all of them in extent.

The economist has little to contribute to the explanation of the growth of Communist ideology into a Great Fact of the modern world, but Communists are "people of The Book," and The Book is a book on economics, so economists necessarily have something to say about the *content* of Communist ideology even if they are unable to account for the role it has played in history.

Capital is not the only book Marx wrote, and in some interpretations it is not as important as some of his others. It is highly likely that many times more Marxists have imbibed their doctrine from the less than forty pages of the *Communist Manifesto* than from the more than two thousand pages of *Capital*. Nor is Marx himself the sole fountainhead of Communist thought: There are many Marxists whose source of inspiration seems to have been Lenin (especially on the currently important subject of imperialism) rather than Marx. But *Capital* was regarded by its author and by its editor, and has been since regarded by orthodox Marxists, as the essential and definitive source of the doctrine; so it necessarily occupies a special place in Communist theory.

Capital is not an easy book, and Karl Marx was not an easy writer. To begin with, he did not complete the book himself. Only Volume I was prepared by him for the publisher; it was published in German in 1867. When Marx died in 1883, sixteen years later, he left behind masses of manuscript which Engels undertook to put into publishable form in two more volumes. Volume II appeared fairly quickly after Marx's death, in 1885, but Volume III was not ready until 1896. One need only read Engels' prefaces to Volumes II and III to understand what a herculean task it was. Much of Marx's manuscript was more in the nature of notes and jottings than a considered text. He was the kind of person who thought with pen and paper, and a great deal of what he wrote down represented the process of working out a problem rather than the end results of a finished analysis. This is reflected in the published volumes of *Capital* itself, even in the volume which Marx himself completed. There are large sections, for example, devoted entirely to considering the meaning of a simple mathematical statement. Marx will say that $A \times B = C$ and go on for several pages considering the inner meaning of that statement. Then he will draw attention to the fact that this equation implies that $C = A \times B$ and go on for a good many pages more on the significance of that. Then he will note that the original statement also implies that $B = C/A$ and go on at length again on the inner meaning of that, and so on. By the time he has rung all the algebraic changes that are possible on a simple mathematical statement, which is often purely definitional to begin with, dozens of pages of text have been covered and the reader is faint with ennui and pleading for him to get on with it. But, as often as not, he does not yet go on, but says: "Let us now consider some numerical examples," and one has to go through the whole thing again with numbers instead of symbols.

Nevertheless, it is through these many pages in which the same thing is turned inside out and upside down that Marx's picture of capitalism and its economic processes gradually emerges. The opening chapter of Volume II of *Capital*, for example, seems on superficial reading to employ sixty pages to say nothing more than that the objective of the capitalist is to come out of the productive process in which he engages his capital with more money than he puts in, i.e., to realize a profit. Yet in the course of saying so, Marx presents as a model of the economy a set of exchanges constituting a circular flow process, which is a vital part of his general picture of capitalism (and, indeed, is a fruitful device of economic analysis for non-Marxists as well as Marxists). It is for this reason that the efforts of Western economic theorists to describe the pure model of Marxian economics are so unsatisfactory. They are like a *Reader's Digest*-type summary of *The Brothers Karamazov*; the main lines of the story may be told, but the images that make great literature are absent.

This essay is not a general study of Marxian thought—that has become a virtual impossibility because of the vast Marxian and critical literature that now exists in all the literate languages of the world, and that is daily being added to. It is a much more limited appraisal, arising from a rereading of the central book of Marxism, *Capital*, which was stimulated by the occasion of the centenary of the publication of Volume I and the decision of the American Economic Association to notice that occasion at its annual meeting in San Francisco in December 1966.[2] What I intend to do in the following pages is to make a personal tour of this Byzantine cathedral of a book and to visit especially the established stations of the cross that have become the focal points of Marxist orthodoxy.

VALUE AND EXPLOITATION

Our first station must necessarily be the labor theory of value. This is the part of his theory that Marx himself regarded as most fundamental. In Marx's view, it was error on this question that prevented Adam Smith and David Ricardo and others from carrying their great achievements in the science of political economy (which he acknowledged without stint) to the point which would reveal the inner nature of capitalism as an economic system. The labor theory of value pervades *Capital* in its entirety. There is no section of the book that does not appear, from the way the argument is advanced, to depend directly or indirectly upon it. It has become, since Marx's time, the most important theoretical element in the popular ideology of Marxism. Rank-and-file Marxists who know no more about Marxian thought than an Irish bartender knows of Aquinas can recite the essentials of the labor theory of value with as little reflection as is required for a Hail Mary. It was on the value theory that the first full-scale attack on the Marxian system was made from the ramparts of orthodox economics. But there has been considerable skirmishing around this point among self-acknowledged Marxists as well, and some of the disagreement within the ranks would appear to be quite as fundamental as the attacks of hostile critics.

The outcome of the extended discussion by Marxian and non-Marxian economists seems to be that, as a theory of the relative prices of commodities under capitalism, the labor theory of value is inadequate, but that the Marxian system does not operate with, nor does it require, a theory of relative prices; hence this inadequacy is not important. However, this does not mean that the labor theory of value is unimportant altogether. It is, indeed, as fundamental as Marx thought it to be in revealing what he regarded as the inner workings of capitalism. Its real role in Marxian thought, however, does not lie plainly on the surface of the pages of *Capital* and is apparent at all only if one attempts to grasp the subliminal understructure of Marx's thought, which Marx may, indeed, have been as little conscious of as is an altogether literal reader of *Capital*.

It is difficult for a person who is trained in the Western tradition of economic analysis to grasp the real meaning and impact of Marx's labor theory of value. One's immediate proclivity, in attempting to come to intellectual grips with it, is to translate Marx into the concepts of Western analytical economics so that the powerful apparatus of modern economic theory can be brought to bear upon it. Marx was sufficiently concerned in the text of *Capital* with problems of value theory which correspond to those of Western neoclassical economics to make such a translation appear to be a fruitful approach to the understanding of Marxian economics, as well as posing a challenge to the intellectual ingenuity of the theorist.[3] In making such a translation it is necessary to discard some of Marx's comments as being merely obiter dicta or reflecting his partisan political viewpoint, or his normative predilections, or his unfortunate tendency to employ Hegelian-like verbiage or to be concerned with "metaphysical garbage," in order to restrict the model to those elements with which modern Western economics is able to deal. But, if one reads *Capital* as it is, without any methodological preconceptions as to how wheat is properly separated from chaff in a book dealing (apparently) with economic processes, one should begin to wonder whether the matter which these translations typically discard does not contain elements that are fundamental to Marx's thought. At any rate, that is the distinct impression which a centennial reexamination of *Capital* has had on this writer. But it is not easy to describe these neglected aspects of Marxian value theory in a way that makes them stand out as something more than footnotes to a typical Western-style model of the Marxian system.

In an effort to come closer to what I believe to be the real spirit of Marx, I will proceed by translating between Marx and modern Western economics, but in the opposite direction from what is usual. If we begin with a statement of the Western sort and then modify it to take account of special Marxian constraints and propositions, it is possible to build up a picture of those elements of Marxian thought that seem, to this reader at least, to be fundamental.

We begin with a production function, a general statement which says that the output of final goods and services (by a firm, an industry, or the economy as a whole) is a function of the various inputs of factors of production which are used in the production process,

$$O = O(A, B, \ldots, N), \tag{1}$$

where O is the output, and A, B, ..., N are the various input factors. This is a physical production function, and Marx would not have disputed its general validity. But a production function of this sort does not appear as a central feature of *Capital* because the relationship that Marx wished to examine is the relationship between physical inputs and the *value*, not the physical quantity, of output. The modification that this requires is that the input factors on the right-hand side of the equation must be restricted, for not all input factors were regarded by Marx as contributing to the *value* of output, however important they may be to its production in a physical sense. First, according to Marx's view, it is necessary to eliminate all natural resources from the right-hand side; these resources help to create useful things, but they do not create value. If a factor of production "is not the product of human labour," says Marx, "it transfers no value to the product. It helps to create use-value without contributing to the formation of exchange-value. In this class are included all means of production supplied by Nature without human assistance, such as land, wind, water, metals in situ, and timber in virgin forests."[4]

Capital instruments, which appear as independent factors of production in the production function of modern Western economics, have no place on the right-hand side of the equation in the Marxian version. On the crucial problem of the time-dimension of the capital-using production process, Marx rejects the notion that any difference of value is to be attributed to one time-shape of production compared with another.[5] All real capital used in the production process is simply reducible to the antecedent labor that went into its own creation: It cannot *create* new value; it merely *transmits* the value already embodied in it to the commodities it helps produce and only in such a form can it appear in the production function. Engels summarized this succinctly in his preface to Volume III: "The law of value is aimed from the first against the idea derived from the capitalist mode of thought that accumulated labour of the past, which comprises capital, is not merely a certain sum of finished value, but that, because [it is] a factor in production and the formation of profit, it also produces value and is hence a source of more value than it has itself; it establishes that living labour alone possesses this faculty."[6] Our function then has become:

$$O = O(L), \qquad (2)$$

where O is the value of output and L is the input of labor.

This statement embodies, in essence, the doctrine which is the cornerstone of Marxian political economy, in the broad sense of that term. As presented above, the doctrine is simply an assertion, not a theoretical argument or an empirical generalization. Marx does not arrive at it by way of a *Gedankenexperiment,* or by any other process of reasoning that could be called a theoretical analysis; nor does he put it forward as an extraction from statistical or other empirical information. (I shall consider later whether it is simply a way of measuring value rather than a theory of value creation, a line of interpretation which is generally used by economists who have interpreted Marxian economics in terms of Western-style economic theory. But, in the present connection, one must interpret it as a functional statement: The value of output has the nature of a dependent variable, with physical labor input being the only independent variable in the function.)

Some insight into the significance of equation (2) is obtained by considering why Marx used the terms *variable capital* and *constant capital* to refer, respectively, to the labor power and to the materials, machinery, etc., that the capitalist purchases and brings together in the process of production. The words *variable* and *constant* have no relation whatever to the concepts of variable and fixed cost in the neoclassical theory of production, and an attempt to interpret them in such terms will only lead one astray. *Variable* and *constant* refer to different *inherent properties* of the two types of things that the capitalist purchases. Raw materials, machinery, buildings, etc., are constant capital because they are devoid of creative power, because they are inert physical substances; they can never be put on the right-hand side of a functional equation because they are purely passive agents in the production process. Labor, on the other hand, is the creative force of the productive process. It is variable in the sense that it produces more value than is consumed in its own creation and maintenance. It is the source of positive net output.

Marx conceived the problem of value production in the same analytical framework as that of the French Physiocrats (whom he spoke of with a degree of respect not exceeded for any other group of economists referred to in *Capital*), and his solution to the problem posed was similar to but importantly different from theirs. Both used the analytical device of conceiving the economy as a closed circular flow process. A central problem for such a system is to provide for a net output (and thereby for growth in the system), since in a closed model the inputs and the outputs would appear to be perfectly balanced against one another. The solution is to endow one of the inputs with power to create more value than it uses up. In the Physiocratic scheme, such a *produit net* was conceived to enter the circular flow in the agricultural sector of the economy, where, uniquely, "nature labors along with man." In Marx's scheme, it is in the whole sphere of production, not only in agriculture, that "surplus value" is generated because this is due to the special properties of "living labour." Labor, in the Marxian system, has the mystical endowment of creativity, which is not shared by other elements in the productive process: "By the purchase of labour-power, the capitalist incorporates labour, as a living ferment, with the lifeless constituents of the product."[7] Raw materials are useless unless acted upon by labor: "Living labour must seize upon these things and rouse them from their death sleep. . . . Bathed in the fire of labour, appropriated as part and parcel of labour's organism . . . they are . . . consumed with a purpose. . . ."[8] Thus, the assertion that labor is the sole source of value is based on a conception of labor's unique, inherent qualities.

In Marx's treatment, not all of the economy's outputs and not all of its labor inputs were to be included in the value statement, so equation (2) was restricted on both sides.

First, Marx restricted his value analysis (by and large) to the commodity production sector of the economy. This is related to the significance he saw in the practice of commodity production for sale as essential to the understanding of capitalism as an historical economic stage. It means that neither side of the above equation includes the production of services for direct consumption.

Second, there are certain types of labor which Marx regarded as being useful to the capitalist in that they help him sell his products and realize his surplus value, but Marx believed they are not useful to society at large and do not create new values. This category includes all labor devoted to the selling of commodities—not only such activities as advertising and other efforts to gain purely commercial advantage but also the labor of packing, sorting, storing, and distributing commodities.[9]

Third, labor that is expended in a wasteful or inefficient fashion does not create value, in Marx's view. The only labor that counts on the right-hand side of the equation is that which is necessary to the production of the commodity in question, given the social and technical conditions of production obtaining in the economy at the time the commodity comes to market. Wasted labor, that which creates no value, is considered to include labor expended in creation of excessive quantities of a commodity, in the sense that the total output of it cannot be marketed without lowering the price.[10] (This, of course, inserts the demand side of the market into the theory of value, but Marx does not follow his logic in this direction.[11]) The equation can now be written, with these further modifications, as:

$$O_c = O_c(L_n), \tag{3}$$

where O_c refers to the total value of commodity production, and L_n to the "socially necessary" labor required for this production.

The next set of modifications is due to the fact that L_n is not a homogeneous substance; laborers differ from one another, both qualitatively and quantitatively, in their skill and training. Marx's conceptual method for handling this problem is to consider all specific labor inputs as multiples of an "abstract, undifferentiated human labor." He does not say how the conversion factors are arrived at and is content to refer, rather mysteriously, to a "social process that goes on behind the backs of producers." Some of his argument (the part suggesting that the conversion factors reflect the different market values of the commodities produced by different kinds of labor) constitutes circular reasoning. Just as serious perhaps is his failure to recognize that the training of labor takes time and that capital as an independent production factor and interest as a cost have therefore crept into the input side of the production function even though it appears to be composed exclusively of labor.[12] The equation now can be read as:

$$O_c = O_c(L_{n,a}),   (4)$$

$L_{n,a}$ being not real labor actually expended but socially necessary labor measured in abstract homogeneous units—like horsepower, or BTU's, but, unlike them, having no operational procedure specified by which the conversion of the concrete to the abstract may be obtained in specific cases.

We must now move back to the left-hand side of the equation and consider the terms in which the physically heterogeneous output of commodities is measured and aggregated. This leads us to the celebrated Transformation Problem, which was for many years the chief focal point of attack by non-Marxians on Marx's system, before it became apparent that Marxism was a much grander theory than a mere model of the economy.

The Transformation Problem arises out of an inherent incompatibility between Marx's value theory and his conception of capitalism as a competitive economy.[13] For any particular commodity or class of commodities, the total value produced is divided into three parts: $C = v + s + c$. C is the total gross value of output of this industry or segment of the economy; v and s, variable capital and surplus value, are, taken together, the net output or value added by this segment, as divided into the portion of that net output received by laborers, v, and by capitalists, s. The value of goods used in this industry, which are the outputs of other industries, is constant capital, represented by c. This consists largely of raw materials used up and the depreciation of capital equipment. (To avoid problems stemming from different turnover rates and durabilities of constant capitals, Marx usually assumes that all periods of production, and the life of all capital equipment, are one year in length.)

Marx's conception of labor is that it is the sole source of value and therefore the sole source of the surplus value, which is the capitalists' profit. In a given society, competition will make wage rates tend to equality in different industries, and therefore, the amount of surplus value that capitalists can extract from each man-day of labor will be uniform throughout the economy, i.e., s/v is uniform. The rate of profit for the capitalist is the ratio of surplus value to his total investment, $c + v$, and competition will tend to make this equal in all industries, i.e., $s/(c + v)$ is uniform. But these two cross-sectional uniformities imply algebraically that the ratio of constant to variable capital, the "organic composition of capital," is also uniform throughout the economy. This is clearly not the case in fact, and Marx explicitly acknowledged the existence of differential cross-sectional, capital-labor compositions in the economy.

This analytical problem was recognized by Marx, but he did not provide any solution for it in Volume I of *Capital*, and it quickly became the focal point for much criticism and debate. When Engels issued Volume II, he called attention to the problem and challenged critics of Marx, especially the followers of Rodbertus, to provide the solution, which he promised would appear in Volume III.[14] The solution which Marx there puts forward involves abandoning the proposition (hitherto implicit) that each capitalist employer obtains the surplus value yielded by the labor he in fact employs. Instead, an overall average rate of profit is struck for the economy as a whole by expressing total surplus value (which is determined by total variable capital) as a ratio of total capital (both variable and constant). This profit rate is then applied to each industry or firm.[15] Symbolically:

$p' = \Sigma s / (\Sigma v + \Sigma c)$, p' being the average rate of profit for the economy as a whole. Thus the "price" of a commodity is equal to $c + v + p'(c + v)$, whereas, it will be recalled, the "value" of a commodity was equal to $c + v + s$. As readers of Ricardo will not be surprised to learn, the only commodities whose prices equal their labor-determined values are those produced with labor-capital compositions equal to the average. Commodities produced with c/v greater than the average sell at prices which are higher than their values, and vice versa. Marx seemed to be impressed by the fact that the positive and negative deviations of prices from values cancel out, but this, of course, is nothing more than an algebraic property of any arithmetic mean.

The solution put forward by Marx in Volume III of *Capital* was not an adequate one. It had the effect of altering the output composition of the economy's production, so that if the demands and supplies of consumers' goods and means of production were in equilibrium when measured in values, they were no longer so when measured in prices. This difficulty, as subsequent investigators discovered, could be resolved by applying the same process of measuring in price terms instead of in value terms to the labor and constant capital input components of the Marxian value equation as well as to the final output component.[16] Thus, values were transformed into prices throughout the whole system.

In constructing an aggregate, we can use as a counting unit anything in which the elements may be individually measured, and there is nothing in nature that decrees that only one such counting unit should exist. We may, for example, aggregate a number of books by weight, using any of a number of systems of weight measurement, or by volume similarly, or we can price them in any of many currencies. We can easily transform one weight measurement into another as long as we know the proper conversion factor, and the same with volume or money aggregations, and we can even transform between weight, volume, and money with the same type of information.

If socially-necessary, abstract, labor is merely a counting-unit for values, we have to make an important alteration in our last version of the Marxian value statement. We cannot say:

$$O_c = O_c(L_{n,a}),\qquad\qquad (4)$$

for the quantity of value output is no longer construed as *functionally* determined by the quantity of labor input; it is simply counted in labor units. Output is measured by input, and it would be as erroneous to write the statement in the form of equation (4) as it would be to say that the weight of an article in grams is a function of the number of gram weights we have to put on the other side of the scales to restore balance. The Marxian value statement would have to be written not as a function, not even as an equation, but as an identity:

$$O_c \equiv L_{n,a},\qquad\qquad (5)$$

which is to say that value has no existence independent of labor input so far as its being measured is concerned. To measure and to aggregate values, one must measure the labor which is the source of value,[17] just as to measure weight we must measure gravitational attraction, for that is what weight "is."

The response of the Western economist to this result is that (5) is not an operational statement. There is no procedure, nor is it conceivable that one can be constructed, by which units of $L_{n,a}$ can be counted, and therefore O_c is not measurable. The alternative, as adopted by Western economics, is to define *value* as market price, which is clearly an operational concept. Moreover, the outcome of the Marxian solution of the Transformation Problem is that while individual prices do not correspond to labor values, the aggregate of all values equals the aggregate of all prices. So if, in Marxian economics, we are not concerned about relative prices, if we are solely in the realm of macroeconomics, why bother with labor values at all? Why not simply measure and analyze in terms of prices? This may seem eminently logical to the Western economist (despite the troublesome index number problem), but the dedicated Marxist's reaction to it, with his soul here in peril, must be *non possumus.* Why is this so?

The Marxian labor theory of value is not primarily advanced as a counting or aggregating unit. Its essential quality lies in its normative content, as a vital part of the Marxian theory of exploitation.[18] Prices cannot be substituted for Marxian values because macroeconomic price calculation is incapable of serving as a vehicle for an argument of this type. The very merit that Western economists claim for it, its positive nature, is its most conspicuous demerit for Marxian theory. To appreciate the significance of Marx's value theory, one must not consider it apart from his theory of exploitation.

The Marxian theory of exploitation can be analyzed as consisting of three statements: first, a statement concerning the creation of value (a value equation); second, a statement concerning the basis of moral right to share in the value created (a distributive rights equation); and third, a statement of the actual distribution of income in society (a distribution equation). The exploitation theory may then be represented thus:

$$O = O(L) \quad \text{(value equation)} \tag{4}$$

$$R = R(L) \quad \text{(distributive rights equation)} \tag{6}$$

$$O = l + p \quad \text{(distribution equation)} \tag{7}$$

The value equation is Marx's labor value function. (The subscripts have been dropped merely to simplify.) It is retained in functional form despite what has been said above about its fundamentally definitional quality, because Marx's exploitation theory uses the labor value statement as if it were a true functional statement, and I am here simply expounding that theory. Labor creates not only value but also the only justifiable right to receive income. This is embodied in equation (6). Equation (7) simply states that in capitalist society, the net national income is shared between those who provide socially necessary labor and those who do not, the latter group obtaining income because of their ownership of means of production or their provision of services to such owners. These two income components are labelled l and p respectively to represent labor incomes and property incomes. Adam Smith's great blunder, in Marx's view, resulted from confusing the value equation with the distribution equation. After having correctly described total value to be the source of all distributive shares (equation 7), Smith turned these "component parts" of income distribution into original sources of value creation, "thereby throwing the doors wide open to vulgar economy,"[19] i.e., the writing of a value creation equation such as (1) above.

For all the great amount of space Marx devotes to it, the theory of exploitation is very straightforward. Only labor creates value and deserves income, but property-owning capitalists get income too, and this can only be regarded as *theft* by the capitalist of what rightfully belongs to labor. It is "the yearly accruing surplus-product, embezzled, because abstracted without return of an equivalent from the . . . labourer."[20] And capitalism as an economic system is merely a disguised form of exploitative society: "The essential difference between the various economic forms of society, between, for instance, a society based on slave-labour, and one based on wage-labour, lies only in the mode in which this surplus-labour is in each case extracted from the actual producer, the labourer."[21]

But it is not yet clear why equation (4), which represents the labor theory of value, is necessary to the exploitation argument. Why cannot equations (6) and (7) above constitute such an argument, since the first of these asserts what distribution *ought* to be and the second, what it in fact *is*? From (6) and (7) above, it would appear that any positive magnitude of p represents exploitation—a gap between the *ought* and the *is* of the economic system. This was the simple line of reasoning of many post-Ricardian socialists, who laid down as an ethical assertion "the right of labour to the whole produce of labour," but there is a technical problem that is not met by a simple proposition of this nature. It is as follows: If rights to income are the result of labor performed, how can we be certain that the sum of rights so acquired is exactly equal to the sum (value) of goods produced? If this requirement is not met, there will be some output with no just claimants, or just claims with no output left to satisfy them. This is where the labor theory of value enters Marxian exploitation theory. If the coefficients of equations (4) and (6) above are the same, i.e.,

$$O = \alpha(L), \tag{4a}$$

$$R = \alpha(L), \tag{6a}$$

then it will necessarily follow that for any given quantity of labor performed in the society $\Sigma O = \Sigma R$, and the total product is exhausted by the just claims made upon it. This is, implicitly, Marx's exploitation theory. In his value theory itself he made $\alpha = 1$, which is what gives (4a) more the character of an identity than a true equation, and this makes his basic ethical statement (6a) more like an identity than a true equation as well. It is impossible for me to conceive of an ethical argument by which the coefficient α could be made different from unity (though pragmatic ones would be easy to construct and could be made the basis of taxation in a socialist state, for example), but it is clear that a value theory of Marx's general type was an essential part of the exploitation theory he wished to advance.

Marx's exploitation theory, put this way, appears to be plain enough, but there has been a great deal of discussion of it and some further examination is necessary here. First, one should note that it is *not* a theory which condemns *inequality* as such. *All* capitalist property incomes are unjustified, regardless of their individual or aggregate size. Property income may in fact be largely responsible for the great inequalities in the distribution of total income, but that is not what tells against them. They are condemned *sui generis*, because they do not result from the labor of the recipient but from someone else's labor. It may be, as some interpreters of Marx's theory of the breakdown of capitalism have argued, that it is inequality of incomes that leads to the contradictions of capitalism and the crises which herald the onset of proletarian revolution, but that also is beside the point so far as the exploitation theory is concerned. The appropriation of surplus value by capitalist owners of the means of production would be condemned (perhaps more strongly) even if capitalism were regarded as a potentially permanent economic system. It may be, too, that under capitalism, inequality tends to grow, because capitalists can devote part of their surplus value incomes to further accumulation of property, but such growing inequality is not what makes capitalism exploitive. It is no less exploitive in the scheme of simple reproduction under which Marx analyzes an economy of zero net accumulation. In no way does the doctrine of exploitation depend upon the inequality of the total income distribution.

Secondly, the labor theory of value and the labor theory of distributive right are not made to rest, by Marx, on a disutility concept of labor. The Marxian theory of the ethics of distribution is not a theory which says that labor connotes pain and sacrifice and that it is pain and sacrifice which confer (proportional) desert. Early in Volume I of *Capital* Marx castigates Adam Smith for erroneously equating quantities of labor on this basis. Smith "has a presentiment," says Marx, "that labour, so far as it manifests itself in the value of commodities, counts only as expenditure of labour-power [the correct view in Marx's opinion], but he treats this expenditure as the mere sacrifice of rest, freedom, and happiness not as at the same time the normal activity of living beings." To this note Engels as editor added the remark that "The English language has the advantage of possessing different words for the two aspects of labour here considered. The labour which creates Use-Value, and counts qualitatively, is Work, as distinguished from Labour; that which creates Value, and counts quantitatively, is *Labour* as distinguished from Work."[22] Marx's celebrated ironies on Nassau Senior's abstinence theory of interest do not mean that he intended only to dispute whether the capitalist who invests incurs a sacrifice by having to wait for his enjoyments. The whole point is irrelevant. Whether he sacrifices or not, the capitalist does not labor, and hence he neither creates value nor earns a place among those deserving of income. Marx's picture of the capitalist is not one of slothful, carefree self-indulgence. The classic Marxian capitalist is busy—buying and selling, calculating, organizing, contriving, contending against other capitalists, full of cares and worries and driven by a compulsion to accumulate wealth rather than enjoy it. But for all his energetic activity the capitalist does not labor, as Marx defines that term. He drives the capitalist engine onward, and he has an essential role in the functioning of the capitalist system, which, according to Marx, generates the greatest increase in productivity known to history, but his activity does not constitute labor, in the Marxian sense of the term.

The position we arrive at in considering Marx's theory of exploitation is the same as the position one arrives at in considering his theory of value. There is no point in asking what are the grounds for the labor theory of value or the labor theory of distributive right. Such a question assumes that labor may be reducible to something even more fundamental. But in Marxian theory it is not. Labor (as Marx defines it) is itself the essence—the elemental, irreducible absolute of the system of both economics and ethics; the *is* and the *ought* are fused, through "abstract socially-necessary labour," into one. The commodity that emerges from the process of production is inert matter into which has been breathed the fire of life. Thenceforth it has *value*. But in the capitalist mode of economic organization, it does not belong to those who have furnished the breath of its being, and it therefore becomes the symbol of the Manichaean conflict that must go on in capitalist society, the class struggle.

THE CONCEPT OF CAPITALISM AND THE ANTINOMY OF CLASSES

"The history of all past society," wrote Marx and Engels in the *Communist Manifesto*, "has consisted in the development of class antagonisms, antagonisms that assume different forms at different epochs. But whatever form they may have taken, one fact is common to all past ages, viz., the exploitation of one part of society by the other."[23]

"Marx," said Maurice Dobb, one of the leading Western Marxist economists, "focused attention on the class relation, expressed in class incomes, as the relation which defined the major rhythm of capitalist society and was crucial for any forecast of the future."[24]

In *Capital*, very little is said, explicitly, about social classes. But very little has to be said specifically, because the whole book is about class relationships under capitalism. This is one of the major reasons why the Western economist finds it difficult to come to grips with Marxism. Large sections of *Capital* appear to be irrelevant to any analysis of economic processes, but they take on a central importance when one remembers that the focus of the analysis is not on the processes in themselves but on their class content and implications.

This aspect of Marxian theory, like so many others, has respectable parentage in the writings of the great classical economists. Adam Smith and David Ricardo spoke about the categories of factors of production and of income distribution as corresponding to the great established social classes in their society, and they had judgments to offer, flowing from their analyses, on the question of conflict of interest among these classes and their future relations. But such concerns did not really occupy a fundamental place in the analytical system which evolved as classical economics. The social class content of the classical trinity of landlords, capitalists, and laborers became steadily more and more attenuated in the work of post-classical economists, and by the end of the century they were classes only in the taxonomic sense, i.e., analytical or accounting categories, representing economic functions rather than identifiable groups of flesh-and-blood people.

In the introduction of his *Theory of Capitalist Development*, Paul Sweezy is very critical of modern Western economics for having no social content, for not dealing with the question of the relation between classes. The point is important to any proper understanding of Marxism and its relation to Western economics, and especially so because of the efforts that have been made by Western economists to "translate" the Marxian system into Western analytical categories. Marxian economics is not to be understood without holding in the forefront of one's consciousness that the whole apparatus of Marxian concepts—capital and its various categories, commodity, value, surplus value, etc.—are deliberately invested with social class content and are designed to serve the needs of a normative sociological analysis, just as modern Western economics cannot be understood without apprehending that the categories with which it operates are designed to be devoid of such content, so that a *Wertfrei* analysis of economic processes may be carried out, the economic phenomena being treated by the economist with the same detachment as physical phenomena are by the physical scientist.

We enter this world of special Marxian concepts in the very beginning of Volume I of *Capital*, and what one finds there should be held in mind as one reads the rest of this mammoth work. The act of exchange is the main social fact of capitalism, the main relation between persons. The fact that it takes place at arm's length in a market and that the object of exchange is a physical commodity separated from the men who made it with their labor merely obscures the social relations between those engaged in the production process; a commodity-exchanging capitalism is not so obviously a system of exploitation as is a society of slavery or feudalism. But below the surface appearances of things, Marx says, the same sort of relationship exists—a dichotomy of classes, of exploited and exploiters; laborers who must sell their labor to live and capitalists who own the means of production. The position of the capitalist is the same as that of the feudal lord or member of the slave-owning aristocracy. His role in society is crystallized in the concept which Marx regarded as so central that he used it as the title of the book—*Capital*.

Now "capital" is a complex and sometimes bewildering concept in *Capital*, and especially so if one attempts to translate Marx's use of it into the categories of Western economics. Marx speaks of constant capital and variable capital, fixed capital and circulating capital, money capital and commodity capital, and more besides. Almost everything becomes capital in some sense; even labor becomes capital, and one wonders at times whether Marx does not use the term as a substitute for *thing*. But there is, in fact, a unifying concept, if one allows oneself to stop translating for a bit in order to enter into the spirit of the book. All categories of capital are values in the possession of the capitalist class. The labor power that the capitalist purchases and has the use of for the contracted time, the raw materials, money, buildings, machinery—all are capital because they are the *property* of and are at the command of the capitalist class. Marx's long discussions of the circular flows of economic activity and the systems of simple reproduction and expanded reproduction are designed to elaborate the theme that the capitalist class owns all and controls all. Whenever things move in the economic process, whatever stages they may go through, they never leave the possession of the capitalist class until sold to the final consumer. Whatever may be the external appearances of a commodity-producing, division-of-labor economy, it is not, to Marx, the atomistic, individualistic world of open and arm's-length exchange pictured by the Western economist. Beneath the appearances there still remains the antinomy of ruler and ruled.

This helps to explain what otherwise seems to be an inconsistency, or at least a mystery, in Marx's concept of capitalism, while, on the other hand, it exposes (in this writer's view) one of the most serious weaknesses in the Marxian analysis. The apparent inconsistency is that Marx's conception of the capitalist economy whose functions he is analyzing in *Capital* is the competitive economy of classical and neoclassical economics, and yet the capitalist class is represented as being a unified entity so far as its position vis-à-vis the workers is concerned. It is important to be clear on this point. Marx's analysis of capitalism is not an analysis of a monopolized economy. His picture of the capitalistic economy is one which does not possess central organizing institutions, either of goverment or of business itself.

His conception is, in this respect, the same as that of the Western perfect competition theorist. His theory of value, when treated as a theory of price, is solely a supply-side theory; and if one were to allow monopolistic elements in the analysis, the value theory would have even more difficulties than we have noted above. What monopoly elements enter Marx's discussion of capitalism are treated as extrinsic phenomena, and even his occasional suggestion that monopoly will grow under capitalism is not woven intimately into his picture of the evolution of capitalism. His analysis, then, is of a world of competing capitalists who, nevertheless, *as a class*, stand in unified antinomy to the workers *as a class*.

This opposition of classes is not simply a matter of institutional arrangement; it is the product of the functioning of the competitive economy itself. What differentiates capitalism from preceding social systems is that the relation of classes as exploiters and exploited is *not* a matter of law or custom or any other plain and simple structure of power and subordination, for, as Marx called it, the *differentia specifica* of capitalism is that laborers are free of all such formal constraints and sell their labor in free markets. "The Roman slave," says Marx, "was held by fetters: the wage-labourer is bound to his owner by invisible threads. The appearance of independence is kept up by means of a constant change of employers, and by the *fictio juris* of a contract."[25] *Plus ça change, plus c'est la même chose—mais pas si évidemment!* This is a conception that is inherently exhilarating. Only a dullard could fail to respond emotionally to an analysis that promises to pierce the mysteries of modern economic life and expose its hidden meaning in terms of the classical dramatic categories of hero and villain.

But when we begin to examine and dissect rationally what has been disclosed, we begin to have difficulties. It is not sufficient simply to assert that the competitive economy works out to be a system of class exploitation. One must explain how this comes to be. What is the mechanism by which the competition of profit-hungry individual capitalists leads to the extraction of surplus value by capitalists as a class from laborers as a class? Why does such competition not, instead, lead to the shaving away of profit, as envisaged in Western economic theory? Why does not the fact that laborers are the sole source of surplus value lead to the bidding up of wages as capitalists vie with one another to acquire this source of profits?

Marx himself recognized this to be a crucial problem in his general theory of social classes and exploitation. His argument was that while capitalists compete against one another, the total amount of their profit depends upon the exploitation of the total mass of labor by the total mass of capital, and he spoke of this as "a mathematically precise proof why capitalists form a veritable freemason society vis-à-vis the whole working-class, while there is little love lost between them in competition among themselves."[26] But what is meant by *proof* in this connection is simply that it is inherent in the logic of Marx's total system that capitalists and laborers are to be treated as unified classes even in a competitive economy with free labor markets.

The question must be turned the other way around, however. Unless one can demonstrate that there is some mechanism in competitive capitalism that keeps laborers from sharing in the surplus value which they are regarded as creating, then the theory of class identification and exploitation cannot stand. This is the way in which the Marxian theory of the "immiserization of the working class" must be regarded. It must be proven that there are forces at work under capitalism which keep pressing wages down; otherwise, the gap between value and cost of production does not necessarily flow into the pockets of the capitalists. The immiserization theory is not merely a *prediction* that the Marxian analysis generates concerning the course of capitalist evolution; it is part of the fundamental logic of the Marxian theory of class exploitation.

Marx rejected the theory of the classical economists that would have filled this crucial place in his own analysis—the Malthusian theory of population. He regarded Malthus with contempt, as a sycophant and plagiarist who had committed, in his population theory, "a libel on the human race." In place of the infinitely elastic long-run supply curve of labor of Malthusian theory, he employed an infinitely elastic short-run supply curve based on the existence of unemployment. Capitalists can buy labor in the marketplace without causing wages to rise because the existence of a "reserve army of unemployed" prevents any such rise.

The theory of the reserve army of unemployed is one of the mysteries of the Marxian system. Schumpeter has interpreted it[27] as an argument along the lines of Ricardo's chapter "On Machinery," which was added to the third edition of his *Principles*. There is some evidence for this view in *Capital*, including a laudatory reference to Ricardo as evidencing his scientific impartiality and love of truth by the change in view on the unemployment question which this added chapter represented.[28] There are a number of passages in which the Ricardo argument is put forward in terms of Marx's categories of constant and variable capital, technological change being taken to constitute a rise in the ratio c/v which reduces, relatively at least, the demand for labor, since this arises from v only.[29] But the argument, on this plane, is never advanced in any clear-cut way. Moreover, Marx rejected the wage-fund theory, with its view of wages being "advanced" by capitalists to laborers out of a previously accumulated fund, which was the crucial conception underlying Ricardo's "Machinery" argument. His own mode of economic analysis, including his discussion of wages, ran entirely in terms of *flows*, and it is impossible to invoke a *stock* concept argument such as Ricardo's in explanation of his theory of unemployment.

The limitation of the demand for labor by capitalists that is necessary to Marx's wage theory could be derived by regarding the organic composition of capital, c/v, in the aggregate as a fixed technical coefficient of the economic system at any point of time. Capital (in the Western sense) and labor would then be nonsubstitutable factors of production, and the aggregate demand for labor would be determined uniquely by the quantity of capital the economy possessed. This is a line of approach adopted by some modern interpretations of the Marxian system, but it does not fill the need that is involved here; for there is nothing in such a line of argument that demonstrates whether the aggregate demand for labor so determined is less than, equal to, or greater than the existing supply of labor.

If we pursue this matter with some tenacity while reading *Capital*, we find that, like the theory of value, Marx's theory of wages depends upon constraints that are definitional and doctrinal, rather than analytical. Let us examine, as an example, the dicussion of the matter which one finds in Volume I.[30] If we assume, says Marx, that the organic composition of capital is constant, then the accumulation of capital may be such as to make the demand for labor exceed its supply and thus wages will rise. But, he goes on, "wages, . . . by their very nature, always imply the performance of a certain quantity of unpaid labour" (which is the surplus value of the capitalist class). The increase of wages may reduce this surplus value, but this "can never reach the point at which it would threaten the system itself." The rise in the demand for labor which raises wages, if it proceeded to a certain point, would mean that accumulation would be checked. But wages cannot even proceed *to* this point (which would be a stationary state equilibrium), Marx insists. Why? "The rise in wages," he asserts, is confined within limits that not only leave intact the foundations of the capitalist system, but also secure its reproduction on a progressive scale. . . . It cannot be otherwise in a mode of production in which the labourer exists to satisfy the needs of the self-expansion of existing values" (i.e., to serve the capitalists' passion for incessant accumulation).

Thus we find not that capitalism is a class exploitation system because there is some explained mechanism functioning within it that keeps wages down, but that it is argued that wages *must* be kept down by some mechanism (which in the final analysis is left unexplained in *Capital*) because capitalism is, by definition, a system of class exploitation. What cries out for explanation turns out to be embedded in doctrinal assumption, and like the great Omar's seeker of enlightenment we are forced to come out by the same door wherein we entered.

I have here focused on a particular section of *Capital*, but there is in fact, no way out of this problem provided by the work as a whole. The theory of classes as identifiable economic groups which are related to one another in a fashion that is a clear juxtaposition of exploiter and exploited is not made coherent with Marx's conception of capitalism as a competitive economic system. The theory of wage determination that is necessary to such a view is not provided.

To most Marxists, and to a great many non-Marxists as well, the chief merit of Marx as a social scientist is considered to lie in the fact that he provided a sociology which was founded upon the solid bedrock of economics. Just as physics, and the phenomena with which it deals, are regarded as the ultimate to which all other natural phenomena, and therefore all other natural sciences, are reducible, so economic phenomena and economic theory are regarded by some as the fundamental bases of all social science. Thus the Marxian theory of social classes is regarded by many to be immensely revealing because it cuts through the complex web of intricately articulated social relationships of the modern highly differentiated society and discloses the fact that these relationships are merely elaborations of a simple antinomy of economic class interests.

As an empirical generalization of the society Marx used as the chief focus for the analysis of *Capital*, this view is of undeniable merit. Who can deny that a major feature of the maturing industrialism of mid-nineteenth–century England was the division in society between those who lived by the sale of their labor power and those who owned and directed the means of production? But Marx did not put this forward as a mere empirical generalization; he derived it as an ineluctable conclusion from a general theory of economic organization and evolution. This theory, in its effort to demonstrate the inevitable antagonism of classes via the theory of the immiserization of the proletariat, was technically deficient, as I have tried to demonstrate above, but its chief demerit must be considered to lie in the misplaced focus it gave to political thought.

The dramatis personnae of the Marxian view of society derive from a simple Manichaean division into bourgeois capitalists and proletarian workers, and, operating with such a political sociology, Marxists have been unable to grasp the immense significance of the changes that have taken place in the developed economies of the world during the past half century. The flow of power into the hands of bureaucrats and managers, the rise of a class of people who are the "trustees" of property rather than the direct owners of it, the growth of centers of power and influence in the mass media and in the education industry, the development of the intense solidarity of the professions—these and many other developments have left Marxism behind as an archaic theory whose proponents often fall into a ridiculous doctrinairism in their efforts to squeeze the modern world into the framework of the Marxian theory of classes.

What Marx was really trying to come to grips with was the problem of oligarchy, and he did have the great insight to see that oligarchy alters its form and content as society changes and develops. But his view that oligarchic relationships are predictable outgrowths of predictable patterns of economic evolution was a major misdirection which has prevented some of his more ardent followers from perceiving the fact that entrenched oligarchies can develop in society in a variety of ways and their membership is not necessarily confined to persons who are "owners of the means of production." Under some forms of society, bishops can be the leading oligarchs; in others, the chieftains of the Communist Party. Marxism is, on account of its theory of classes, a potentially conservative ideology— a potential that is realized wherever and whenever Marxist parties come to power. For countries such as the United States and those of Western Europe, which have undergone great changes since the last century, Marxism remains a radical ideology but, again because of its erroneous theory of classes, irrelevant to the understanding of the problems of political and economic power with which these societies are faced.

CONTRADICTIONS, CRISES, AND BREAKDOWN

Contradiction, crisis, and *breakdown* are terms that have to do with what many regard as the most fundamental and/or the most distinctive feature of Marx's thought—his theory of history. About Marx's view of history as representing the actions of definite laws of development and the particular theory of these laws that he advances, I shall have little to say, despite the fact that I am inclined to agree with those who regard this aspect of Marxism as being of central importance to the Marxian system of thought. The reason for neglecting this important question is that this essay does not deal with Marx and Marxian thought in general but is basically restricted to what one finds in *Capital*, and in that book very little is said about the laws of history or the dialectical process. Little, indeed, is said even about the stages of economic evolution, which is the overall framework in which Marx conceived of capitalism as a particular economic system. (The last sixty pages or so of Volume I, for example, where such matters are discussed, is presented largely as an addendum to the volume, and its main purpose seems to be to criticize those who justify private property by tracing its origin back to the original persons who saved from labor income, rather than to discuss the stages of economic evolution as such.) *Capital* is indeed so completely concerned with the inner workings of capitalism as an economic system that a reader who knew nothing of the rest of Marx's thought could, unless he was very attentive, miss the essential fact that Marx conceived of capitalism as an inherently transitory system of economic organization and social relationships. But capitalism is inherently transitory in Marx's view, and this means that the examination of the structure and functioning of capitalism, with which *Capital* is concerned, should be expected to disclose these endogenous forces of change.

Remembering the nature of Marxian historical theory, we must pay special attention, in reading *Capital*, to what Marx has to say about the so-called contradictions of capitalism, for it would seem apparent that the forces of change work through such a route. But the nature of these contradictions does not emerge from Marx's writing with a satisfactory degree of clarity, either in the brief passages here and there in which such phenomena are referred to, or in the more extended discussion of the matter that one finds, for example, in Chapter 15 of Volume III. In some passages the inherent contradiction seems to lie in the fact that the distribution of income is, due to the greed of capitalists, kept so unequal that the output of industry cannot find buyers and the capitalists, as a consequence, cannot "realize" the profits after which they hunger. In other passages, it is the growth of concentration resulting from the predatory competition of capitalists among themselves that transforms capitalism so fundamentally that it cannot be sustained.[31]

Another theory, and the one that has come in for most attention, is bound up with the idea that capitalism experiences periodic "crises." It is not clear whether these crises are thought of as being contradictions in themselves, or merely as illustrating or reflecting contradictions of a more fundamental sort, but, at any rate, Marx repeatedly called attention to economic crises and to the cyclical character of economic activity in *Capital*. There is however no single clear-cut theory of cycles and crises to be found in *Capital*. Some suggestions are very general, such as that capitalism is by nature a system in which growth is discontinuous or that capitalists, because their greed is for money profits, lapse from time to time into fits of financial speculation. Other suggestions are fairly specific, such as the development of structural disproportionalities between the demand side and the supply side of the economy: the rise of raw materials prices during a period of boom cutting into profits, the rise of wage rate having similar effects under similar conditions, the lack of savings-investment synchronization resulting in hoarding and consequent deficiency of effective demand, etc. However, none of these suggestions is developed in *Capital* into a definite theory, and even dedicated Marxists such as Sweezy and Dobb have had to acknowledge that a distinct theory of cycles and crisis is not advanced by Marx. Marx himself at one point remarked that such phenomena "fall beyond the scope of our analysis,"[32] but whether he meant that he expected to take the matter up in a further work or that he regarded cyclical phenomena as not being a fundamental part of the mechanism of capitalism (even though ever-present), it is impossible to say.

In the same way, and perhaps for this reason, we do not find in *Capital* any clear theory of the mechanism by which the breakdown of capitalism is supposed to occur. Sometimes it appears as if the forces of breakdown are regarded as primarily political: A revolutionary upheaval is expected to be carried out by workers who have achieved class consciousness and solidarity and are aware of their fundamental conflict with the bourgeois class. In other versions the breakdown mechanism seems to depend on economic forces which sap the viability of capitalism. The lengthy debate over Marx's "law of the falling rate of profit" has been regarded by many Marxists and non-Marxists as of crucial importance because the theory of breakdown was considered to depend upon it, but much of this debate ascribes to Marx a much more rigid "law" than one actually finds in *Capital*.[33]

It is necessary to agree with Sweezy that Marx did not provide an economic theory of the breakdown of capitalism. But this does not mean, as Sweezy seems to believe, that such a theory is necessary to the view that capitalism is a transitory economic and social system.[34] The point at issue is the method and pattern of transition, and on this matter Marxism has proved to be a doctrinaire scholasticism rather than an aid to the interpretation and understanding of what has been going on in the most economically advanced countries during the past hundred years. The changes that have occurred have been so great that it is doubtful whether *capitalism* is a useful term if it must stretch to cover the socio-politico-economic system of these countries both today and in Marx's time. And the forces of change are by no means spent as yet; we may see even more fundamental developments in the forthcoming century.

But these forces of change have not been Marxian, and the pattern has not been in accord with the Marxian model. The immiserization of the working classes, the solidarity of the working classes, class conflict, the increasing difficulty of capitalists in finding profit opportunities, revolution, and the dictatorship of the proletariat have not been the actors in the scenario of change in the economically advanced countries. The center of the stage has been occupied by science and technology, industrial management, communications, education, democracy, and the changing role of government. Doubtless these forces and developments can be squeezed and pummeled into Marxian categories, as doctrinaire Marxists are wont to do, but that only demonstrates (once again) the infinite elasticity of the scholastic mode of reasoning. It does not offer an acute perception of the forces that are at work in the modern world or give promise of the creation of useful techniques for their direction and control.

NOTES

1. J. M. Keynes, *Laissez-Faire and Communism* (New York: New Republic, Inc., 1926), pp. 47–48.

2. See *Papers and Proceedings, American Economic Review*, vol. 57. no. 2 (May 1967), pp. 594–641, for the papers that were presented at this meeting.

3. There are quite a number of such translations. To mention a few representative ones: Paul Davidson, *Theories of Aggregate Income Distribution* (New Brunswick, N.J.: Rutgers University Press, 1960), chap. 2; Irma Adelman, *Theories of Economic Growth and Development* (Stanford: Stanford University Press, 1961); Martin Bronfenbrenner, "*Das Kapital* for the Modern Man," *Science and Society*, vol. 29, no. 4 (Fall 1965), pp. 419–38; Paul Samuelson, "Wages and Interest: A Modern Dissection of Marxian Economic Models," *American Economic Review*, vol. 47, no. 6 (Dec. 1957), pp. 884–912.

4. Karl Marx, *Capital*, I, 204. (Moscow: Foreign Languages Publishing House, 1961). All references to *Capital* in this paper are to this edition.

5. See, e.g., *Capital*, II, 121–22.
6. Ibid., III, 12.
7. Ibid., I, 185.
8. Ibid., 183.
9. See, e.g., *Capital*, II, 130 ff.
10. Ibid., I, 107.
11. In one place, his analysis seems to imply a picture of the demand side of the economy as consisting solely of demand curves of unitary elasticity. (See *Capital*, I, 524). This would mean that expenditure of labor in the creating of "excessive" quantities of commodities would leave total market value produced unchanged.
12. Sweezy's suggestion for arriving, theoretically, at the conversion factors for labor would avoid circularity of reasoning, but would not meet the training time problem. P. M. Sweezy, *The Theory of Capitalist Development* (London: Dobson, 1946), 42–45. But this is perhaps no more and no less serious than the general elimination of the production time dimension in Marxian economics.
13. In *Capital*, capitalism is treated as a competitive economy essentially like the world of perfect competition of neoclassical economics. None of Marx's arguments are based on the existence or growth of monopolistic elements, and where such elements are introduced they are used to make *a fortiori* a proposition already established for a competitive economy. The two leading modern American Marxist economists, however, have attempted a reconstruction of Marxian theory along monopolistic lines: P. M. Baran and P. M. Sweezy, *Monopoly Capital* (New York: Monthly Review Press, 1966).
14. The tone of Engels' challenge, and his subsequent evaluation of the attempted solutions in his Preface to vol. III, are of interest. The criticisms are not used as a test of Marxian theory, but the theory is used as a test of the quality of the critic, and accolades are awarded in varying degrees depending on the similarity of the writer's solution to what is contained in Marx's notes. These prefaces are clear foreshadowings of the characteristic that was to become the dominant feature of Marxian politics, its passion for legitimized doctrinal orthodoxy.
15. In his analysis, in chap. 9 of vol. III, Marx distinguishes between "used-up c" and "total c," but this does not affect the result in any substantial way.
16. See Sweezy, chap. 7, for an excellent discussion of this problem.
17. To understand this, the opening pages of vol. I of *Capital* should be read with care and not dismissed as mere metaphysical obscurantism.
18. The argument made in this and the next paragraph is taken from my paper "Why Does Marxian Exploitation Theory Require a Labor Theory of Value?" *Journal of Political Economy*, vol. 76, no. 1 (Jan./Feb. 1968).

19. *Capital*, II, 372.

20. Ibid., I, 611.

21. Ibid., 217.

22. Ibid., 46–47n. (Engels' italics).

23. Emile Burns, ed., *A Handbook of Marxism* (New York: International Publishers, 1935), p. 45.

24. M. H. Dobb, *Political Economy and Capitalism* (London: Routledge, 1937), p. 70.

25. *Capital*, I, 574.

26. Ibid., III, 194.

27. See J. A. Schumpeter, *Capitalism, Socialism and Democracy*, pp. 35–36.

28. *Capital*, I, p. 438n.

29. See, for example, *Capital*, I, chap. 25, sec. 3.

30. Ibid., chap. 25, sec. 1.

31. This seems to be the argument in the passage from *Capital* that is most frequently quoted on this point: "Centralisation of the means of production and socialisation of labour at last reach such a point where they become incompatible with their capitalist integument. This integument is burst asunder. The knell of capitalist private property sounds. The expropriators are expropriated." (vol. I, p. 763.)

32. *Capital*, III, 353.

33. The counteracting forces to the falling rate of profit noted by Marx in chap. 14 of vol. III are such as to render the proposition weightless as a prediction of a long-term tendency, since at least some of these counteracting forces could easily recur without limit.

34. Sweezy, pp. 191–92.

9

Macroeconomic Models and Central Price-Setting in the Soviet Economy

ROBERT W. CAMPBELL

In the socialist countries and in the literature produced in other countries on centrally administered economies, two issues have exerted great fascination—the proper principles to follow in price formation and the appropriate design for a fiscal system that would achieve macroeconomic equilibrium and the desired redistribution of income. These are two perennial subjects for disagreement to which economists and policy-makers return over and over again, and today both are receiving special attention as aspects of the economic reorganizations being carried out in the socialist world. In the centrally administered economy these two problems are closely interrelated: Indeed they may be said to be but two faces of a single problem. Where prices are administratively determined and the entire economy is under central direction, the rules of price formation simultaneously generate certain fiscal flows. At the same time, the choice among alternative fiscal instruments and the resulting differences in the incidence of certain macroeconomic magnitudes among different sectors and products have an important impact on the sys-

Robert W. Campbell is Professor of Economics at Indiana University.

tem of relative prices. Unfortunately, these two questions are often considered in isolation from each other; people are likely to elaborate their ideas about the fiscal system without systematic consideration of the implications of fiscal flows for the problem of price-setting, and the issues of price-setting are discussed without due attention to the fiscal problem. This situation has given rise to a great deal of confusion and misunderstanding. The goal of this paper is to formulate an approach to these problems which will encompass them both in their mutual relations, and establish the simple fundamental conditions for their rational coordination.

SECTORS AND FLOWS IN THE CENTRALLY-ADMINISTERED ECONOMY

As a basis for this kind of analysis, it is necessary to set out a simple macroeconomic conceptualization of the centrally administered economy. The scheme proposed is a better representation of the early stages of the centrally administered economy and its strategy of development (such as the Soviet economy in its first two decades of industrialization) than it is of present realities.[1] We recognize that things have changed, but by first formulating the scheme in relation to the characteristics of that kind of economy, it will then be possible to analyze better the macroeconomic and pricing problems as they are affected by contemporary economic reorganizations.

Macroeconomic thinking more or less implies the notion of the circular flow as a point of departure. The form of this conception as developed to analyze the market economy requires considerable modification in application to the Soviet-type economy. Figure 1 preserves the basic idea, but modifies the sectoring and flows to make the system more relevant for macroeconomic reasoning in the centrally administered economy. The principal sectors it is necessary to distinguish are what we will call the state production establishment (SPE hereafter), an urban household sector, and a rural household sector. The diagram also shows a rest-of-world sector, but its nature is obvious and we will not comment on it at length in this paper.

The SPE is the analogue of the business sector in the capitalist form of the circular flow diagram, but has many differentiating features. Unlike the multitude of firms that make up the business sector in the bourgeois form, the SPE can best be considered as a single gigantic firm under the unified direction of the planners. Its physical manifestation is the aggregate of state property or production facilities, including natural resources. It can also be thought of as an organization—a hierarchical administrative system designed to pursue the production goals set for it by the party and governmental leaders of the socialist society. As the name suggests, it thus combines state functions with production activities.

The urban households sector is likewise inspired by the households sector of the usual circular flow diagram, but in central planning of the Soviet-type economy this sector is distinctive in that households do not exercise ownership of productive property—property belongs to the state production sector.

Given the historical fact that central planning has usually been aimed at transforming relatively underdeveloped economies with a large agriculture sector into a more modern form and given the many differences between agriculture and nonagriculture in relative growth rates, susceptibility to effective administrative control, legal status, etc., it is useful to consider rural households separately from urban. In concrete institutional terms, the rural household sector is made up primarily of collective farm households, both in their role as private producers and as participants in the collective production of the kolkhoz. Such private agricultural production as is carried on by urban workers and by workers on state farms also belongs in this sector conceptually. Note also that this splits agriculture between two sectors—the state farm production and Machine-Tractor Stations, when they existed—being of the SPE. The rural households sector differs in an important way from the urban households sector—it is

FIGURE I
Macroeconomic Sectors and Flows in a Centrally Administered Economy

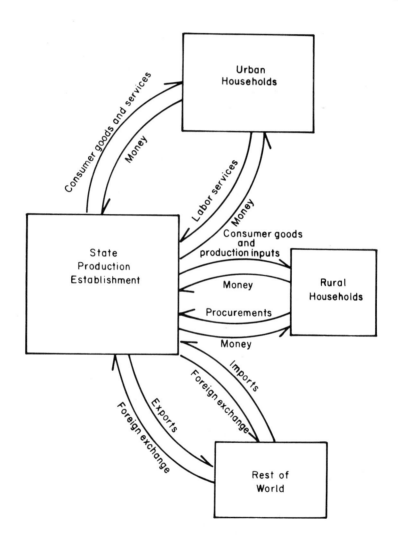

not purely a consumption sector, but carries on production activity as well.

These sectors are connected by exchange to the SPE. The urban household sector is linked with the SPE in two kinds of exchange relationships. In the upper loop (see fig. 1) households exchange their money incomes for a flow of consumer goods and services from the SPE, and in the lower the SPE gives them money incomes in exchange for their labor services. In the real world these flows include not only requited exchanges, but also transfers in kind and money in each direction such as medical and educational services, voluntary and involuntary unpaid work, and taxes and social security payments, but we are not especially interested in these here.

The transactions between the SPE and the rural households are somewhat different. In return for part of the money incomes it pays out, the SPE receives not labor services, but procurements of agricultural produce. Similarly, in the other half of the exchange it supplies, for money from the rural households, not only consumption goods and services but also inputs to be used in production. By virtue of their private production and consumption in kind, rural households are less dependent than urban households on the SPE for their subsistence, a circumstance with important consequences. We might note in passing one other important exchange—not explicitly shown in figure 1—that between urban and rural households in the form of the collective farm market.

There are a number of interesting problems connected with this exchange, but they are peripheral to our main interest and will not be elaborated on in this paper.

The rationale behind the flows presented and the particular exchanges chosen for consideration is that these exchanges exhibit to a large extent the characteristics of market relationships, i.e., that each side has some autonomy in decision-making. This is especially true in the case of the urban household sector. These households are generally free to make their own decisions about responses to the exchange terms offered by the SPE: They can spend or save, choose their occupation, and allocate their spending among goods as they see fit. The outcome of these exchanges (by which we mean the allocational results—i.e., the level of skill acquired and the level of effort put forth, the allocation of labor services among occupations and regions, and the allocation of welfare among households) is determined by the reactions of decision-makers on both sides to the terms of exchange (price relationships) established for these transactions.

The link between rural households and the SPE is less clearly a market one: The SPE attempts to control allocation and decision-making in this sector by direct administrative commands. Such devices as procurement quotas and acreage allotments are designed to limit the autonomy of this sector's responses to the terms of exchange presented to it by the SPE. In fact, however, the conditions under which rural households work have always permitted them considerable discretion in the effort they exert and the kind of production decisions they reach, and these decisions have been quite sensitive to the price relationships they face.

One very important category of exchanges is not explicitly revealed in this scheme; namely, the intra-SPE transactions, those between the component enterprises and sectors of the SPE. But these exchanges, lacking the market characteristics of those between households and the SPE, are of less interest from the point of view of pricing and macroeconomic equilibrium. In the centrally administered economy, the SPE is controlled administratively: Its varied parts are coordinated and its internal exchanges effected by administrative rather than market means.

In this scheme one can visualize a kind of real output or income accounting in physical terms that at the same time embodies a strategy of development. The SPE, drawing in labor services from urban households and a stream of agricultural inputs from rural households, operates its production facilities. The exchanges within the SPE—when labor services are transformed into successive forms of intermediate goods, moved from one sector to another for further processing, and ultimately transformed into final goods—are extremely complex. Anyone trying to develop a theory about the strategy of Soviet development will immediately find his attention drawn to the kind of internal sectoring that the planners have imposed on the SPE—the designation of leading links; the preoccupation with the division into industry A and industry B, the tendency to treat the numerous sectors that border on or effect the exchanges with households as loosely planned, low priority, buffer sectors peripheral to the attention of the planners. But as already indicated, that sectoring is of limited interest from the point of view of macroeconomics and pricing.

Ultimately the circular flow is completed, as a portion of the output produced in the SPE returns to households either as consumer goods and services to urban households, or as consumer goods *and* production goods and services to rural households. But this return flow far from exhausts the total output of final goods turned out by the SPE. In short, there is a surplus, which in physical terms gets accumulated in the form of new production facilities and stocks of intermediate goods or is drained off for military use, foreign aid, and other such objectives determined by the directors of the SPE. Another way of interpreting this surplus is as the *income* of the organization we are calling the SPE.

VALUATION OF AGGREGATE FLOWS

All the intersectoral flows described may be visualized in physical terms, or interpreted in value terms, according to whatever theory of value one is partial to. The Marxian theoreticians could evaluate and compare the two flows making up each loop between the SPE and another sector in the common denominator of socially necessary labor expenditures. Such an evaluation implies, of course, an unequal exchange in the sense that the labor hours provided by households to the SPE far exceed the labor hours embodied in the form of the goods they receive in return. According to this interpretation, the income of the SPE arises as the appropriation of surplus value. The western value theorist would have a different interpretation;

he would consider some of the value of the output of the production establishment to be attributable to the contribution of the capital stock, natural resources, etc., used in cooperation with labor. But even in this more sophisticated version, the value of the return flow to households is much less than the value of their contribution to the SPE. Most economists, from the pioneer Marxian theorists of industrialization in the Soviet Union in the twenties to contemporary Western students of centrally administered economies, have seen the achievement of this unequal exchange as one of the central elements in the Soviet strategy of growth.[2]

On this skeleton we can hang still another garment, i.e., a pricing and fiscal system. That is, we now shift from the evaluation of the various flows of goods and services according to some theory of value to an evaluation in terms of the prices actually used in transactions. The outstanding feature of the pricing and fiscal systems established in the centrally administered economy is the use of these systems to cope with the macroeconomic disequilibrium associated with the unequal exchange between the SPE and households. In its fiscal guise this system accumulates in financial terms the real income accruing to the SPE. (The fiscal system also has the function of distributing this income, but the relationship of that function to pricing introduces some new issues that we will consider only later.)

We are thus ready to deal with the second problem posed by this paper: What are the fundamental requirements to be met by this fiscal and pricing system? Any given level of income could be collected by a great variety of fiscal measures, differing from each other in their incidence on the price system. It could be collected exclusively in the exchanges with households by setting prices on consumer goods above their factor cost. Alternatively, it might be collected by setting high, profit-generating, transfer prices on intermediate goods exchanged within the SPE. Ultimately, of course, these would be passed on to households. In either case, it could be collected at a uniform markup rate on all goods—or heavily on some, lightly on others. One can examine this system in the light of both the demands of macroeconomic equilibrium and the demands of rational pricing. Each has its own conditions, and the interesting question is how these two sets of demands can be coordinated and reconciled.

The condition for macroeconomic equilibrium is obvious. The general level of prices on what the SPE sells to households relative to those on what it buys from households must be set so as to equate the two flows. The total paid to households must be sufficient to buy back the consumer goods and the productive inputs for agriculture offered in the other half of the exchange: The appropriation of surplus value by the SPE in physical terms must be reinforced by a fiscal and pricing system which assures financial equilibrium. To do the job by direct taxes would have adverse effects on morale and incentives. The regime has worked hard to create the money wage incentive system, and it would not make sense to dilute it by too obvious a tax bite.

In the practical reality of an economy, of course, price setters do not establish general price levels. They set individual wage rates, prices for each consumer good, and procurement prices for specific commodities. What considerations should govern the allocation of the tax burden among individual kinds of goods? This question can be answered at two levels of sophistication. Given the autonomy mentioned above which households have about allocating their incomes and choosing their employment, the price setters will want to differentiate the markup to achieve "micro-balance." Relative prices must be set to clear individual markets; they must be juggled to ensure equality of supply and demand for each consumer good and for all the different categories of labor. It would be undesirable to have the prices on shoes so low that there was a shortage of shoes and the prices of sardines so high that the supply turned out by the SPE could not be sold. Prices that are too low produce deficits in the consumer goods markets which are wasteful of people's time and create the conditions for speculation and black markets. Surpluses are an obvious waste; resources tied up in unsalable sardines make no contribution inducing households to provide labor services. All these symptoms of failure to achieve micro-balance are so obvious that it doesn't take any great economic sophistication to recognize the validity of this rule in pricing, although it has certainly not been consistently honored in centrally-administered economies.

There is a second requirement to be met in pricing exchanges with households that is less widely appreciated, but equally important from the point of view of economic efficiency. This is that the mark-up rate on all consumer goods over their factor cost (or over the socially necessary labor expenditures for their production if we are thinking in Marxian terms) be identical. In other words, micro-balance for each market must be achieved by adjusting the relative outputs of goods rather than by differentiating the rate of markup among goods. The reasoning behind this principle can be understood from the following simplified example.

Imagine that there are only two consumer goods—shoes and sardines—and that they are priced as shown in table 1.

Table 1

	Shoes	Sardines	All Consumer Goods
Number of units sold	2,000 pairs	4,000 kilos	
Actual cost per unit	15 rubles/pair	5 rubles/kilo	
Turnover tax	15 " "	10 " "	
Selling price per unit	30 " "	15 " "	
Aggregate value	30 × 2,000 = 60,000	15 × 4,000 = 60,000	120,000

Assume that these prices assure both micro- and macro-balance—i.e., that demand just equals supply for each good—and that the aggregate retail value of 120,000 rubles for consumer goods output just exhausts the purchasing power of households. The resulting allocation would still be wasteful in the sense that the income of the SPE would not be a maximum. Consider the effect of reducing the production of shoes and increasing the production of sardines. Given the relative prices, decreasing shoe production and sales by one pair would mean a loss of revenue of 30 rubles. To maintain macrobalance, that 30 rubles would have to be made up by producing and selling more sardines to the population—2 kilos more, to be precise. But this shift has saved the SPE some resources. The resource cost of the extra sardines (10 rubles worth) was more than covered by the saving of resources in shoe production (15 rubles worth), and the SPE has saved itself 5 rubles worth of resources which can now be appropriated as income and devoted to one of its objectives such as investment. This gain is made without diminishing the welfare or impairing the incentives of households. Their behavior shows that they are just as well satisfied as before. They were perfectly willing to give up one pair of shoes to get two kilos of sardines. As this shift continued, of course, the market-clearing price for sardines would fall and that for shoes rise, by lowering the rate of turnover tax in the one case and raising it in the other. The advantage of further shifts would vanish just at the point suggested above, i.e., where the ratio of price to cost is just equal for both goods.

The principles of micro-pricing, indicated above in relation to consumer goods, have their counterparts in the various other exchanges between households and the SPE. In the labor market, prices must equate the supply of each category of labor with the requirement for that kind of labor and must also be proportional to the value of the services of the various workers, i.e., their productivity, to the SPE. Raising pay to whatever level is required to attract enough workers to man the coal mines of Vorkuta does not by itself guarantee efficiency: It might turn out that the wage rate required was so high that the cost of the coal would be excessive compared to alternative ways of meeting fuel needs. Just as in the case of the consumer goods market, rationality through the market approach requires adjustment in the quantities of different categories of labor demanded until the market-clearing prices are in proportion to the contribution that each worker makes toward production. We can trust the workers' own reactions to make these wage rates proportional to the relative attractiveness of different jobs.

All this is based on the assumption that prices are signals to which decision-makers are free to react, an assumption largely justified in the exchanges between the SPE and households. An equally important implication of our discussion, per contra, is that if decision-makers are not free to respond by making quantity adjustments in the amounts of goods offered for exchange, then the subtleties of price formation become unimportant, and the price system can be left to be the instrument of macroeconomic considerations alone. As long as decisions within the SPE—i.e., about what to produce or how to produce, where to ship, etc.—are not made on the basis of prices, but in accordance with a plan, we can manipulate the fiscal tools and collect the surplus in any arbitrary way without affecting the behavior of decision-makers within the production establishment. Of course, that has never really been the case. The decision-makers within the SPE are sensitive in various ways to prices. Decision-making is not a fully centralized function, but is split up into many spheres which are carried out by many different people. In each of these spheres, and in some more than others, decisions are taken by comparisons of price-based aggregates. In conformity with this reality, the designers of price-fiscal systems in centrally administered economies have groped toward the kind of price system that the Western theory of value suggests. Even in the old, unlamented days of dogmatism in economic theory, the planners were often led by purely empirical administrative considerations to collect part of the income of the corporation by profit markups and turnover taxes— not at the border between the SPE and households, but at various points of exchange within the SPE. The most common examples are found in the juggling of prices of substitutable materials to equate the cost to the user of comparable use values. The philosophy of the reforms discussed and initiated since the mid-1960's is to acknowledge the freedom that decision-makers in the SPE already had and to enlarge this freedom. In consequence, it becomes necessary to redesign the pricing and fiscal system as these apply within the SPE in order to offer rational guidance for this enlarged scope of decision-making.

PRICE-FISCAL RELATIONS WITHIN THE SPE

Having explored the fundamentals of price-fiscal coordination in the simpler kind of macroeconomic model system developed so far, the issues in the new setting ought to be clear. The main difference is that although the pricing implications in those links were about the same whether we started with a Marxian theory of value or a Western theory of value, in the practical design of a pricing system for the intra-SPE problem, the two theories have very different implications, and we will get very different kinds of behavior, depending on which theory we take as inspiration. The issue is whether to establish prices equal (or proportional) to cumulations of the labor input valued in money terms at the prices established in the wage market of my model or, believing that some of the income of the SPE is generated by other scarce resources, to motivate the stewards of the state domain to conserve those resources by introducing fiscal devices to make them financially accountable for their use, which would pass these costs on to the users of the output and accumulate the income of the SPE for allocation by the leadership.

Apparently most Marxian theorists have now become convinced that the price system must include such charges as interest, rent, and quasi-rents if decision-makers are to be motivated to maximize the output of the SPE. This consensus has now been embodied in price reform schemes.[3] The officially accepted formula for prices under these schemes will be something like

price = cost of labor + cost of purchased materials + eK + rent + profit,

where K is the stock of capital in a given production process and e is the norm for the capital charge. But there remain controversial points. As L. V. Kantorovich said, "the important thing is how one understands this price building formula." There is still a big division of opinion over whether the charge for capital and the profit rates should be uniform, and there is much confusion as to how rent will be determined. Two comments on the debate over this problem are worth making.

First, in the reforms and in the thinking of many economists the real function of prices has not yet been properly understood. Even after the reforms, prices are going to be administratively set by adding to the traditional cost calculations a number of new fiscal charges; the rationale for these charges comes from the Marxian macroeconomic idea of allocating of surplus value among sectors and commodities. That is, the macroeconomic income-collection point of view still predominates over the pricing point of view. The problem is that a large portion of the surplus to be collected in socialist economies today is price-determined, not price-determining. In an economy like that of the USSR, which has a big legacy of misallocated resources, there are tremendous rents and quasi-rents side-by-side with zero productivities. In this situation prices need to be fixed by mutual negotiation, or by some machine manipulation of this process that will reveal what capital is productive, what resources are scarce, what materials are being produced in such quantities that in some of their uses their contribution to production does not justify their cost. If the full power of prices is to be brought to bear on the task of improving economic performance, the new charges must be varied so that they take account of past errors. Kantorovich has given us a very instructive insight into this issue in his assertion that machinery prices should not be burdened with a full charge for the capital invested over the years in that branch both because of the low productivity of this capital and because of the low marginal cost of output that would accompany the demand pressure and profit squeeze which would be generated by relatively low machinery prices.[4] A mechanical attempt to include profit and interest charges at uniform rates can make no contribution to this problem. The charge on assets in use and the profit charges that are being introduced are useful motivating devices of managerial behavior—from a business accounting point of view—but not an adequate solution of the pricing problem.

Second, much of this literature is imbued with the erroneous notion that the fiscal-pricing system should be responsible not only for determining the prices and for collecting the surplus that is the income of the SPE, but should also play a very large role in allocating that surplus to specific uses. There has always been in Soviet writing the idea that prices for a given branch should be set so that it will have enough revenues to cover its need for investment. This idea has again been repeated in the guidelines for the price reforms of the late 1960's.[5] Unfortunately, that is simply one function too many: The price system cannot channel profits precisely to those sectors and firms which should expand and still perform its other functions properly. There may be some correlation between the profitability of various activities and the desirability of expanding them, but there is no neat quantitative correspondence between the surplus earned in a given activity and the need for investment to expand that activity. This could be made into a complex theoretical argument, but a couple of examples may be sufficient to convince.

For instance, technological progress, in its groping advance, may lead to rapid obsolescence in certain sectors, and this calls for replacement investment. But the innovations that have made its capital obsolete have cut the opportunity cost of its output, so that its prices, rather than being raised to assign profits to the industry, should be lowered. Funds for expansion will have to come by transfer from other sectors. Often, surpluses are in the form of a rent, generated by the fact that marginal costs are far above the average. These high marginal costs are a good indication that output should not be expanded, but that the rent should be transferred for the expansion of some other sector, not kept in this one.

It is one of the tenets of bourgeois economics that efficiency and normative notions of distributive justice are not jointly resolvable by the price system. It is recognized that the prices that will maximize the output of an economy may result in an income distribution that is inequitable according to some social criterion. But the way out of that dilemma is seen to be not to distort prices, but to redistribute income by some means outside the system of exchange prices. This idea would take some reinterpretation to apply directly to the problem of letting the exchange prices within the SPE allocate the surplus, but it is applicable. It may be easier to show its relevance to familiar pricing problems in centrally administered economies in terms of SPE-household exchanges. One use to which the directors of the SPE have put its surplus in recent years is to raising household consumption levels and mitigating the degree of inequality in their exchanges with households. In the early postwar years they mostly used cuts in prices of consumer goods for this purpose; more recently this method has been supplemented with a great deal of juggling of the wage structure. In the process, there have been many allusions to the normative goals of using these changes in prices to improve distributive justice, to improve the distribution of income. The important point is that they can do the latter only by sacrificing adherence to the efficiency-pricing rules described above. Suppose that these rules are currently satisfied, and one then attempts to reallocate a part of SPE income in the direction of a particular group of households, say to lower-income groups by cutting the price of bread, or to the elite by cutting prices of consumer durables. The result will be all those symptoms of disequilibrium mentioned earlier. The argument working through the labor market is the same. In fact, most of these price changes have been designed to meet the efficiency conditions, and it is only a confusion of thought that attributes equity considerations to them. Another practical problem that the planners would be in a better position to understand if they were accustomed to this kind of analysis is the effort to conduct separate income policies for urban and rural households. The market link between these two sectors that we have mentioned, though not elaborated on, makes that effort difficult and productive of mischief.

In conclusion, some further justification may be in order as to why the title brings together price-formation and macroeconomics and why the paper has also had to touch on so many topics too cursorily and unrigorously. A macroeconomic model is a kind of strategic vision, a kind of gross somatic atlas on which we can localize the functions and disorders of the *corpus economicus* and display the articulations that both set off problems for separate analysis and show their mutual ties: The analysis of the centrally administered economy, whether by socialist economists and policy-makers or by outside observers cries out today for some simple, but clear-cut macro conceptualization. The kind of macroeconomic models on which we instinctively rely in thinking about these economies have been developed for other purposes and have big deficiencies for analyzing the centrally administered economy. The principal Marxian macroeconomic model is inappropriate in its concentration on the division into Department I and Department II; as we have tried to show, the operational problems of macroeconomic equilibrium and pricing have been in the relationships between households and the SPE. The Keynesian analysis and national income accounting assumes sectoring and exchange relationships that mirror a very different institutional reality where saving and investment decisions are split between households and business and where government and business are institutionally separate. Input-output is useful, especially its southeast quadrant, which considers the relationship with households and the SPE, but that is the least developed part of input-output analysis; it is a mere blank in most tables! Linear programming is mostly concerned with intra-SPE pricing and allocation rather than with the macroeconomic relationships with households.

The purpose of this paper has been to suggest a scheme that would display what there is of macroeconomics in the centrally administered economy and that at the same time would illuminate the practical pricing problems that go with that kind of economy and abstract some fundamental principles for thinking about the problems of macroeconomics and pricing—particularly as these problems may appear within the SPE when the character of exchange relations within the SPE begins to change. Those acquainted with early Soviet literature may think that this paper is essentially a novel presentation of old Preobrazhenskii constructs or, more crudely, Preobrazhenskii plagiarized. But no one need apologize for so honoring that fertile thinker. If the standard texts of socialist political economy contained something analogous to this model, much of the controversy over issues of pricing and of macroeconomic relations in centrally administered economies could be clarified and resolved.

NOTES

1. See notably E. A. Preobrazhenskii's discussion "On Primary Socialist Accumulation," in *Foundations of Soviet Strategy for Economic Growth*, ed. N. Spulber (Bloomington: Indiana University Press, 1960), pp. 230–57.

2. See, for instance, Naum Jasny, *Soviet Industrialization, 1928–1952* (Chicago: University of Chicago Press, 1961), pp. 1–34.

3. See notably Morris Bornstein, "The Soviet Price Reform Discussion," *The Quarterly Journal of Economics*, vol. 78 (Feb. 1964), p. 15ff.

4. For a discussion of Kantorovich's ideas on prices, see Benjamin Ward's review "Kantorovich on Economic Calculation," *Journal of Political Economy*, vol. 68 (1960), p. 545ff.

5. Cf. *Ekonomicheskaia gazeta* (The Economic Journal), no. 45 (1965).

E

R//OPF

ESSAYS